Quality Whitetails

Quality Whitetails

The Why and How of Quality Deer Management

Karl V. Miller and
R. Larry Marchinton, Editors

STACKPOLE
BOOKS

Published by
STACKPOLE BOOKS
5067 Ritter Road
Mechanicsburg, PA 17055

Printed in the United States of America

Cover photograph by Robert Clark, courtesy of *South Carolina
Wildlife Magazine.*

Computer graphics by Appalachian Prepress.

First edition

10 9 8 7 6 5 4 3

Library of Congress Cataloging-in-Publication Data

Quality whitetails : the why and how of quality deer management /
   Karl V. Miller and R. Larry Marchinton, editors.
      p.   cm.
   Includes bibliographical references.
   ISBN 0-8117-1387-3
   1. White-tailed deer hunting. 2. Wildlife management. 3. White-
tailed deer. I. Miller, Karl V. II. Marchinton, R. Larry.
SK301.Q35   1995
639. 9'797357—dc20   95-18450
                                                          CIP

To all the sportsmen, landowners, and biologists who recognize the importance of wise stewardship of all our natural resources

There is value in any experience that exercises those ethical restraints collectively called sportsmanship.

—ALDO LEOPOLD
A Sand County Almanac

Contents

PART IV
THE QUALITY HUNTING EXPERIENCE

Foreword

The problem, then, is how to bring about a stirring for harmony with land among a people many of whom have forgotten there is any such thing as land, among whom education and culture have become almost synonymous with landlessness. This is the problem of "conservation education."

—ALDO LEOPOLD
Conservation

A quality deer herd, increasingly desired by individuals and organizations but experienced by too few, is necessary, worthwhile, and rewarding. Everyone, regardless of the level of involvement, should help ensure that deer populations within his or her sphere of influence are maintained or restored to a level of quality as outlined and explained in this text.

A quality deer herd is based on a healthy habitat. More is involved in deer herd management than the manipulation of numbers and ratios of bucks, does, and fawns. Herd management is highly complex, with many factors affecting the effort.

Successful management is rewarding and beneficial, not only to the herd itself but to all other animals that share the deer herd's habitat. To succeed in influencing proper herd management, though, one must have a base of current, correct, and relevant information on as many phases as possible of the management plan. This information should be written in an easily understood format and presented in one text.

There is a wealth of information on how to hunt deer, what to use, and where to go, complete with a myriad of gadgets, gimmicks, and advice. Many dollars, hours, and thoughts are expended in the pursuit of harvest success each year; yet, all hunters should devote equal effort in the management of this renewable resource. It is time, if not imperative, for every wildlife enthusiast (and particularly those interested in white-tailed deer) to help improve deer herds through proven management techniques.

This publication is the result of hundreds of thousands of man-hours expended by the foremost deer researchers, biologists, and managers in the nation. It has been compiled, edited, and presented to influence everyone who reads it to become more knowledgeable, aware, and active in improving the quality of deer herds nationwide.

—AL BROTHERS

Introduction

Few biological arts depend as much on ingenuity and resourcefulness as the art of game management.

—ALDO LEOPOLD

In a provocative address at the 1982 Southeast Deer Study Group Meeting in Charleston, South Carolina, Al Brothers warned hunters about the deterioration of American deer hunting. He pointed out that many good hunting areas "are exhibiting or beginning to exhibit symptoms of deer herd and habitat deterioration. These symptoms include lowered reproductive rates, widening buck-doe ratios, poor nutritional levels, and, in far too many instances, a buck harvest composed mostly of yearling age-class bucks. . . . Yet at the same time, the regulations [often] allow landowners and hunters to literally and legally rape the antlered segment of the herd. Isn't it time we attempt to practice total deer herd management with respect to harvest by giving the antlered segment of the herd the same consideration we have given the antlerless segment?" He argued that "quality deer management involves quality bucks, does, and fawns, quality habitat, and thus quality hunting experiences."

These words ring even truer today. Many deer ranges suffer from problems associated with past management practices. Habitat degradation, urban deer problems, and deer-automobile collisions have increased. Body weight, antler development, and reproductive output have declined in many areas. In some areas, high deer densities

1

adversely affect forest regeneration and even other wildlife, such as songbirds and rodents.

In *Producing Quality Whitetails*, published in 1975, Al Brothers and Murphy Ray declared, "A revolution is needed! A revolution in deer management concepts, in range management concepts, in deer harvest and production concepts, and . . . in methods used to disseminate research, management and status information." This revolution is well under way. A change in the way deer are being managed is spreading across our country. It is a grass-roots change led by sportsmen and landowners.

The *real* managers are the landowners and the hunters who make a management decision every time they harvest an animal. These managers need to know the implications of their decisions. Currently, however, most information on wildlife management and research is published in obscure journals that are read exclusively by wildlife professionals. Rarely does it get to the people who can use it most directly to benefit wildlife. Even when it does, it usually is not in language that can be understood. For landowners and hunters to fully appreciate their potential role in deer management, they must have the benefit of research and management research results. If proper wildlife management (and deer hunting in particular) is to survive, hunters, managers, and professional biologists must manage the resource in consideration of the entire wildlife community.

This book is intended to span the gap between professional biologists and the deer hunter-manager. We hope it provides information and understanding of one technique, quality deer management. If the book by Brothers and Ray was the manifesto of quality deer management, then this is an updated battle plan aimed at moving quality deer management out of the realm of the large landowner and into that of the average hunter all across North America. Each chapter was written by authorities on various aspects of deer management and biology. They explain deer management in general and quality deer management in particular. Our goal is not to criticize current or traditional management but to present an alternative where social and biological constraints allow. The deer-hunting tradition has changed in recent years and will continue to do so. In many regions, hunters are no longer satisfied with the status quo. They are better educated and more sophisticated than ever before. Managers also are realizing that deer herds are only one portion of the wildlife resource that must be considered in management decisions. Only a common understanding can guide deer management into the twenty-first century.

Quality deer management clearly is not for everyone, nor will it work equally well in all regions of the country. Some areas need management more and the benefits of quality deer management will be more pronounced in some regions than others. Quality management works only where hunters have the desire and ability to assume the role of manager. Regardless of whether you choose to participate in management, however, we hope that this book will make you a more knowledgeable hunter and a more responsible wildlife steward.

This book is divided into four parts. In part I, the philosophy and practice of quality deer management is described. The five chapters explain how to begin a management program and evaluate it. Part II focuses on white-tailed deer biology and management. Chapters cover basic population dynamics, habitat management, deer behavior, and nutritional requirements. Although the idea of quality deer management originated in the South, part III discusses its potential in other regions. Chapter 13 presents the special problems and potentials of quality deer management in poor habitats, where "textbook" management does not apply. Finally, part IV discusses hunting, its mystique, and the importance of ethics in maintaining the tradition for future generations.

We would like all readers to know that the contributors to this book have donated their efforts. All royalties from sales will be donated to the Quality Deer Management Association, a nonprofit organization dedicated to promoting hunter education, proper deer management, and hunter ethics. An application is included at the end of the book if you would like to join this growing organization and help preserve the sport for future generations.

—KARL V. MILLER AND
R. LARRY MARCHINTON

PART I

Theory and Practice

CHAPTER 1

How Quality Deer Management Works

Quality deer management is first and foremost an attitude. . . . The self-imposed restriction of taking antlerless deer while allowing young antlered bucks to pass provides the hunter opportunities to study deer, learn their behaviors, and sharpen hunting skills. The success of the hunt is no longer measured merely as a filled tag or the number of antler points.

—David C. Guynn, Jr.

Quality deer management is the voluntary use of restraint in the harvesting of young bucks combined with an appropriate antlerless deer harvest to maintain a healthy deer population in balance with the habitat. Quality deer management promotes healthy animals, a good habitat, and good hunting. It is not an indictment of traditional methods of managing deer. In fact, traditional methods have produced the abundant herds that are now enjoyed by hunter and nonhunter alike. In many cases, quality management is simply taking the next step in the management of the herd where you hunt.

Probably the most important aspect of quality deer management is changing hunters from consumers into managers. Respect for the quarry bestows an obligation upon the hunter to practice sound management. Quality deer management (QDM) is becoming widely accepted in the eastern United States. The philosophy began during the late 1960s in Texas. *Producing Quality Whitetails,* a 1975 landmark book by Al Brothers and Murphy E. Ray, Jr., outlined the management concepts. More recent research around the country has shown the importance of age structure and sex ratio in herd management. QDM is receiving increasing attention in magazine articles, in seminars, and through the Quality Deer Management Association. A desire for the opportunity to hunt mature white-tailed bucks has led many hunters to ask, "Should I consider QDM on my lands?" Clearly, quality deer management is not appropriate for everyone or in every situation. This chapter examines the pros and cons of QDM to help you determine whether it's right for your situation.

BENEFITS OF QUALITY DEER MANAGEMENT
The chance to hunt mature white-tailed bucks initially attracts most hunters to QDM. Research has shown that QDM can increase the number of older bucks, especially 2½- and 3½-year-old animals. This is only one of the potential benefits. Many hunters have discovered that QDM provides experiences that are far more valuable than simply harvesting a buck with large antlers. Often, the greatest satisfactions are provided by monitoring changes in the condition of the deer, improved hunting safety and ethics, and opportunities to learn about deer behavior and management.

Changes in Herd Condition
Reducing herd density through antlerless harvests (when necessary) and increasing the age structure of bucks by restraint in harvest of immature bucks (1½-year-olds) typically improves the overall condition of the herd. Increases in average body weights, antler size, and reproductive rates generally can be detected after two to three years. Less obvious benefits may include having mature bucks for breeding and thereby placing less stress on yearlings, an earlier and more defined rut, and a more balanced adult sex ratio. These factors create a natural social balance within the herd where mature bucks will do most of the breeding. The presence of older bucks and their signposts (rubs and scrapes) may suppress the competitiveness and libido of younger bucks. Lower testosterone levels should result in decreased weight loss during the rut and allow young bucks to grow to greater size before they begin breeding. The philosophy of maintaining a natural density and social balance within deer herds should appeal to non-hunters as well as hunters. This represents sound stewardship of a valuable natural resource.

Changes in Hunting Experiences
Many sportsmen practicing QDM will remember the first time they did *not* shoot an antlered buck that they normally would have taken. Most often this will be a yearling, but sometimes older bucks must

For hunters just beginning quality deer management, the frustration of not taking a buck often is eased by seeing deer as never before. Breeding season behaviors, such as rubbing, scraping, and sparring, may become common sights under quality deer management. COURTESY UNIVERSITY OF GEORGIA, WARNELL SCHOOL OF FOREST RESOURCES.

be passed depending on harvest guidelines. The frustration of not taking the buck often is rewarded by observation of deer behavior never before seen by the hunter. The "unshootable" buck may make a rub or scrape, spar with another buck of similar size that magically appears, or submissively retreat at the approach of a mature buck. QDM allows the hunter to learn about deer, their habits, and the interaction between hunter and quarry. It represents a change in philosophy for many hunters as they begin to measure the success of the hunt in terms of the experience, the enjoyment of nature, and the appreciation of man's role in its processes.

Increased Skills for Hunters
Selective harvest of does and antlered bucks under QDM requires hunters who can identify individual animals and understand deer behavior and ecology. Hunters must be able to distinguish does, fawns, yearling bucks, intermediate aged bucks (2½ and 3½ years old), and mature bucks (4½ years and older). This requires an understanding of how body size, shape, and other features are related to sex and age of the animals. Understanding behavior related to age, sex, breeding status, and social status also aids identification and increases opportunities to observe and harvest animals.

A more knowledgeable hunter is not only able to select appropriate animals for harvest but is more capable of understanding the biology and management of the species. This understanding likely will foster communication between the hunter and the biologist who manages the resource. The more knowledgeable hunter also is better able to communicate the importance of proper deer management to nonhunters. This is critical if hunting and proper deer management are to survive for future generations.

Promotion of Hunter Ethics
Quality deer management requires that hunters identify individual deer before deciding whether to shoot. This should greatly decrease the chance of mistaken identity or hitting the wrong target. As deer populations continue to increase and spread into areas where crop and yard depredations and automobile accidents are common, society's need for deer management will increase. Under QDM, herds usually are kept at lower densities than under traditional management practices, thus reducing crop damage and collisions.

As deer populations in many parts of the United States have increased over the past several decades, deer-vehicle collisions and crop damage have become significant problems. Quality management, with its emphasis on antlerless harvests to maintain healthy populations, can ease these problems. PHOTOGRAPH BY JOE HAMILTON.

QDM affords hunters the opportunity to learn about deer, their habits, and the interaction between hunter and quarry. The more a hunter knows, the more he or she respects the animal and the greater the focus on the experience rather than the number or size of animals harvested. Conversations with fellow hunters become focused on what is seen and left rather than what is killed. Landowners and clubs can be better neighbors when they unite to have areas large enough for QDM. The pride and feeling of giving provide a satisfaction that is the most important value fostered by QDM.

POTENTIAL DRAWBACKS TO QUALITY DEER MANAGEMENT
A common misconception under QDM is that fewer deer will be taken. Fewer antlered bucks will be taken initially, but the harvest of antlerless deer will, in many cases, exceed the usual numbers. Depending on the current condition of the herd, the change in harvest generally should balance the sex ratio and reduce density. Herd reduction often results in increased reproduction and fawn recruitment. The annual harvest of bucks should increase with time while the harvest of antlerless deer is stabilized or decreased. Ultimately, desired herd and harvest sex ratios will be established.

Many hunters initially worry that management success will invite illegal hunting. A property's reputation for big deer entices poachers. Isolation and access control help, but other measures can secure property. Boundaries should be marked clearly. Make sure all hunters and landowners report violations. Most conservation officers will go the extra mile to help hunters who report and prosecute violators. Get to know your local officers and inform them of your management program.

In areas where hunting rights are leased, a common fear is that more affluent hunters will take over once a quality herd is established. There is no guarantee that this will not happen, but most landowners recognize the importance of having a quality management program and ethical hunters on their property. There are obvious advantages to the landowner in having a sustained financial yield from a group with long-term, vested interests in the property and the deer herd. Some landowners have sought top dollar for hunting rights, only to have their herd quality eliminated in one or two years. These unethical hunters abandon the property to seek other unsuspecting landowners. "Puddle jumping" has hurt quality deer management and hunting in general.

Quality deer management is designed to produce a more balanced adult sex ratio and usually a lower herd density. These changes often result in increased reproduction and fawn recruitment. Under favorable conditions, most adult does should produce and raise two fawns. PHOTOGRAPH BY GERALD MOORE.

QUALITY DEER MANAGEMENT FAILURES

The most common failure of quality management occurs when groups with small tracts surrounded by heavily hunted areas try to go it alone. Even under optimum conditions, the return on passing up young bucks is not 100 percent. Dispersal, natural mortality, and illegal hunting lower the return. This "cost" varies with management conditions.

Quality management also fails when a group decides during the summer to begin a quality management program, then reverts to a traditional buck harvest during the season. Good intentions are abandoned quickly without strong leadership.

Quality management sometimes does not appear to have improved the herd because the group did not allow enough time to accomplish objectives. The lag time between initiating a plan and obtaining obvious results often creates dissension within a group. Patience is necessary among quality deer managers because a plan may require five years or more to yield full benefits.

One of the goals of quality deer management is to reduce hunting mortality of young bucks like this yearling. On small tracts surrounded by heavy hunting pressure, this may be impossible unless you can persuade hunters on adjoining properties to join the management program. PHOTOGRAPH BY KENT KAMMERMEYER; COURTESY UNIVERSITY OF GEORGIA, D. B. WARNELL SCHOOL OF FOREST RESOURCES.

DEFINING REALISTIC OBJECTIVES

Realistic expectations should be stressed. Harvesting a record-book buck is the dream of nearly every hunter, but quality management goals should be set with the local herd in mind. Managing a deer herd to produce bucks like those in the stories told by the old-timers from your area is a more realistic goal. Remember too, though, that recollections of big "mossy-horned" bucks are often exaggerated; as a quality herd is established, participants should avoid letting expectations exceed the capabilities of the habitat.

Quality management participants are confounded by normal fluctuations in harvest success and deer activity during a hunting season and from year to year. Hunters must understand the dynamic nature of deer hunting and the activity patterns of deer. For instance, during periods of minimal or nocturnal activity, hunters might assume that deer have been overharvested. Lulls in deer activity during daylight can result from the effects of season, weather, abundant food supplies, or hunter activity. For example, deer are not active around food plots or openings when acorns are plentiful, so hunting in those areas is not productive. Understanding deer behavior and habitat use is critical to reaching quality management goals.

There have been numerous attempts at QDM across the United States in recent years. Many have been successful and greatly increased the quality of hunting; others have been equally disappointing. Disagreement over goals and unrealistic expectations are usually to blame. Biological, land use, and legal constraints also can diminish effectiveness. These factors must be considered in the development of QDM programs so that realistic objectives can be set and proper assessments made.

Biological Constraints

Soil fertility, land ownership patterns, genetic composition, and other factors can limit antler development. Nearly everyone who begins a QDM program does so with the hope of increasing buck age structure and antler size. The relative potential increase in antler size varies greatly by locality.

Area-specific biological constraints must be considered, especially in terms of antler development. In managing for a natural herd structure and quality hunting, however, biological constraints are less important.

Land Use Constraints

The most common question is "What is the minimum acreage necessary for participating in this type of program?" Minimum acreage is based on a variety of factors including shape of the property, access (public and private), access control, degree of illegal hunting, membership, method of hunting, habitat diversity, habitat quality, land use, and hunting pressure on neighboring properties. Each factor should be considered before initiating a quality management program.

Even on good range with the genetic potential to produce large antlers, QDM can be limited by land use. Some of the most fertile soils in the United States are farmed, inundated by reservoirs, or developed. In agricultural areas, deer commonly cross property boundaries, feeding on crops of one owner and bedding in thick areas of another. Thus, hunting on one property may have a tremendous impact on the density and age structure of the deer herd on another.

The physical characteristics of the land where you hunt will dictate the involvement in quality management and its outcome. Management depends upon long-range planning and should be compatible with land-use practices and goals of the owner. Forest management practices such as harvesting, prescribed fire, and thinning can affect the nutrition and behavior of deer. In particular, harvesting large areas (50 acres or more) can have a major impact on deer movement. Layout and extent of roads and access control also can be problems associated with land use.

Properties involved in quality management can be hurt by activities on neighboring tracts. Therefore, a relatively small tract with all the right circumstances can be managed as successfully as a large tract with marginal elements or poor habitat. The size and shape of a property should be viewed from a number of perspectives before a quality management plan is initiated. Hunters using quality deer management guidelines should maintain communication with other hunters and neighboring groups. Hunters who are aware of a successful quality management program are more inclined to adopt similar guidelines. This is the beginning of a "cooperative," the value of which is obvious. All deer hunters desire the opportunity to hunt a mature buck. It is in the best interest of adjoining groups to employ similar guidelines when they have a common goal.

A number of cooperatives in the Southeast have grown to 100,000 acres. Cooperatives are appearing in other regions as well. Management objectives and regulations may vary from one group to another, but all share the quest for better-quality deer.

Legal Constraints

Hunting regulations can hamper QDM efforts. Season lengths, bag limits, and antlerless seasons vary by state and within states and can dictate options for achieving QDM objectives. In many southeastern states, deer seasons last several weeks with bag limits of five or more, and there are liberal antlerless deer seasons. Several states have deer management assistance programs administered by wildlife and fisheries agencies that allow the harvest of antlerless deer by permit over a period of several weeks. This is ideal for QDM on hunting club lands. Club members and guests generally can harvest an adequate number of antlerless deer to change the herd. In many northeastern, north central, and midwestern states, seasons may be one or two weeks long with a one- or two-deer limit. These regulations can target antlerless harvests on a regionwide or even countywide basis, but they can leave little room for more precise harvest quotas on small land holdings.

Archery and muzzle-loading seasons also are set for antlerless harvests in some states. Regulations may need to be evaluated and modified for QDM to work on most private properties in some of these states. Such changes are often difficult to implement and will require sustained broad-based support by a large number of sportsmen.

QDM on Public Hunting Areas

Although QDM is most easily practiced on private lands, the philosophy has such broad appeal that it is beginning to appear on public lands. Mississippi, South Carolina, Georgia, and Wisconsin have public areas under quality management. The Sandhill Wildlife Area near Babcock, Wisconsin, has been managed as a research area since 1974, exploring innovation in managing deer and hunters (see chapter 14). Georgia is experimenting with QDM on a countywide basis. Regulations state that bucks must have a minimum 15-inch outside spread to be legal game in Dooly County. These regulations will be enforced for three years beginning with the 1993 season to determine whether they will increase the buck age structure. This remarkable experiment may be a landmark in the QDM movement, since law enforcement officials, the judiciary, local politicians, landowners, and sportsmen have united in a large-scale management effort. In a survey of landowners and sportsmen, 70 percent of the respondents favored restricting buck harvest to mature animals.

THE BOTTOM LINE

So, should you consider QDM on the land where you hunt? If you can answer yes to the following questions, then QDM may be right for you:

1. Do you have enough acreage to manage your deer population without being severely affected by hunting pressure on adjacent properties? If not, will your neighbors join you and possibly others in forming a cooperative quality management area?

2. Is the habitat on your hunting property good enough to produce and maintain healthy deer? If not, do you and your hunting companions have the funds, equipment, and commitment to manage it?

3. Do the deer-hunting rules and regulations in your state allow you enough leeway to manage your herd? Does your state wildlife agency have a deer management assistance program, an antlerless deer quota program, or similar programs that encourage sound deer management and allow some flexibility in obtaining adequate female harvests?

4. Do you and your companions have realistic expectations regarding a quality deer management program?

5. Are you and your companions prepared to commit to a long-term management program?

If your answer is yes to all of these questions, quality deer management may be for you.

—Joe Hamilton,
W. Matt Knox, and
David C. Guynn, Jr.

CHAPTER 2

Starting Out

If our profession can give valuable service on strings of quail preserves, why not to other game species . . . ? At least one reason harks back, I think, to a lack of respect for private property. In most regions the public puts all landowners, large and small, under moral suasion not to post. The public does not realize that this is moral suasion not to manage.

—ALDO LEOPOLD (1940)
Journal of Wildlife Management

Wildlife management is a three-legged stool. One leg represents habitat management, the second population manipulation, and the third people management. This chapter will discuss how to begin a QDM program, including habitat evaluation and planning, record keeping, and assessing initial herd and habitat conditions.

GOAL SETTING

The goal of QDM is to maintain a healthy and productive deer herd with natural sex and age structures. But because of the realities of management, it often is not possible to totally achieve this goal. Nevertheless, it is important to assess each situation and establish realistic objectives. In many areas, sex and age structures have been skewed by years of high buck-only harvest rates, which often exceed 70 percent of the total buck population annually.

The first step in QDM is a firm decision on goals. No management program will succeed otherwise. Then you should turn to dealing with the three aspects of management.

HABITAT

From the time of Aldo Leopold, textbook definitions of wildlife management always include the phrase "the art and science of." No aspect

19

of the field demands more the artisan's hand than habitat management. Habitat is the key to white-tailed deer management, and being able to understand its role is paramount to achieving your goals.

A respected range scientist once remarked, "There are a great number of animal husbandrists, but very few range managers!" This meant that it is one thing to understand the basic husbandry of a species but another to fully understand how that species functions in its ecosystem.

This certainly is true with white-tailed deer. In spite of many years of research and extension effort, many hunters still do not draw the connection between habitat and herd health. Habitat generally is thought of as "space," rather than assemblages of food and cover. This "parking lot mentality" causes many problems for professional managers and hunters. If space remains, there must be room for more deer!

One common question is "How many deer will this land carry?" Even some biologists think of deer in terms of so many per square mile, rather than stocking level. Two parcels within a mile's distance may have two disparate population densities, yet in both cases be fully stocked. Assessing stocking level will be discussed later.

Whether it be corn, wheat, timber, or white-tailed deer, the real resource we must work with is the land. Land is the one unchanging commodity in resource management. Yet, there often is a poor understanding of the land-vegetation-animal relationship. In Germany, Ueckermann (1951) developed a site index for roe deer *(Capreolus capreolus)*. Although a site index is a common concept in forestry, used for rating productive potential of various soils and sites (Sharpe et al. 1986), prior to Ueckermann it had not been applied to wildlife.

For timber, a ninety site index, with a base age of fifty years, means a forester can expect the average tree planted today to be 90 feet tall at fifty years of age. Another area may have a site index of only seventy, indicating a tree of only 70 feet in height at the same age. Obviously, a higher site index indicates greater productive potential and allows the forest manager to set management strategies. In fact, the difference between a seventy and ninety site index is a tremendous increase in potential income.

Applying this concept to roe deer, Ueckermann examined several site and habitat conditions, relating these to abundance, weights, and antler conditions. He found forest type, soil fertility, and land use as the major factors in determining productivity, body size, and antler development. Many years later, Jacobson et al. (1981) reported a similar relationship, where body weights of whitetails in Mississippi were

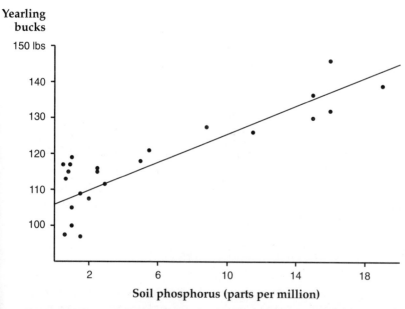

In twenty-three areas in Mississippi, average deer body weights correlated with soil phosphorus levels. This relationship led to the development of a "site index" management concept for deer. If the manager knows the inherent potential of a site, he should be able to predict the average weight of the deer on that area. Weights below the predicted line mean the herd is overpopulated (Jacobson et al. 1981).

related to phosphorus in the soil. Numerous other researchers have reported on relationships between soil and site conditions and herd productivity, body condition, and antler quality. Hence, the site index, as applied by Ueckermann, has merit with whitetails.

Site quality is directly reflected in forage quality. The amount of quality forage is directly related to the number of deer that can be produced on a specific property (Adams 1984). In fact, some deer biologists suggest whitetails need no more than 30 percent cover; once this is provided, habitat quality is best evaluated by the amount of nutritious forage available year-round. For example, the Midwest supports plenty of high-quality whitetails, while the predominant land use is agriculture, interspersed with small woodlots and fencerows.

The high productivity of some southeastern states can be directly related to soybean agriculture, so the amount of high-quality food, natural and cultivated, will determine the productive capacity of land. The use of agricultural plantings specifically for whitetails has increased in popularity (Evans 1989, Higginbotham and Kroll in press).

Goals should depend on the evaluation of habitat. Ranking of habitat will first depend on the site index, since highly fertile soils can be the most productive deer habitat. Next are land use considerations, such as type of forest cover and forest stand species composition, stand age and density, and agricultural practices. Cover types also are important. In general, the greater the diversity of habitat, the better. Certain cover types can be extremely important in different regions of the country. In the Far North, winter yarding cover such as white cedar swamps may be a key habitat. Water placement and prickly pear cactus may be key habitats in the arid Southwest; bottomland hardwood and streamside management zones elsewhere. Lands with the greatest agricultural and timber values also have the highest value for deer. It is land use that ultimately determines deer stocking levels.

DEVELOPING A RECORD-KEEPING SYSTEM

Landowners often make two management mistakes. First, few have well-defined goals for their management programs, often changing activities to suit the immediate situation. Second, there seems to be a general reluctance to keep adequate records on the deer herd and habitat practices. Record keeping is tedious, yet except for goal setting, it is the most important aspect of whitetail management.

If possible, to assess progress toward goals, you should acquire the following:

1. Harvest records, including age, weight, antler measurements, and evidence of lactation.

2. Census and incidental sightings of sex, fawn crop, approximate age, and antler quality.

3. Annual records of forest management practices, agricultural plantings, and so forth.

Often it is not possible to obtain all of this information. At the very least, you should obtain harvest data and maintain records of habitat treatments or changes.

Other biological data such as kidney fat index, fetal and *corpora lutea* counts, abomasal parasite counts, and blood chemistry also can aid in decision making but require special equipment and expertise.

Harvest Data

To acquire accurate harvest data, a check station should be constructed in a convenient location on the property or in a place convenient to

SEASON: 19___ –___   CONTACT PERSON:_____

HUNTING CLUB:_____   PHONE: AC_____-_____

| Deer # | Date | Sex | Age | Weight (pounds) | | Antler Measurements (inches) | | | | | | Doe in Milk (Yes/No) | Hunter | Comments |
				Live	Dressed	Points	L. Beam Circum.	R. Beam Circum.	L. Beam Length	R. Beam Length	Inside Spread			

Data on white-tailed deer harvested from management areas keep the program on track.
Courtesy Institute for White-tailed Deer Management and Research, College of Forestry, Stephen F. Austin State University.
All other rights reserved.

hunters from two or more neighboring properties. A check station can be as complex as a screened building with walk-in cooler or as simple as a tree with a small metal roof, scale, and record-keeping materials. Still, the management program is only as effective as the quality of data collected. Materials and equipment needed at a check station include the following:

1. Scales or weight tape.
2. Jaw spreader and extractor.
3. Shears.
4. Marking materials for jawbones.
5. Weather-proof storage for jaws.
6. Record-keeping forms.

Age Structure

It is important to age whitetails, for many reasons. Harvested deer must be aged to obtain a reasonable representation of age structure. Vital statistics such as body weight, antler measures, fetal numbers,

Guidelines for a Successful Hunting Club

In many areas, deer hunters use private lands where hunting rights are either leased or tightly controlled. The individuals hunting on such property usually form hunting clubs. Club organization varies from group to group; however, for quality deer management to be successful, a number of guidelines should be followed.

HUNT CLUB CHARACTERISTICS

The number of participants (hunters) and the hunting schedule should be considered when establishing harvest goals. Strong and impartial club leadership is important; dissension can occur when management guidelines are vague or when rules are routinely disregarded. Visiting hunters or guests lacking a vested interest in the management program are likely to impede progress toward quality management objectives.

The focal point of hunting activities is the clubhouse or hunt camp. Facilities range from simple to elaborate and usually reflect club size, season length, and the number of deer harvested. They may contain walk-in coolers, large freezers, and equipment for processing venison.

The meeting location is also the setting for harvest data collection. A quality management program should be run like a business with accurate harvest records used to monitor management results. Items needed include jawbone shears, jawbone extractor, and an accurate set of scales.

Harvest data should include the date, time, weapon, hunt

method, sex, live weight and dressed weight, number of points of one inch or more, antler spread (inside or outside), main beam length (right antler), main beam circumference (circumference one inch above the antler burr), age (jawbone), reproductive data (from adult females), hunter's name, and any appropriate comments. Harvest data should be collected from each deer harvested on the property, especially on those bucks that will be mounted.

CLUB BYLAWS

Quality management groups should draft and adopt a set of bylaws. Items to be addressed include membership requirements, annual dues, payment dates and methods, hunt schedule, hunt method, property maintenance, guest policy, expulsion policy, harvest guidelines (antlered buck and antlerless deer harvest criteria), habitat management guidelines (what to plant, when, and where), and a list of penalties to be imposed for harvesting an incorrect deer, for misses, and for crippling.

Although fines are punitive in action and may appear unnecessary, some mechanism should be established that deters hunters from harvesting "protected" animals. During the first several years of a quality management program, fines are often the most effective deterrent. The higher a fine, the greater the effect. As the program gains momentum, peer pressure will begin to replace fines as a strong preventative. The financial penalty assessed for harvesting a button buck will become much less painful than the good-natured ridicule of fellow hunters. Money generated from fines should be put into the treasury and used for special projects and purchases (e.g., gates, boundary posting, or habitat development).

—Joe Hamilton,
W. Matt Knox, and
David C. Guynn, Jr.

and lactation have little meaning unless matched to age class. In time, knowing the age structure allows the reconstruction of deer populations to help set harvest goals. Finally, hunters and managers alike must learn to recognize different age classes of bucks in the field. As the hunter-consumer becomes the hunter-manager, his role in maintaining a more natural deer herd increases.

Severinghaus (1949) first reported white-tailed deer could be aged with reasonable accuracy by tooth wear and replacement patterns. Deer and other mammals also can be aged by counting the *cementum annuli* in cross sections of teeth, either incisors or molars (Gilbert 1966, Lockard 1972, Sauer 1973, Bell 1974). After years of testing these procedures, however, the Severinghaus technique remains the most common, since the *cementum annuli* method requires laboratory procedures and equipment. This discussion will be limited to aging by tooth wear and replacement.

Aging by Tooth Wear and Replacement

The lower jaws should be removed from every harvested animal as soon as possible. It is tempting for hunters to take an animal from the premises with the intention of removing the jaw later, but few of these jaws ever are returned to the manager, reducing effectiveness of record keeping.

Removal of the lower jaw is simple and best accomplished by having the equipment available at the check station. Jaws may be removed with the extractor and shears or simply by cutting the lower jaw from the skull. The jaw extractor (Marshall et al. 1964) can be fabricated from quarter-inch iron reinforcing bar or obtained commercially from a vendor such as Forestry Suppliers, Inc., in Jackson, Mississippi. Once jaws are extracted, they should be cleaned of most tissue, tagged, and dried. Each jaw should be given a number corresponding to that recorded in the field data record book. They can be labeled by writing directly on the jaw with an indelible marker or by attaching a waterproof paper or metal tag. Jaws should be aged by the local biologist at regular intervals or after the hunting season. In either case, they should be stored in well-ventilated containers—no plastic bags or sealed containers. A wire screen-covered box or fish basket protects jaws while providing adequate drying conditions.

The teeth on each side of an adult lower jaw consist of three incisors, one canine, three premolars, and three molars. The eruption and wear on the premolars and molars normally are used to determine age

(Severinghaus 1949). Fawns are born with (or obtain shortly after birth) three deciduous premolars known commonly as milk teeth. All permanent teeth are acquired by 18 to 24 months of age, depending on geographic location and condition of the deer.

Since most deer are born in the late spring or early summer and hunted in the fall, ages usually are assigned in increments of half years. Although there are published studies showing eruption and wear patterns in younger individuals at monthly intervals, this is unnecessary. The following aging discussion as published by Kroll (1991) is limited to half-year age classes.

If the lower jaw has fewer than five "jaw teeth" (three premolars and two fully erupted molars), the deer is less than 1 year of age and should be classified a fawn. This age class also is easily distinguished by the small size of the jaw. If the deer is not a fawn, examine the third jaw tooth (last premolar). In fawns and yearlings, this tooth is unlike any other, containing three cusps. The soft, deciduous nature of these teeth may cause confusion, since they often are worn smooth by 18 to 20 months. Therefore, even if the first three jaw teeth are well worn, look carefully at the third tooth. If it has three cusps, the deer is a yearling, called so because it is about 18 months of age. Occasionally, late fawning dates or poor nutrition result in some yearlings not having a fully erupted third molar. If, however, the deer has three premolars and two fully erupted molars, it should be classified as a yearling, not a fawn.

Deer with six jaw teeth where the third tooth does not have three cusps are normally older than 1½ years. The first three teeth generally are replaced with permanent teeth containing the normal two-cusp structure between 18 and 30 months of age. Frequently yearlings are harvested with two cusped molars that have just replaced the three-cusped third premolar. These are distinguished from two-year-old deer by the lack of stain and wear on the premolars, compared with the molars in the mouth. Additionally, the premolars may not be completely erupted. Since the fourth tooth (first molar) is added before shedding of the premolars, it is the oldest jaw tooth and will remain so throughout the life of the deer. This is the tooth to examine next.

The jaw teeth of deer, and all mammals, have two layers (Weichert 1970)—an inner core of brownish dentine covered with a hard white enamel layer. The teeth become increasingly worn as the deer chews. Since the cusps are cone shaped, wear exposes more and more dentine. The relative amount of dentine exposed can be used as an indicator of

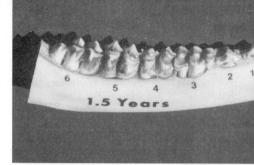

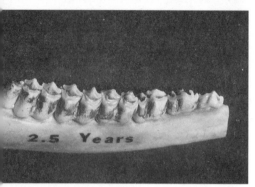

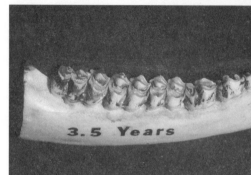

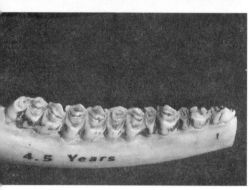

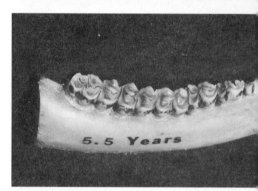

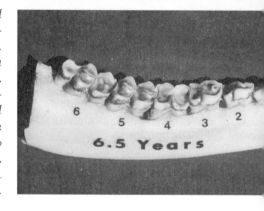

White-tailed deer are best aged using the tooth wear and replacement method of Severinghaus (1949). Generally, deer are aged in one of seven categories: fawn, yearling, 2½-year-old, 3½-year-old, 4½-year-old, 5½-year-old, and 6½ years old and older.

age in older deer. For example, if the third tooth has only two cusps and is stained, the deer is not a yearling. Examine the oldest tooth, the fourth (first molar), comparing the relative widths of dentine (brown) and enamel (white) of cusps on the lingual (tongue) side of the jaw. If the dentine is not wider than the enamel, wear has not progressed and the animal should be classified as 2 ½ years old.

If, however, the fourth tooth shows considerable wear, the deer is older than 2 ½ years. Examine the next oldest tooth, the fifth (second molar). Again, relative widths of dentine and enamel on the lingual side cusps should be compared. If the dentine is not wider than the enamel layer, the animal is 3 ½ years old. If the dentine of the fifth tooth is wider than the enamel on the lingual side cusp, examine the sixth tooth (last molar) using the same criteria. If the lingual side cusps are sharp, with dentine not wider than the enamel, the deer is 4 ½ years of age. If not, the deer is at least 5 ½ years old. Return to the fourth tooth and examine the relative amount of enamel remaining in the center of the tooth. If the tooth has become so worn that little enamel remains in the center of the tooth, the deer is 6 ½ years old. If not, the deer is 5 ½ years of age.

It is possible to age a deer beyond 6 ½ years but this is rarely necessary. Many managers combine all deer 6 ½ years or older into a single classification.

Age-class categories used to evaluate a deer population should be based on intensity of management. Decisions for QDM, in most situations, can be made using three age categories: fawn, yearling, and 2 ½+ years. Accuracy for these limited classifications is high. For intensive management programs, however, aging individuals through the 6 ½+ category can be helpful, particularly if population reconstruction is used.

Problems in Evaluating Harvest Age Structure

Age structure of the herd is important in making management decisions. A herd composed primarily of young animals usually indicates either a growing deer population or a heavy harvest. A very old age structure most likely indicates an inadequate harvest. For more intensive management programs, age data collected over many years can even be used to reconstruct minimum populations at a given time. These estimates include only harvested animals, not deer that died of natural causes. Population reconstruction can be used, however, to determine whether one sex is being underharvested in relation to the other in order to obtain a minimum population estimate and to establish harvest goals.

There are limitations presented by hunter-harvested animals. Do they represent a true picture of population age structure? The accompanying figure presents a comparison of age structure determined from Texas Parks and Wildlife Department storage locker surveys, hunting club reports, and random deer collections by the Institute for White-Tailed Deer Management and Research for the Pineywoods Ecological Region of Texas (Kroll unpublished data). Hunting club and random collection data were obtained from the same privately managed properties in East Texas.

Note that age structure from TPWD and hunting club records is strikingly similar while age structure obtained from random collec-

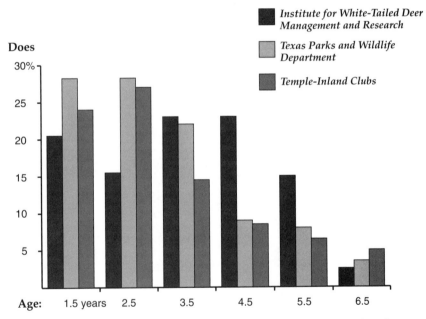

Population age structure of harvested animals in an area can be strongly influenced by sampling method. In this example, three sources of data were used to depict doe age structure in East Texas: hunting clubs on Temple-Inland, Inc., lands, Texas Parks and Wildlife Department cold-storage data, and random collections by the Institute for White-tailed Deer Management and Research. Note the disparity among results from the three types of data.

tions is completely different. Clearly, older animals (4 to 5 years) are better at evading hunters than younger, naive ones. When coupled with hunter inexperience, bias must be considered.

Hunter bias is determined by many factors, especially hunting techniques common to an area. For example, hunting from blinds over bait is not only legal but acceptable in Texas. In other areas, hunting over bait is illegal although hunting over food plots or salt is not. These methods tend to bias harvest in favor of younger deer—both does and bucks. Still, age structure data can be very useful in making management decisions, especially when combined with other tools. Decisions should never be based on a single factor, no matter how much confidence you may have in it.

Weight Data
Weights are a good indicator of herd condition, especially weights of fawns and yearlings. Live weight is much more variable than "field-dressed" weight. Since the rumen of deer is relatively large, a full rumen can add several pounds to live weight. The same animal would weigh considerably less if taken with an empty rumen. Because live weight can be more variable, it requires larger sample sizes than dressed weight to establish similar confidence in the data for management interpretation. Dressed weights can be estimated from live weights by using the following conversion factors: fawns, 0.73; adult females, 0.76; and adult males, 0.78. Conversely, to determine live weights from dressed weights, multiply fawn dressed weights by 1.37, adult female weights by 1.32, and males by 1.28.

Probably the most useful piece of equipment for deer management is a good weight scale. Periodically recalibrate your scale with a known weight. Stress placed on a scale by repeatedly dropping or hoisting a deer carcass can alter accuracy by as much as 10 pounds.

Heart-girth equations and tapes can be used to estimate both live and dressed weights (Smart et al. 1973, Urbston et al. 1976). Several commercial tapes are available. They are geographically limited, so check the source of the data before relying on such devices.

In general, does reach peak body weight (maturity) by 3½ years, while bucks do not reach mature weight until 4½ years. Although mature body weight is a good indicator of herd health, it is far more revealing to examine dressed weights of fawns and yearlings. Each geographic area appears to have different optimum weights for these

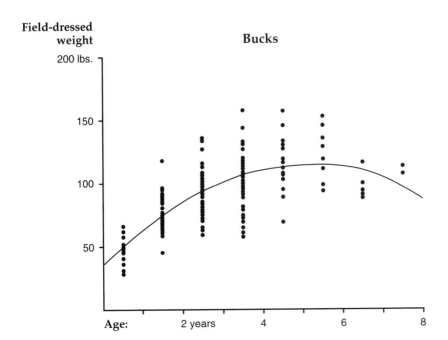

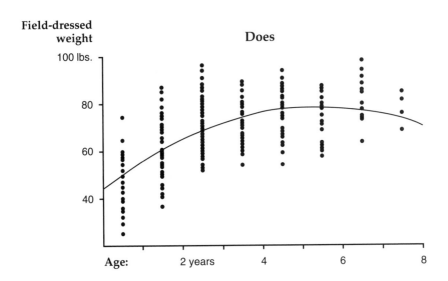

Does generally reach mature weight at around
3½ years. Males mature at about 4½ years.
(Data from Kroll, unpublished)

age classes. For example, in northern deer, it is not uncommon for a yearling buck to field-dress at 120 pounds, while the same age class for some areas in the South may weigh only 80 pounds. In both situations, weights represent healthy individuals, realizing their true growth potential. It is important to know what average dressed weights for healthy fawns and yearlings from *your* area should be. The state conservation agency can help, since most evaluate herd condition as part of routine studies.

The manager can compare trends from year to year by maintaining records on weights. This is yet another decision-making tool. Use of a chart for evaluating management progress based on dressed weights is recommended (Kroll 1991). QDM participants should establish a "quality zone" for their area and aim management goals at maintaining dressed weights within the zone. Again, goal setting is the key to success.

Problems in Interpreting Weight Data

As with other indicators of herd health, weight data can be biased. *When* the animal is harvested has a great impact on its dressed weight. In many areas, the season occurs early in the fall (October and November) and lasts only a few days or weeks. Dressed weights present little problems to interpretation in such areas. But in areas such as South Carolina, where the season may extend from August to late winter, weight data can vary greatly over the hunting season; therefore, you should select a consistent time frame to compare weights from one year to the next.

Another problem is selective harvesting. On properties where selected bucks are being removed as part of a culling program, weights will not be typical for the herd. There also may be an inherent bias in doe harvest data. Hunters often pick the largest doe to harvest, presumably to get more meat or to reduce the risk of taking a button (fawn) buck. If these biases remain constant from one year to the next, they are not serious problems.

Antler Development and Measurements

The record-keeping form discussed earlier allows collection of antler measurements. Size of antlers increases rapidly until about 5½ years (see chapter 7), after which most antler measurements tend to level off. Average number of points is perhaps the poorest indicator of age; beam length and antler spread are the best (Kroll 1991).

Basic antler measurements should include number of typical and nontypical points, basal circumference, beam length, and inside and outside spread. These should be taken for each antler and designated on the record form as left and right.

Additionally, many managers collect the standard measurements used in trophy-scoring systems. The Boone and Crockett (B&C) and the Pope and Young systems remain the standards for most deer hunters; there is little indication this will change. Other systems have been developed, but they have gained little acceptance, although they may better reflect herd condition within individual areas than the B&C system.

Scoring forms for the Big Game Awards publications (Nesbitt and Wright 1985) are obtained from the Boone and Crockett Club. Bucks are arbitrarily classified as "typical" or "nontypical," based on the number and length of their abnormal antler points. Bucks usually produce an antler with a main beam and several typical points or tines growing upward from the beam. Abnormal points may grow from these tines or from the main beam.

In measuring antlers by the B&C system (Nesbitt and Wright 1985), a tape with ⅛-inch increments should be used. Measurements should be rounded to the nearest ⅛ inch. Each antler is measured separately for symmetry comparison with the corresponding antler measurement. The first two measurements are inside spread and greatest spread at the widest points. Inside spread is taken at a right angle to the centerline of the skull at the widest point between main beams. This can be aided by using a carpenter's square. Greatest spread does not figure into the final score, rather serving for identification if necessary later. Often, there will be abnormal points (kickers, stickers, cheaters, and so forth) protruding from the primary tines. These should be included in the greatest spread.

The next measurement is beam length, taken from the point of attachment with the pedicel ("burr") to the center of the beam tip. The measurement should be taken along the outside curve of the beam, as this gives the animal the most credit for length.

Primary tines are measured from a line inscribed across the base of the tine in line with the dorsal surface of the main beam. The measurement extends from this line to the center of the tine tip along the broadest curve of the tine. Primary tines are designated as G tines, derived from the designation on the scoring sheet. The brow tine is G1, while the remaining tines are numbered sequentially G2, G3, and so forth. Only tines more than an inch long and longer than they are wide are considered points.

There are four circumference (H) measurements taken from each antler, whether the buck has eight, ten, twelve, or more primary tines. Erroneous reports of "new world record bucks" originate from a poor understanding of this point. A buck with twelve primary tines is killed and an untrained individual measures circumferences for the base and between all six tines, grossly inflating the score. Circumferences should be measured near the midpoint between each tine (or, in the case of H1, between the burr and G1 tine), but at the point of least circumference. In other words, a pronounced tubercle or swelling on the beam usually is avoided.

When scoring of typical measurements is complete, each side's measurements are compared with the other and any difference is recorded as a deduction. The sum of all deductions then is subtracted from the total score to give a gross typical score.

Abnormal tines are measured after all normal tines and, except for designated nontypical bucks, become deductions to the gross score. In nontypical bucks, the nontypical score is added rather than subtracted to the final score for a total net score. Net score for typical bucks is calculated by subtracting the sum of all extra points from the gross typical score, then adding the inside spread measurement. For nontypicals, the sum of all abnormal points is *added* to the gross typical score and summed with the inside spread for a net score.

To qualify as an official B&C record-book buck, a typical animal must score at least 170, whereas a nontypical must score 195 or greater. Nevertheless, B&C *does* acknowledge lesser bucks in its periodically published record books (Nesbitt and Reneau 1986).

Use of a record-book scoring system, be it B&C, P&Y, Buckhorn, or another, is controversial. There are many who feel use of such systems focuses competition on the wrong aspects of hunting, causes cheating and unethical conduct, and eliminates from competition regions where record bucks cannot be produced.

Consensus will have to come from debate within the scientific and hunting communities, but one point needs comment. Some regions of the country simply do not have the environmental or genetic conditions to produce large-antlered bucks (see chapters 12 and 13). Does not a 110 B&C buck harvested in southern Florida deserve the same credit as a 145 B&C taken in Montana? Although the B&C system probably will remain the standard, a new method may emerge based on geographic potential. Precedent exists in the separation of the Coues' deer *(Odocoileus virginianus couesi)* in the B&C system. This diminutive desert subspecies has small antlers, with a score of 90 B&C being excellent. The point is that QDM participants should establish realistic goals for their area, based on the antler potential of the average, well-nourished mature buck in that region.

Comments on Gross Scores

From a biological perspective, use of a net score is not as useful as gross score, as it is important to measure the amount of antler produced by a particular buck. Since B&C focuses on symmetry rather than antler production, a buck with higher gross score may be rated much lower than one with fewer inches yet greater symmetry. In evaluating bucks and making management decisions, gross score seems more practical.

Antlers as Indicators of Herd Condition

Once goals are established, they can be used as standards or "quality zones" (Kroll 1991) against which to gauge management success. Often the percentage of spike-antlered yearlings has been used as an indicator of herd health, but geographic limitations must be considered. In regions such as south Florida, the vast majority of yearlings always will be spikes, irrespective of the amount of population control and management. Antler quality, like weights, indicates herd health but must be evaluated according to site potential.

Goodrum (1990) presented an excellent example of using antler scoring in evaluating management progress. On the North Boggy Slough Hunting and Fishing Club in Houston County, Texas, the goal of a mature buck with a gross B&C score of 125 was established for QDM. From 1980 to 1990, management strategies were set to reach this goal. In addition to gross B&C scores, lactation rates, dressed weights, and sex and age ratios were used in decision making.

Reproduction Data

Occasionally, biological data should be collected directly from the herd to determine reproductive success and breeding chronology. In most cases, deer must be collected outside the hunting season. Highway kills are used in some states for this purpose and sometimes a scientific collecting permit can be obtained. In some areas, however, does may be far enough along in gestation to allow collection of reproductive information from hunter-harvested deer.

Biologists obtain two types of information from pregnant does.

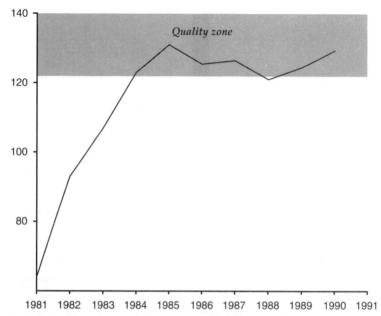

A quality deer management program was initiated on North Boggy Slough Hunting and Fishing Club (Houston County, Texas) in 1980. One goal was for the average harvested buck to score 125 B&C. Additional data such as lactation rates, dressed weights, sex, and age ratios were used in the decision making (Goodrum 1990).

First, crown-rump length (Armstrong 1950) can be used to determine the age of a fetus. Charts and measuring devices are available for determining fetal age, conception date, and parturition date. Backdating to conception, a graphic representation of breeding chronology for the herd can be done if there is an adequate sample size. The width of the breeding curve sometimes reflects herd health. For example, a prolonged breeding period (rut) suggests a herd with distorted buck-to-doe ratios or in poor physical condition. In most cases, well-managed herds will present a definite peak in breeding, lasting only a few weeks. Areas with severe site limitations may always have a prolonged breeding period, no matter the intensity of management.

Ovaries also can be examined. Gross sectioning of the ovary shows *corpora lutea* and *corpora albicans*, both indicators of reproductive performance (Cheatum 1949, Mossman and Duke 1973). *Corpora lutea* (CL) are glandular structures formed after ovulation. Each time an egg is shed, a CL is formed. The CL supports pregnancy. A *corpus albicantium* (CA) is scar tissue from earlier CLs. CLs help estimate breeding timing and reproductive success before fetuses become visible. Since the uterus does not become noticeably swollen until about the twentieth day of pregnancy, CLs provide early indicators of reproduction. CAs sometimes are used to estimate reproductive success of the previous year.

In many cases, it is better to measure reproductive success indirectly, such as by counting harvested does that are lactating. In most areas, deer are harvested during or shortly after the weaning period, so the percentage of lactating does represents a conservative estimate of fall recruitment, assuming each lactating doe has produced at least one fawn. Exceptions would be southern Florida and other portions of the Southeast, including Mississippi and Alabama. In Florida, fawns are born over a long period beginning as early as December; in the other states, fawns are born in late summer to early fall, with spotted fawns commonly seen by hunters during the hunting season.

In regions where fawns are born in May and June, lactation should be recorded for does harvested through mid-December. There is a lot of observer error after this time. In regions where fawns are born later than June, lactation data should be recorded for all does harvested throughout the hunting season.

A lactating doe is identified easily by the appearance of her udder. Glandular tissue is swollen and the teats are enlarged. The teats may be red or callused. Milk is easily seen when the udder is cut.

After all harvest data are collected, the number of lactating yearlings is summed and divided by the number of yearling does harvested, and the total number of lactating does at or more than 2 ½ years of age is divided by the total number of does at or more than 2 ½ years harvested. Biologists differ on interpretation of these data. Some present lactation as a percentage of all does harvested; others prefer the percentage of all mature lactating does (at or more than 2 ½ years). One of the best indicators of herd health, however, is yearling lactation rates. They indicate fawn breeding. Usually, the higher the rate, the better the herd condition. Percentage of lactating does also can be compared with incidental sightings, providing better recruitment estimates.

INCIDENTAL SIGHTINGS

It is easy to maintain records on incidental sightings. When fawns begin to travel with their mothers, record every identifiable deer. This may be

INCIDENTAL DEER OBSERVATION FORM

Club: Boggy Slough Observer: KROLL

County: Houston

DEER SIGHTED

Date	Does	Fawns	Bucks*	Unknown	Remarks
3 Sept	3	2	1	3	8 pt (seeback) - 3-year-old
5 Sept	7	5	2	2	6 pt (1.5); 9 pt (2.5 yrs)
6 Sept	1	1	2	1	10 pt (4.5); 3 pt (1.5 yrs)
9 Sept	8	9	1	0	8 pt (3.5 yrs) - Thin
10 Sept	4	4	0	2	1 fawn spotted

*Record whether spiked or forked

Incidental sightings are excellent for obtaining estimates of doe-fawn and buck-doe ratios as well as herd condition, antler quality, and buck age structure. Data from forms such as this one can gauge the progress of a management program.

January in southern Florida, mid-June in east Texas, or as late as mid-September in the Mississippi Delta. Proper timing should be determined for each area.

At a minimum, record the number of does, fawns, and bucks along with date, time, and any other pertinent information on each visit. This will allow monthly calculation of buck-doe and doe-fawn ratios. Even on small properties, several hundred to a thousand observations can accumulate over a single season.

An experienced hunter-manager also often records the estimated age of bucks, information about antlers, and condition of individual animals. This allows assessments of relative buck age structure and antler quality.

Aging Whitetails in the Field

As noted earlier, it is important to age white-tailed deer in the field as part of population monitoring and decision making. Good luck in hunting is nice, but the hunter always should remember his role as manager. To maintain a quality herd, some animals should be harvested and others left to breed. The decision to harvest a specific buck should be based on more than the size of his antlers.

The QDM hunter should know at least the relative age of each animal taken. Each hunter should ask himself *before* firing the shot or releasing the arrow, "Is this a proper deer to harvest?" A large part of the answer lies in the age of the animal. The ability to age a deer only *after* it is harvested reduces the role of the hunter as a proper deer manager.

Unfortunately, there have been no scientific studies on aging live white-tailed deer; the only available information is anecdotal. With a little practice, the average hunter can distinguish at least three age classes—fawn, yearling, and 2½-year-olds and older.

Fawns. Fawns, especially bucks, often are mistaken for older deer. Lacking fear of humans and being naturally more aggressive than females, "nubbins" are taken in disproportionate numbers. Antlerless harvest figures reported by game agencies include mature does, doe fawns, and buck fawns. Since QDM involves passing up buck fawns as well as yearling bucks, the hunter must learn to recognize fawns. In a well-managed herd, few buck fawns should be taken incidentally as part of the doe harvest.

Fawns are aged by appearance and behavior. Fawns have shorter faces and ears than mature does. The legs of fawns are relatively short compared with depth of body, while does have much longer legs. A fawn's neck also is proportionately shorter than a doe's.

Behavior also is characteristic. Fawns are less wary than mature does and often expose themselves to easy shots. They will almost always be the first to appear on green fields. Further, fawns are much more playful than adults, running and chasing one another in openings while their mothers feed.

Yearlings. Yearlings also are easily identified. These deer, especially bucks, are like human teenagers. Yearling whitetails give the appearance of having abnormally long legs, slender bodies, and long, thin necks. In fact, yearling bucks often look like does with antlers, showing few masculine attributes. Antlers may have two to ten points but rarely exceed 3 inches in basal circumference. Also, yearlings seldom have outside antler spreads or beam lengths greater than 14 inches. The tip-to-tip distance between the ears (held in alert position) of most young bucks is 14 to 15 inches. If a buck has antlers outside its ears, it probably is not a yearling. These measurements may vary from area to area, so set antler criteria for your location.

With enough experience, professionals as well as lay people can age white-tailed deer in the field. This buck was photographed in the wild at 2½ years (a); 3½ years (b); 4½ years (c); 5½ years (d); and 6½ years (e). PHOTOGRAPHS BY MIKE BIGGS.

Yearling bucks seldom have well-developed neck muscles, even during the rut. In herds with balanced sex and age structures, yearling bucks rarely demonstrate dominance except toward other yearling bucks and fawns in feeding areas.

Two-and-one-half-year-old bucks. Bucks change noticeably by 2½ years of age. In many cases, outside antler spread exceeds tip-to-tip ear width. Neck muscles become enlarged and the buck exhibits aggressive behaviors—vigorous antler rubbing, head-up antler displays, elevation of body hair, presentation of the side of the body, and stiff-legged walking. But dominance displays generally are limited to bucks of the same age or younger. These quickly change to submissive postures on approach of an older buck. Also, 2½-year-olds lack the full body development of older bucks.

If the goal is to harvest bucks 2½ years of age or older, the most effective criteria for distinguishing these bucks are outside antler spread and antler beam length. To reduce yearling buck harvests, we recommend a combination of either beam length greater than a certain length (13 to 15 inches in many areas) or antler spread greater than 14 inches. Antler spread is easily judged, but mature bucks may have narrow spreads and a beam length criterion allows these to be harvested. Alternatively, a point rule, such as six points or greater, may protect yearlings in some areas; however, it doesn't protect the best antlered yearlings so we don't recommend it in most situations.

Three-and-one-half-year or older bucks. In management programs in which harvest of older age-class bucks (at or more than 3½ years) is desired, hunters must discriminate among additional age classes. Bucks 3½ years of age look like Thoroughbred racehorses, with well-muscled bodies, thin waists, and long legs. Southern deer with light coats especially reveal body structure. The thicker coats of northern races make it more difficult to determine their body conformation. At any rate, study the base of the neck. In 3½-year-old bucks, although the neck is well developed, there is a distinct separation or structure between the neck and shoulders that is lacking in older bucks.

In most regions, bucks approach mature body size by 4½ years. They have fully muscled bodies with waists equal in width to their chests. For the first time, length of the legs appears equal to body depth and the neck is fully developed. The structure apparent at the point where the neck joins the body for 3½-year-old bucks disappears by 4½ years.

Older bucks present themselves as being mostly shoulders and neck. The abdominal region looks "potbellied" and legs appear to be shorter than the body is deep. Five-and-one-half-year-old bucks are highly dominant and move slowly, swinging their front legs to the side in a slow, stiff-legged walk. In snowy areas, the tracks of an older buck give the impression he is dragging his front hooves in an arched, sideways fashion.

Bucks 6½ years old or older generally look like an old Hereford bull. Their legs appear abnormally short and they walk with a peculiarly slow gait, swinging the front legs to the side. As the buck walks or runs, skin on the shoulder and neck swings loosely. Facial skin also begins to sag and the eyes have a squinty appearance. As with 5½-year-old bucks, the abdomen sags, but there may also be a sway in the line of the back.

CENSUSING WHITE-TAILED DEER

Few aspects of deer management raise greater criticism than census. The general public never has been convinced about the validity of census results. In most cases, census techniques are nothing more than indices to population size, rather than absolute population size. To present them as anything else is improper.

A number of census methods have been studied and proposed for use in white-tailed deer management, including drive, spotlight, strip, time-area, aerial, thermal, and infrared scanning counts; mark-recapture and change-in-ratio estimators; population reconstruction; harvest correlations; browse surveys; and guesses (Downing et al. 1965, Downing 1980). All of these methods are limited in some way.

Perhaps the most common methods are track and spotlight counts (Tyson 1959, Thomas et al. 1964). Track counts require little equipment and manpower but give less information per unit effort than spotlight counts (Kroll 1991). A track count may be more appropriate in some situations, and a spotlight count in others.

Track counts. Track counts are excellent where unpaved roads and sandy soil provide for good tracking. They are especially useful if dense habitat renders spotlights ineffective. A track count is conducted by dragging roads or rights-of-way with a device to smooth the soil, waiting twenty-four hours, then walking or driving the line slowly and counting the number of crossings per mile (Tyson 1959). Track counts assume that deer usually return to the same general location to spend the day and that nocturnal activity is confined to a cruising radius of about one mile. Reports by Thomas et al. (1964), Marchinton and Jeter (1966), Marchinton (1968), Marshall and Whittington (1968), and Downing et al. (1969) suggest average distance between extreme movements ranges from 0.68 to 1.5 miles, with deer seldom leaving their home range even in response to increased food availability or temporary disturbance.

The average population per square mile is derived by dividing the average number of crossings by the average cruising radius for deer in the area. Most managers simply use 1 mile for this value. Therefore, population density estimates are derived using the formula $X_a = T/D_t$ where

X_a = average population per square mile,
T = total number of tracks, and
D_t = total number of miles counted.

Spotlight counts. These also are simple to conduct. A road or right-of-way is traversed by a slow-moving vehicle. One or more observers search for deer with spotlights, usually from the back of the vehicle. The number of deer observed in each 0.1-mile segment is recorded.

The total area sampled may be calculated by two methods. First, an observer can travel the anticipated transect, recording the estimated distance a deer could be seen on each side of the vehicle before the census. Some researchers conduct this portion of the census during daylight, but this may bias results. Second, the driver of the vehicle can call "mark" at each 0.1 mile, at which time each observer records the estimated distance visible on each side of the vehicle. Whatever the method employed, all visibility distances are summed and divided by the total number of estimates to derive the average visibility. From here it is a simple calculation based on number of miles driven and average visibility to determine the total area sampled. Number of deer seen divided by area sampled will provide an estimate of density.

It is important to conduct spotlight and track counts several times to obtain an average. It is also extremely important to conduct surveys at the same time of year, over the same routes, and at approximately the same time at night.

Harvest trends. Harvest trends also have been used in evaluating populations. Creed (1964) discussed use of harvest trends in making management decisions, especially for antlerless harvests. Game agencies often base bag limits on trends in estimated harvest per square mile for each management unit. On smaller, privately owned lands, use of average harvest per square mile probably is not realistic, but monitoring total harvest by age *is* useful. By plotting total number of bucks, does, and fawns harvested each season, you will be better able to assess the results of management.

SUMMARY

Implementation of QDM means setting and adhering to strict goals. They should be based on the productive capacity of the land, land use, and realistic expectations of hunters. QDM is predicated on passing up young bucks and maintaining the population at a moderate stocking level through adequate harvest of females. The age at which bucks are harvested can be adjusted to accommodate demand for older age-class bucks with larger antlers. Once goals are established, record keeping is essential, with established baseline data for the habitat as well as the herd. Records should include habitat quality, harvest age and sex structure, productivity indices, and browse utilization to determine stocking level.

Habitat quality is assessed by delineating types and evaluating utility to deer by ground-truthing and habitat analyses. From these data, detailed prescriptions should be written for each management unit, including recommended practices, detailed instructions on implementation of prescriptions, and a timetable for activities. Forest and grazing management and crops should be considered as integral parts of habitat management. Population control also is significant, as deer can destroy their own habitat. Supplemental plantings, where feasible, should be conducted with specific stress periods in mind and should include mixtures of plant varieties, as no single species is suitable for all situations.

Harvest data should be acquired from *all* animals taken from the property and processed at a check station convenient to hunters. Accurate records should be stressed at all times. Important records include age at harvest, dressed weight, antler measurements, lactation, and body condition indices. Deer should be aged by tooth wear and replacement to construct an estimate of herd age structure and to evaluate herd condition by age class.

Deer also should be aged during incidental sightings. This allows the hunter-manager to evaluate age structure of bucks available for harvest. Being able to estimate the age of live deer in the field also is important and permits the hunter greater selectivity. The "best" buck to harvest may not be the one with the largest antlers.

Production is measured directly and indirectly, using fetal counts (when possible), lactation rates, and incidental sightings of does and fawns. Data then are compared to goals of the management program.

There are several ways to census white-tailed deer, few of which have proven accurate. Nevertheless, censuses are useful in providing indices to population density. The two most useful methods to date are track and spotlight counts, but new technology may soon permit infra-red camera census.

Management progress is assessed and decisions made using the above information as "diagnostic" tools. By setting goals, the manager can monitor progress and population responses to management.

Finally, no management program ever will succeed without realistic expectations and full commitment. A QDM program *always* should include an initial assessment of these hunter-landowner values.

—JAMES C. KROLL AND
HARRY A. JACOBSON

CHAPTER 3

Harvest Strategies

A peculiar virtue in wildlife ethics is that the hunter ordinarily has no gallery to applaud or disapprove of his conduct. Whatever his acts, they are dictated by his own conscience, rather than by a mob of onlookers. It is difficult to exaggerate the importance of this fact.

—ALDO LEOPOLD (1949)
A Sand County Almanac

Before a biologist or manager can recommend specific harvest strategies for quality deer management, he or she must have a reasonable idea of the herd's status. Recent harvest data (as described in the previous chapter) allow an assessment of herd condition. Data on *all* animals harvested during the previous two or three years are needed to set harvest objectives by sex and age class.

Without this kind of information, biologists or managers must rely on intuition and knowledge of other deer herds to produce a "best-guess" QDM plan.

Some hunters may become frustrated with their first attempts under QDM. With traditional management, hunters are accustomed to identifying deer simply as antlered or antlerless and harvesting according to which group is "in season." Under QDM, hunters must learn to identify bucks by age class (or at least consider antler characteristics such as number of points, beam length, and spread) and identify antlerless deer as mature does and fawns. This requires a very different way of thinking. Considerable field experience is required to develop observation and identification skills. The following recommendations are offered to aid in identification and harvest of specific sex and age classes of deer.

ANTLERED BUCK HARVESTS

Management recommendations for buck harvests often must deal with a limited supply of older bucks (2½+ years) resulting from years of heavy harvest. The first objective of a quality management plan likely will be to decrease the harvest pressure on young antlered bucks. This is accomplished by setting antler size limits or establishing buck quotas. Here are some techniques that can help to minimize the harvest of young bucks.

1. Select minimum antler characteristics that will protect the younger age classes.

Antler size generally increases with age, but some antler characteristics are much better predictors of age than others. The number of antler points, in most cases, is not a good predictor. In some well-nourished herds, yearlings may have eight-point or even ten-point racks. The number of points may increase little, if at all, as the deer ages. In other herds, particularly herds in poor or overpopulated habitats, virtually all of the yearlings may be spikes.

Other measurements, such as antler mass (beam diameter), beam length, or antler spread, tend to increase consistently among age classes, at least until maturity. Some measurements may be difficult to field judge (beam diameter or length); others can be judged fairly accurately with a little practice. Antler spread can be field estimated by

Antler points are not a good indicator of age. In healthy herds on good range, yearling bucks may sport small racks with multiple points like the one on the left. In poor or overpopulated habitats, nearly all yearlings may be spikes, like the one on the right. PHOTOGRAPHS COURTESY OF THE UNIVERSITY OF GEORGIA, D. B. WARNELL SCHOOL OF FOREST RESOURCES.

Many quality management clubs use antler spread restrictions to protect young antlered bucks. Antler spread tends to increase between classes, at least until maturity, and can be accurately field estimated. When a buck faces you with his ears cupped forward, the distance from ear tip to ear tip is 15 to 16 inches. The antlers of the buck on the left are well inside his ear tips and the spread is less than 12 inches. The antlers of the middle buck are equal to his ear tips and therefore the spread is 15 to 16 inches. The antlers of the buck on the right are well outside his ears and the spread is more than 20 inches. PHOTOGRAPHS BY KENT KAMMERMEYER (LEFT AND MIDDLE) AND MIKE BIGGS.

assessing it relative to the buck's ears. When a buck faces you with ears cupped forward, the distance from ear tip to ear tip is about 15 inches. If the antlers extend beyond the ear tips, the spread exceeds 15 inches.

Regardless of criteria, it is critical to gather data on the antler characteristics of the deer in your hunting area for each age class. If you cannot gather enough on your area, try to get the information from nearby areas or from your local biologist. Once you have this information, you can establish minimum antler guidelines that will protect certain age classes of bucks. For example, if you determine that the average antler spread of yearling bucks in your area is 11½ inches and that some yearlings may reach 14 inches, establishing a harvest guideline that only allows the harvest of bucks with an antler spread of more than 15 inches will allow yearlings to grow another year.

Harvest criteria must be established for each area. What works in one area may not work in another and may even be counterproductive. Over time, as a quality deer management philosophy takes hold in a group, harvest criteria may no longer be necessary. Hunters will limit themselves and readily pass bucks that would exceed minimum standards. "Think of what he will be like next year!" becomes more important than "Does he make the minimum?" Tales of deer passed become more important around the campfire than tales of deer taken.

2. Establish buck harvest quotas.

Another means of limiting the pressure on bucks is to limit the number that can be taken from an area. Quotas ensure a portion will be protected. This works well in areas where hunters have little experience at field judging deer.

3. Establish buck refuges.

On large tracts, protected areas can help limit the buck harvest. Also, a large property can be divided into hunt units with low to moderate harvests allowed by rotation. Areas protected during one year can be hunted during the following year.

4. Culling.

This should be avoided by beginning participants in QDM. Even biologists disagree on what they consider a cull. Some QDM programs have been hurt by the misdirected culling of young bucks with abnormal antler characteristics, including broken main beams, broken points, mismatched points, and slight deformities. Many of these young, culled bucks could have developed into quality animals.

The more categories of antlered bucks available for harvesting, the more difficult it is to attain an adequate antlerless harvest. Traditionally, hunters have taken bucks in descending order of antler quality. For example, an eight-point buck was preferred over a six-point, which was preferred over a four-point, which was preferred over a spike, which was preferred over an antlerless deer. Initially, quality bucks will be scarce. As the management program takes hold, mature bucks should become more plentiful. The difficulty of harvesting these animals will prevent overharvest. Most hunters have become accustomed to harvesting young bucks and do not know how, when, or where to hunt mature ones.

Terrain, vegetation, methods, and hunter activity can affect the harvest of older, more elusive bucks. Once a buck progresses to 2½ years and beyond, his behavior patterns change and his ability to elude hunters improves markedly. Mature bucks are creatures of habit. Hunters who can read deer sign can determine movement patterns and preferred habitats. This scouting ability, combined with patience and determination, usually results in success. Methods of hunting mature bucks depend on season length, timing of the season, and hunter activity. Long seasons may provide more opportunity, but hunting pressure can force mature bucks to become reclusive and nocturnal. After all, mature bucks, and does too, can distinguish between the clamor of hunting season versus the off-season solitude.

This buck has respectable antlers, but his emaciated appearance shows that he is past his prime and could be culled. During the early phases of a quality deer management program, emphasis should be placed on balancing the sex ratio, building the buck age structure, and reducing herd density. Culling should not be considered until the deer herd has been fine-tuned. PHOTOGRAPH BY WYMAN MEINZER, JR.

When pursuing mature bucks, hunt when other hunters are out of the woods, around midday. Consider hunting out-of-the-way areas where there is less hunter activity. Mature bucks quickly find such areas, which are often dense, offering limited visibility to the hunter.

Rutting bucks are preoccupied. Hunting during this "window of

Traditionally, hunters have taken even yearling bucks in decreasing order of antler quality. For example, the little eight-point at the left was preferred over the spike, which was preferred over the doe. Many quality management clubs reverse this practice, with the most eligible for harvest being a mature doe. PHOTOGRAPHS BY DAVID OSBORN (TOP LEFT AND RIGHT) AND KENT KAMMERMEYER.

opportunity" has the highest success rate for harvesting mature bucks of the entire season, including opening day. Plan your hunting trips accordingly.

Calling bucks with rattling antlers or grunt calls can be very effective as the breeding season approaches. Grunting works best during the peak of the breeding season. Rattling also is useful after the peak, but not as productive. When calling bucks, choose a location with good visibility and face downwind. Incoming bucks will usually travel upwind. Some will approach with abandon, but most will sneak toward the sound. Always wear blaze orange to signal other hunters of your presence.

Expect only marginal success when hunting in food plots or over bait. Mature bucks seldom visit such areas during daylight. Patient hunters often observe a number of intermediate bucks before encountering a mature one. Shooting a "lesser" buck signals older ones that their evening activity should wait until darkness.

ANTLERLESS DEER HARVESTS

The second objective of quality management is to adequately manage the doe population. In many areas, this means increased antlerless harvest. The antlerless harvest is the most important component of a quality management plan. It can help accomplish some or all of the following objectives:

1. Balance the sex ratio (Brothers and Ray 1975).
2. Reduce herd density (Brothers and Ray 1975, McCullough 1979).
3. Increase reproduction and recruitment (Brothers and Ray 1975, McCullough 1979).
4. Reduce yearling buck dispersal (Holzenbein and Marchinton 1992).
5. Shorten the breeding season (Gruver et al. 1980, 1984; Guynn et al. 1986).
6. Shift the breeding season earlier (Guynn et al. 1986).
7. Improve quality of yearling bucks (Knox et al. 1991).
8. Provide reproductive data.
9. Provide additional high-quality venison.

Considerations for Selective Antlerless Harvests

Antlerless deer include all females and 6-month-old male fawns, commonly called button or nubbin bucks. Some hunters refer to fawns, male and female, as yearlings. Technically, a yearling is 1½ years old. In some states, yearling bucks with small spikes (2 inches or less) are considered antlerless.

There are two seemingly conflicting objectives in harvesting antlerless deer. First, remove enough antlerless animals to lower or maintain herd density. Second, avoid the harvest of male fawns. When producing mature bucks is a management objective, harvesting high numbers of button bucks is a mistake. In some states, 20 percent or more of the antlerless harvest may be button bucks. In these areas, not only are antlered males being heavily harvested, but many of the males are harvested before they grow their first antlers. Through education and an understanding of the management impact of each deer harvested, adequate antlerless (female) harvests can be achieved while minimizing harvest of button bucks.

For example, in the coastal plain of South Carolina, the percentage of button bucks in the antlerless harvest has been reduced through selective harvest techniques by nearly half, from 16.2 percent in 1982 to 9.7 percent in 1989. This was accomplished during the same period that antlerless harvests increased by 172 percent (Hamilton et al. 1991).

Here are some recommendations for selective antlerless harvest. Hunting scenarios vary and there are exceptions to every rule.

1. Size and shape are the most important factors in identifying adult does and fawns. An adult doe has a long head and neck; its body is large and rectangular. Fawns have short heads and necks and are small and square. Compare these two descriptions with luggage. A suitcase is rectangular and a briefcase is square. The head of an adult doe could compare in shape to a 12-ounce drink bottle and a fawn would match a 6-ounce bottle. Consider size and shape before shooting and use the best scopes and binoculars available to observe deer.

2. Avoid harvesting "lone" antlerless deer. Wait until other deer arrive to provide comparisons. During the fall, lone deer often are button bucks that have become separated from their dam because of rutting activity, hunter activity, or normal dispersal patterns. During the peak of the breeding season, it is common to encounter small groups of temporarily abandoned fawns. If all the deer appear similar in size, wait for a behavioral clue.

3. When deer are traveling in single file between feeding and bedding areas, their positions often are determined by social rank and thus age. The lead doe often is the correct one to take. Be careful when hunting food plots, however, as button bucks often will enter the field first.

4. When spooked, deer frequently will return to satisfy their curiosity. They will circle the "problem" to get downwind so they can confirm whether danger exists. With few exceptions, the dominant doe will initiate and lead the investigation.

5. When watching antlerless deer, pay attention to the dominant animal that holds its ears back and rushes other deer. Often the front legs are used to strike or flail subordinate animals. Fawns often buck and chase. Watch for aggressive adult body postures and adolescent behavior.

6. Hunt antlerless deer as early in the season as legally permitted. Late in the season, there is less of a size difference between adult does and button bucks. Button bucks are more adventuresome as they get older, but they are still careless and inexperienced.

7. Don't shoot in poor light during the early morning or late after-

Size and shape distinguish between adult does and fawns. Mature does, like the animal on the right, have long heads and necks and are large and rectangular. Fawns have short heads and necks and the body is more square. COURTESY OF THE UNIVERSITY OF GEORGIA, D. B. WARNELL SCHOOL OF FOREST RESOURCES.

noon, don't take long-distance shots, and avoid a moving target, especially when other deer are nearby.

8. The bottom line in harvesting antlerless deer is this: When unsure, always give your quarry the benefit of the doubt.

KEEP THE FUN IN HUNTING!

Harvesting deer under QDM guidelines requires new attitudes and observation skills. Allowing legal antlered bucks to pass, judging antler size and age of bucks, and identifying mature does and button bucks can be difficult even for the experienced hunter. Many clubs strictly enforce rules and assess penalties such as fines or loss of membership. Peer pressure can be so extreme that some hunters cannot enjoy hunting. Disagreements and dissension can unravel well-conceived plans after the first or second year. In some situations, it is wise to phase in QDM guidelines over three or more years, allowing attitudes and skills to evolve with the changing herd.

Protection of button bucks is often overemphasized during the initial years of QDM. In most situations, the primary objectives will be to

Quality deer management requires changes in attitudes and skills. In many clubs, rules are strictly enforced and peer pressure can be extreme. Adopt reasonable guidelines instead, allowing hunter attitudes and skills to evolve over time and keep the fun in hunting, especially for young, inexperienced hunters. PHOTOGRAPH BY JOE HAMILTON.

protect yearling bucks and increase the harvest of does. Concerns for protecting button bucks can hamper harvest of mature does if hunters who make honest mistakes are chastised or fined. These mistakes will occur even with seasoned QDM hunters, but their frequency should decrease with time.

Another concern is young hunters who have never taken a deer. Many QDM clubs will allow an inexperienced hunter to take any antlered buck or antlerless animal for their first deer, but thereafter they must adhere to the same rules as experienced hunters. Other clubs argue that patience and restraint are valuable lessons and that inexperienced hunters should be given no special considerations. The same arguments can be applied to archery hunting.

Every QDM situation is different. People hunt for many reasons, but they all hunt because they enjoy some aspects of the experience. The experience, skill levels, and opportunity to hunt vary greatly among and within clubs. QDM cannot create the desired herd density, sex ratio, and age structure in a single season. QDM is a long-term relationship between hunters and deer that becomes stronger with time. These factors should be considered when developing QDM harvest guidelines to ensure that hunters enjoy their current experience, as well as the expectation that as their relationship with the resource grows stronger so will their enjoyment of the hunt.

—Joe Hamilton,
W. Matt Knox, and
David C. Guynn, Jr.

CHAPTER 4

Common Misconceptions

The greatest obstacle to discovering the shape of the earth, the continents, and the ocean was not ignorance but the illusion of knowledge.

—DANIEL J. BOORSTIN
The Discoverers

Misconceptions about quality deer management abound and can hinder successful herd management. Exactly what QDM can and can't do is the subject of much debate among hunters, managers, and wildlife biologists. In most cases, poor communication is to blame. This may influence some clubs to make management decisions based on incomplete or poorly understood information.

Two situations can result from this. For one, misconceptions create unrealistic expectations of what quality management can achieve. Clubs trying QDM might become discouraged when their dream of harvesting Boone and Crockett bucks is not fulfilled. Also, clubs considering switching to quality management may be hampered by nagging doubts about what they can expect and what it takes to be a quality manager. This chapter should help clear up some misconceptions about QDM so that your club can avoid these situations. Perhaps it will also alleviate some of the miscommunication.

Misconception 1. Trophy management and quality deer management are the same thing.

This distinction is paramount, yet it seems to be ignored, unrecognized, or poorly communicated. QDM is not a euphemism for trophy deer management. The two management philosophies share some approaches but seek different goals.

Trophy management primarily concerns maximizing Boone and Crockett score and stresses the *harvest* of very large antlered bucks. A quality hunt yields a very large antlered buck to the gun. In contrast, quality deer management is broader. Emphasis is not solely on the harvest of bucks, but rather production of quality deer (not just bucks, but all deer), hunting experiences, and hunters through continuing education. It also involves the maintenance of quality wildlife habitat. To completely comprehend and use QDM, all of these goals must be actively sought. If not, QDM cannot achieve its full potential.

Misconception 2. Under quality deer management, your club will harvest fewer deer.

Population control is the keystone to sound deer management. Switching to QDM does not necessarily mean you harvest fewer deer. The opposite may be true. Many deer habitats are overpopulated and initially need increased harvests to reduce herds to manageable levels. Annual removals must maintain the residual (posthunt) population well below the carrying capacity of the habitat. This may require substantial increases in doe harvests. Combined with decreased harvests of young bucks, this produces a population more in balance with its habitat and often a better sex ratio. Population control is the keystone to sound deer management, and adequate doe harvest is the key to population control.

Clubs contemplating switching to QDM should know that lower populations mean *seeing* fewer deer than before. Seeing fewer deer is a necessary sacrifice for increased herd quality as well as increased habitat quality, which benefits all wildlife.

Misconception 3. Even though a club continues to harvest some immature bucks each year, it is managing for quality because it started shooting more does. *Or,* a club is under quality management because it passes all young bucks.

Many clubs believe they are operating under QDM but actually are playing only half the game. They may protect young bucks, yet not adequately control the population by harvesting enough does. In most areas, you cannot pass bucks while maintaining a low harvest of does and expect positive results. If you can't stand shooting does, QDM is not for you.

By the same token, a club may harvest enough deer but continue to take too many immature bucks. Clubs in these situations assure failure. Once you decide to implement QDM, follow through by fulfilling all aspects of a management plan developed after consultation with a

Where young bucks are passed but inadequate numbers of antlerless deer are harvested, deer often are in poor condition (left). The deer on the right, by contrast, was taken from a quality-managed herd. Don't expect good results if you play only half the game. PHOTOGRAPH BY SCOTT McDONALD.

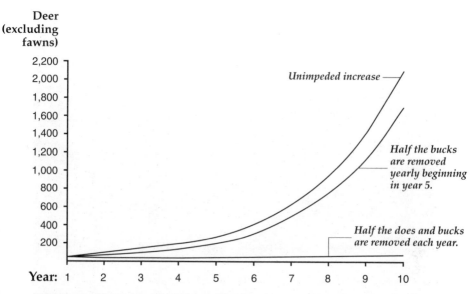

The reproductive potential of white-tailed deer is astounding. If no animals are removed, twenty-five pairs of mature deer can become a herd of more than two thousand in ten years. Although natural populations are rarely unimpeded, the management implications are clear: Does must be harvested at a level that will control populations. ADAPTED FROM LEOPOLD (1933).

biologist. If you play only half the game, don't expect to reap half the benefits because there probably won't be any. Even worse, the impact could be harmful.

Misconception 4. Only a few members of a club will enjoy the benefits of QDM.

Nothing could be further from the truth. Anytime a nice deer is harvested, all the members of a QDM club can feel proud. It takes only one person to pull the trigger, but it takes the patience and persistence of the club to produce that deer. When you take a young buck, you decrease the chances that you or anyone else will kill a large one. The quality of any hunting experience heightens when the possibility of harvesting a mature buck exists, so encourage members to help stack the odds in everyone's favor.

Misconception 5. When a club manages for quality deer, members can hunt mature bucks the same way they hunted yearlings.

Probably not. The two age groups behave differently. Because young bucks make up the majority of the buck segment of a tradition-ally managed herd, few hunters ever see older bucks, much less get the

Pulling the trigger is the easy part. Deer like these result from the dedication of all the hunter-managers on a quality property. Everyone enjoys the harvest when the seeds are well sown. PHOTOGRAPH COURTESY HARRY JACOBSON.

chance to learn to hunt one. Deer learn from previous mistakes and become increasingly difficult to harvest. A hunter also will have to learn and adapt to harvest older bucks. Biologists can tell you how to grow quality bucks, but it's ultimately up to you to grow them and learn how to hunt them.

Misconception 6. Every buck that is passed will be around next year. A club can really stockpile bucks on its property.

This may be one of the most misunderstood aspects of QDM. Some hunters assume that every young buck they pass will be available for harvest next year. Deer also die from disease, malnutrition, parasitism, trauma, automobiles, and poaching. Every herd has some non-harvest mortality, and the immature buck you did not shoot this year may die before next season. Also, just because you let a young buck walk does not necessarily mean he will establish his home range on your property. University of Georgia studies indicated that adult does drive off their male offspring, causing them to wander until they find an area in which they are tolerated. Without the dam around to drive them out of their natal range, the youngsters stay put and are exposed to fewer dangerous situations. The management implication is obvious.

Passing up young bucks doesn't necessarily mean stockpiling deer. Some percentage of each age class is inevitably lost each year to disease, predation, poaching,
and other nonharvest mortality. There aren't any guarantees that a yearling buck
produced on your property will be around next year. Research has shown that
harvesting enough antlerless deer can decrease the number of bucks lost to such
factors. PHOTOGRAPH BY DAVID OSBORN.

Harvesting does may create a situation where fewer yearling bucks disperse from the property.

Misconception 7. A club in South Carolina followed some simple instructions for QDM from a local biologist and it's working great. We'll just do the same thing they're doing on our area in Wisconsin.

Recommendations must be made on a site-specific basis, depending on location and herd status. The best way to determine what is appropriate for your property is to seek the advice of a local wildlife biologist. You also should understand that deer populations are dynamic and harvest recommendations may vary from year to year. QDM is most effective when you follow these guidelines and accept changes in them. By working closely with biologists year after year, you'll gain intimate knowledge of your herd and become more effective managers.

Misconception 8. Quality deer management works equally well in all areas.

Quality is represented by the best that a given herd can achieve. Some hunters become discouraged when their perceptions of a "quality" buck are not realized. Expectations often exceed results possible for an area. Age, genetics, and nutrition influence the quality of deer. If you're passing young bucks, you're taking care of the most important factor, age. Genetics is rarely a limitation anywhere in the United States. In fact, restocking programs moved deer around so much that herds in most regions really may not be genetically separable.

The third limitation is nutrition, which largely depends on habitat. Habitat differences account for many "failures." Differences in flora, water availability, soil, and land uses can influence the quality attainable in your herd. For example, a club surrounded by cropland would probably have better quality than one stuck in the middle of young pine plantations. Although wildlife is a product of habitat, you can improve your habitat through proper management of timber, wildlife openings, and maintaining a low deer population. Keep your expectations in line by setting harvest restrictions in accord with your region, habitat types, and so forth.

Misconception 9. The only effective way to set buck harvest guidelines is through the strict enforcement of spread limits (or limits on beam length, points, and so forth).

Just as there are no blanket harvest guidelines, there is no best way to judge bucks for all areas. Certain methods are better under different circumstances. Point limits were one of the first methods used, primarily because they were easy to understand and use. Spread limits, although a little harder to field judge, have become common and work great under most conditions. Many programs have combined point and spread limits.

South Carolina district wildlife biologist Lewis Rogers suggests that clubs that want better results try limiting the number of bucks that can be harvested by each member. This causes hunters to study deer before pulling the trigger. This works particularly well for clubs that have been under quality management for only a short time and for clubs frustrated by other methods of sizing up bucks.

The important point is to use a method (or methods) that protects young bucks until they can develop to meet your harvest criteria. One method will not work everywhere. If you're having problems, try techniques others have found successful. Deer hunting and management are supposed to be fun, so don't "limit" your pleasures.

Misconception 10. Quality deer management is for everybody.

QDM is not an indictment of traditional management. Certainly there are areas and situations where QDM is not the best option. Some hunters simply prefer a traditional management approach. Others enjoy trophy management and hunting. Such hunters and managers are not inferior to QDM subscribers and vice versa. If you treasure the values and goals held by the quality management philosophy, give it a try. If you don't, keep an open mind.

Misconceptions about quality deer management result from several things, especially poor communication among hunters and biologists. This leads to inefficiency. Some is usually unavoidable, but when it's added to programs trying to control nature, the problems are compounded. The results are disgruntled and frustrated hunters, managers, and biologists. Oddly enough, the search for solutions to these problems was partly responsible for quality deer management.

—MICHAEL D. VAN BRACKLE AND
J. SCOTT MCDONALD

CHAPTER 5

Evaluating the Plan

How futile it is passively to follow a recipe without understanding the mechanism behind it.

—ALDO LEOPOLD (1938)

Quality deer management requires the commitment of all involved—landowner, hunter, and biologist. After two or three years of such commitment, it is reasonable to ask, "Is QDM working for me?" In this chapter, we show how indicators of herd condition and hunter satisfaction can be used to evaluate your QDM program. The interpretation likely will suggest ways to fine-tune it.

USING BIOLOGICAL INDICATORS: AN EXAMPLE
Complete and accurate harvest information is a key to any QDM program. Poor data result in poor management recommendations.

An analysis of harvest data that includes age structure, reproductive performance, and herd health can tell more about overall herd conditions than can more advanced population or census techniques. Basic health indicators include body weight (usually taken as dressed weight), antler characteristics, and lactation.

There are three basic rules in the use of harvest data: The goals of the management program must be clearly stated, the data must be complete and accurate, and examination of harvest data over years is necessary to evaluate changes in herd condition.

We know that quality deer management works in areas with good deer habitat; however, many areas of the country have poor habitat. For example, most Florida herds have relatively poor nutrition because of low-quality, acidic soils with major mineral deficiencies. Florida could be considered the ultimate testing ground for QDM. If it would work there, it should work anywhere!

In the fall of 1988, a QDM program was initiated on a 38,000-acre cattle and sod ranch in Brevard County, Florida, owned and operated by one of Florida's oldest families, the Dudas. The Dudas have a rich tradition of hunting and deer management on their ranch. Either-sex harvest was initiated many years before and good records were maintained on their herd. The Dudas could be considered pioneers in deer management.

Most of the deer habitat on Cocoa Ranch consists of saw palmetto prairie and slash pine flatwoods—habitat that would by Florida standards be considered average to good, but it is poor for most of the white-tailed deer's range. After examining the ranch and harvest records, several recommendations were made. Even though as many does had been harvested as bucks for at least ten years, it was felt that deer density was too high for the habitat. Doe harvest was greatly increased with

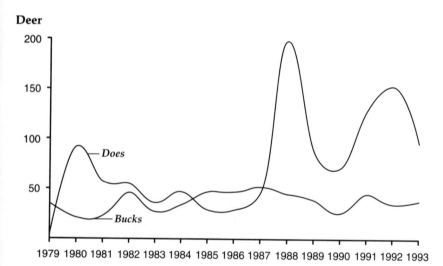

The deer harvest on Cocoa Ranch, Florida, demonstrates that even a balanced either-sex harvest frequently cannot achieve management objectives. At Cocoa Ranch, a quality deer management program was initiated in 1988. It was recognized then that many more does than bucks would have to be harvested initially to achieve objectives. Note that the average number of bucks harvested did not change under the quality management program.

no corresponding increase in buck harvest. Before 1988, an average of 38 bucks and 44 does were taken annually. From 1988 to the present, an average of 38 males and 122 does have been taken annually.

The second recommendation was to improve habitat through intensive management and plantings. Habitat management consisted of timber thinnings, roller chopping palmetto, improved rotational cattle grazing, and controlled burnings. In 1989, 166 acres were set aside for plantings of small winter grains, clovers, cowpeas, millets, jointvetch, and others. They were not aimed specifically at deer but at a variety of game and nongame species.

A third recommendation was related to the Dudas' desire for better-quality bucks. The age structure of their harvest revealed that before 1988, the average buck taken was a yearling or 2-year-old. Few bucks were allowed to live until the age of 3 to 6 years, when they could achieve good antler development. In fact, 50 to 70 percent of the total buck harvest consisted of yearlings.

Since 1988, hunters on the ranch have been asked to restrict their harvest to bucks meeting two of three criteria: a 16-inch outside spread, a 16-inch beam length on one antler, or at least eight antler points. Although a few yearlings with small antlers are mistaken as does and

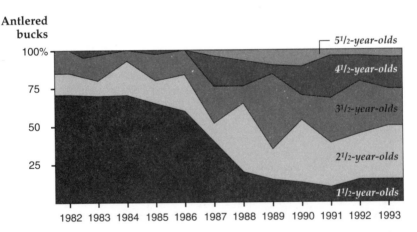

Before 1981, Florida had a 4-inch spike law. Few yearlings on Cocoa Ranch met the criterion for harvest, so most bucks harvested were 2 years or older. After 1980, bucks with any antlers became legal and most bucks harvested on Cocoa Ranch were yearlings until 1988. Since then, self-restraint by hunters participating in quality deer management has dramatically improved age structure, with most harvested bucks 3 years old or older.

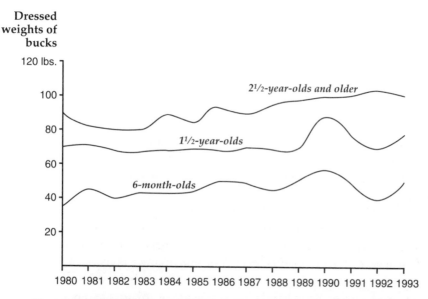

The substantial doe harvests and habitat improvements initiated in 1988 on Cocoa Ranch apparently resulted in a general increase in body weights of all age classes of bucks during subsequent years.

occasional mistakes are made, the age structure of bucks on the Cocoa Ranch has shown dramatic improvement since 1988. Before then, most bucks harvested were yearlings, and since 1988 most have been 3 years old or older. This difference equated to taking home a spike buck with less than 4 inches of antlers, to taking home an eight-point with a 15-inch or better spread. Interestingly, after four years of greatly increased doe harvest and restrictions on the quality of bucks to be harvested, the average buck harvest has changed little from the pre-1988 years.

What has changed greatly is the condition of deer on Cocoa Ranch. Body weights have risen: from 8 to 11 pounds for bucks, and from 4 to 6 pounds for does. Reproduction, although still reflecting the low productivity of Florida deer, also demonstrated a major increase after 1988. The average number of fetuses per pregnant doe increased from 1.01 to 1.14 for yearlings and from 1.11 to 1.32 for adult does, pre-1988 to post-1988. Additionally, for the first time, even fawn does have been documented to breed on the ranch. In 1993, two of five doe fawns examined were pregnant.

Spotlight counts of deer on Cocoa Ranch in 1993 still indicated a surprisingly high density of about 1,100 deer (one deer per 35 acres or nineteen deer per square mile), with an amazing 1:0.8 buck-to-doe ratio. There is no spotlight count data before 1990, but in that year (two years after initiation of substantial doe harvests) the counts indicated about 1,350 deer (279 fawns, 806 does, and 242 bucks) with a 1:3.3 buck-to-doe ratio. It may seem surprising, but there is good evidence that fewer does are now producing more fawns that have better survival rates than in earlier years. In addition to fetal counts, spotlight counts support this. In 1993, the spotlight count estimated 335 does, 327 fawns, and 404 bucks on Cocoa. Half as many does as present in 1990 were producing more fawns in 1993; almost twice as many bucks were sighted.

Can QDM work even in Florida? Just ask the Dudas or any of their employees and guests that hunt on Cocoa Ranch. In 1992, the average buck harvested on Cocoa had 8.4 points, 17.4-inch antler beams, and a 15.7-inch spread. Also, the first ever Pope and Young trophy buck (score of 142) was taken by a bow on the ranch. In 1993, a buck with thirteen points and a gross Boone and Crockett score of 162 was taken. Cocoa Ranch is not a "trophy" management area, however, so don't expect a Boone and Crockett buck to ever be harvested there.

QDM is not about raising Boone and Crockett trophies. It should

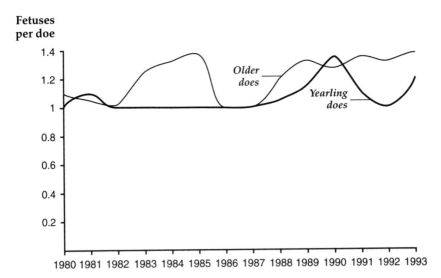

Reproduction in yearling and mature does increased on Cocoa Ranch following heavy antlerless harvests beginning in 1988. First reports of pregnant fawns occurred in 1992 and 1993.

Jeff Andree, land manager for Cocoa Ranch, displays an average buck harvested after quality deer management was initiated. Bucks such as this represent the best animals that can be produced on some poor-quality habitats, such as are found throughout Florida. PHOTOGRAPH BY HARRY JACOBSON.

be aimed at producing quality deer, quality habitat, and a quality hunting experience. At Cocoa Ranch, hunting means a day of riding horseback, with hounds, in the true tradition of an organized southern deer hunt; fathers and sons; chuck wagon lunches; an end-of-the-hunt barbecue; tall tales and loss of shirttails by the fireside; and the great respect and love of the quarry that all have pursued. It is a true experience of quality deer management!

INDICATORS OF QDM SUCCESS: HUNTER OBSERVATIONS
Sightings of deer by hunters can be used to indicate trends in numbers, buck-doe ratios, fawn-doe ratios, and buck age structure. The observations must be conducted consistently and hunters must learn to identify deer as to sex and age. Sighting data should include the hunter's name, date, location hunted, the time hunting began and ended, and the number of deer seen. At first, the number of deer seen should be recorded as antlered deer, antlerless deer, and unknown, since many

hunters will have difficulty distinguishing does and fawns. Any deer without antlers or spots is a doe to most hunters. With experience, hunters can quickly distinguish does and fawns in most situations. Likewise, most can learn to distinguish yearling bucks from older ones by body and antler characteristics. The number of shots taken and the identification number of deer killed should also be recorded. The fawn-doe ratio can be used to approximate fawn recruitment by dividing the total number of fawns sighted by the total number of does sighted. For herds in good conditions with low predation, the fawn-doe ratio can be 80 percent or better. The sex ratio is calculated by dividing the number of does seen by the number of bucks. A ratio of one buck to three does is adequate for most herds. Should the data suggest a higher ratio and if doe age structure and lactation rates are not desirable, an increase in doe harvest may be necessary to improve herd conditions and productivity (Kroll 1991).

Hunter observation data help show what is being accomplished with QDM programs. Sightings by the Koeller Hunting Club in south-central Missouri from 1988 to 1990 are an example (see table). The club hunts on 2,680 acres of hardwood forest; 800 acres were clear-cut in the late 1970s. Before starting QDM in 1988, the club harvested about twenty bucks each year, mostly yearlings. The increased antlerless harvest is reflected in lower total deer sightings in 1989 and 1990. The restraint of buck harvest is also reflected in the increased number of buck sightings and the improvement in the antlered-to-antlerless deer ratio. Note also the consistent pattern in the antlered-to-antlerless deer sighted ratio by month. Buck activity peaked during November as influenced by rutting behavior. All of the six bucks harvested during 1990 were good, with the largest being a 3½-year-old ten-point with a net B&C score in the 130s. The number and size of antler rubs increased noticeably in 1990 and for the first time deer responded to antler rattling.

EXPECTATIONS FOR IMPROVING AGE STRUCTURE

A primary goal of most QDM programs is to allow bucks to mature and to create a more natural age and sex structure within the herd. The number of mature bucks harvested would seem to be the most logical indicator of QDM success. In most QDM situations where bucks have been harvested intensively (50 percent or more of antlered bucks harvested are yearlings) for several years, however, at least five years of management may be necessary before any bucks 4½ years or older are

		Antlered deer sighted (harvested)	Antlerless deer sighted (harvested)	Unknown	Antlered deer sighted per 100 antlerless deer
	October	35	204	63	17:100
1988	November	31	117	43	27:100
	December	12	91	43	13:100
		78(1)	412(33)	149	19:100
	October	41	160	88	26:100
1989	November	47	82	37	57:100
	December	9	39	18	23:100
		97(2)	281(29)	143	35:100
	October	27	79	58	34:100
1990	November	69	154	103	45:100
	December	7	20	9	35:100
		103(6)	253(23)	170	41:100

Observational data can be important when evaluating a quality deer management program. For example, on the Koeller Hunting Club in south-central Missouri, the percentage of antlered bucks sighted increased twofold only two years after a quality management program was begun. Data provided by Grant Woods.

taken. Expectations for older age structure after two to three years of restrained harvest of young bucks are often dashed by unexpected or uncontrollable factors. Harvest strategies that remove a substantial proportion of yearlings (such as shooting spike bucks) can retard an older age structure. Bucks that are protected on a managed property may be fair game on adjoining property, killed by poachers, or lost to other factors.

There are two common questions among QDM participants: What improvements in age structure of bucks can we expect? And, How long will it take before we harvest some mature bucks? A hypothetical example can answer these questions (see figure on next page). Assume a QDM program is implemented on an area where annual adult buck survival has averaged 30 percent. In other words, 70 percent of all adult bucks die each year from combined harvest and nonharvest reasons. On this area, 50 percent of the yearling bucks are spikes and the rest have at least one forked antler. We will harvest bucks such that the

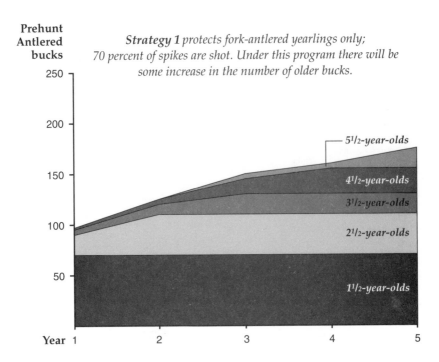

Prehunt
Antlered
bucks

Strategy 1 *protects fork-antlered yearlings only;
70 percent of spikes are shot. Under this program there will be
some increase in the number of older bucks.*

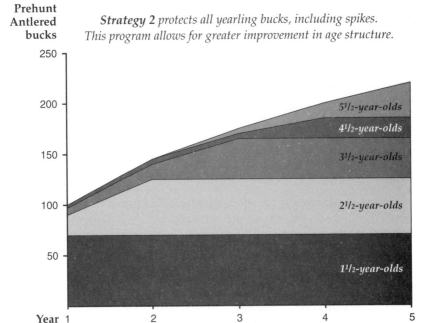

Prehunt
Antlered
bucks

Strategy 2 *protects all yearling bucks, including spikes.
This program allows for greater improvement in age structure.*

Hypothetical change in age structure of bucks created by two quality management strategies.

average annual survival rate of 1½-year-olds is 80 percent, and of older bucks 70 percent. Two QDM harvest strategies are compared: (1) spike antlered 1½-year-old bucks are harvested at a rate of 70 percent, forked antlered 1½-year-old bucks at a rate of 20 percent, and bucks 2½ years and older at a rate of 30 percent; and (2) 1½-year-old bucks are harvested at a rate of 20 percent and bucks 2½ years and older at a rate of 30 percent. This is intended to illustrate the effect of yearling harvest rates on age structure.

Although the predicted numbers of bucks in each age class are hypothetical, the example illustrates several management implications. Under both QDM strategies, the increase in the number of 2½- and 3½-year-old bucks becomes apparent in the second and third year of the programs through sightings and harvest. The change in adult sex ratio of deer sighted should be obvious. Note, however, that detectable numbers of 4½- and 5½-year-old bucks do not appear until the fourth and fifth years of the programs. Remember, we assumed that the survival rate of 2½-year-old bucks was 70 percent. In most QDM situations that use number of points or beam length as the criterion for judging mature bucks, most 3½-year-olds and many 2½-year-olds would be judged as "takers." Thus, the actual survival rate would be lower than 70 percent and the number of 4½- and 5½-year-old bucks would grow at a slower rate than depicted here. Unless harvest is greatly restrained on 2½- and 3½-year-old bucks, it may take many years for any 5½-year-olds to be harvested.

Protecting all 1½-year-old bucks (including spikes) allows for greater improvement in age structure in a given time than selecting against spikes. In most situations of heavy buck harvest (50 percent or more), all 1½-year-old bucks should be protected to improve buck age structure. After the desired age structure has been achieved (five years or longer), a harvest of spikes may be desirable if the total deer population is appropriate for nutritional conditions. Refer to chapter 8 for a more detailed discussion of considerations in the harvest of spike bucks.

HUNTER SATISFACTION

One final measure of QDM is hunter satisfaction. The axiom "Wildlife management is people management" certainly holds true in deer management; hunter satisfaction is perhaps the best test for the acceptance and success of QDM.

Respondents to a survey conducted by Clemson University in South Carolina were asked to rate the characteristics of an enjoyable hunt (Woods et al. 1992). Safety, knowing a mature buck is in the area, seeing deer, seeing other species of wildlife, and seeing lots of deer sign all rated highly. Of all components measured, taking a deer was the least important part of an enjoyable hunt. The responses to a series of statements about the harvest necessary for an enjoyable season showed that harvesting a deer is only a small part of the hunt for those surveyed. Harvesting the limit of antlered bucks regardless of size was ranked as the least important. Bagging a mature buck and several antlerless deer was of moderate importance. Of all the factors participants were asked to evaluate, knowing that the opportunity existed to harvest a quality buck was by far the most important.

This was reinforced by another question in the survey. When asked, "During the 1990 season, how many possible shots at antlered bucks did you not take?" the average response was eight! Overall, the opinions and attitudes of hunters on QDM were probably best summarized by a single question toward the end of the questionnaire (results are expressed in percentages):

	Yes	No	No Opinion
For your club, do you feel QDM:			
A. Has improved deer herd quality?	88.3	6.6	5.1
B. Increased the opportunity to harvest a quality buck?	84.8	9.6	5.6
C. Is preferable to traditional deer management?	78.0	12.3	9.7

Eighty-seven percent of the survey participants who expressed an opinion and 78 percent overall preferred QDM to traditional management. The impact and significance of QDM was perhaps best illustrated by a final question: "Would you prefer your child's first hunting experience to be in a QDM or traditional deer management club?" Ninety-one percent of the respondents selected QDM. These responses reflect a high level of hunter satisfaction with QDM.

In the past, most management was directed toward the hunter as a consumer. Deer hunting and management will be better served if efforts are directed toward the hunter as a manager and more emphasis placed on the experience rather than the harvest. QDM is not the answer for all hunters, biologists, or situations. But for ever increasing numbers of hunters, the natural progression from exposure to education, to awareness, to understanding, and finally to respect for the quarry fosters a change in attitude and whets desire for a QDM experience. This "new" management ethic denotes the hunter as a manager and emphasizes QDM values other than the actual harvest. While hunters should still know the biological benefits of QDM, they should also recognize that a successful hunt is not the same as harvesting an animal; it is the realization of a quality, memorable experience.

—JAMES F. BULLOCK, JR.,
DAVID C. GUYNN, JR., AND
HARRY A. JACOBSON

PART II

White-Tailed Deer Population Biology

Chapter 6

A Primer

The disquieting thing in the modern picture is the trophy-hunter who never grows up, in whom the capacity for isolation, perception, and husbandry is undeveloped, or perhaps lost. . . . who consumes but never creates outdoor satisfactions. For him the recreational engineer dilutes the wilderness and artificializes its trophies in the fond belief that he is rendering a public service.

—Aldo Leopold (1938)
Conservation Esthetic

It is relatively easy to provide food and habitat for optimal growth and development of one deer, but providing these same needs for an entire population of deer requires more complex management. To understand population management, hunters and managers must recognize that no two areas and no two populations are alike.

Many factors regulate deer numbers, health, and population structure. How a population responds to changes in habitat, harvest, predator populations, or climate depends on what factors are regulating it. The previous chapters should help you begin deer management and solve some common problems. In this chapter, we describe how and why deer populations respond to management, but this book should not be considered a substitute for professional advice. You should consult a wildlife biologist before entering into a deer management program. If in doubt about an individual's qualifications, ask if he or she is certified as a wildlife biologist by the Wildlife Society and how much experience he or she has with deer. Your state wildlife agency or extension wildlife specialist can help you find professional advice.

DEFINING THE POPULATION

Defining the population is the first step. Often this is based on land holdings (for example, a landowner wants to manage the deer on 1,000 acres). Unfortunately, unless there is a deerproof fence, deer don't recognize property boundaries and will spend time on adjacent properties. Thus, the manager has to consider not only his property but practices on adjoining lands as well. Barriers such as highways, rivers, or terrain help to define the management areas. Property shape also is important. A 1,000-acre tract that is long and narrow is very different from 1,000 acres in a square block. The larger the unit, the more likely the manager will be able to directly impact the population, although someone with 100 acres of winter cover surrounded by farms may be able to influence a deer population more significantly than a landowner with 1,000 acres whose habitat differs little from that of neighboring properties.

Properties of fewer than 2,000 acres often are too small for effective regulation of population sex and age structure because of the influence of neighboring lands. If there are cooperative arrangements with adjoining landowners or if geographic barriers exist, however, population management can be effective on smaller properties.

A recent development in some areas of the United States has been the formation of deer management associations. These groups of adjoining landowners or hunting clubs establish goals and agree upon harvest practices. Some of these cooperatives are effectively managing deer over large areas.

POPULATION GROWTH CHARACTERISTICS

Management of white-tailed deer means the manipulation of habitats, populations, and, most important, people. Harvest strategy defines how many, by what method, where, and when to harvest deer. The effects of harvest strategies on populations can be understood by knowing how deer populations grow.

A classic example of deer population growth occurred on the Edwin S. George Reserve in southeastern Michigan. In 1928, 6 white-tailed deer (2 bucks and 4 does) were introduced into the 2-square-mile fenced area (McCullough 1979). Six years later, the first drive census showed 160 deer. The growth of the George Reserve deer herd resembles that of a mathematical model used by biologists to describe population growth, called the logistic equation (Caughley 1977).

The logistic model can be used to illustrate basic principles of harvest management. The S-shaped growth curve reflects the impact nutrition has on reproduction and mortality in a deer herd. At the pioneer stage of growth, deer numbers are low and plenty of food is available. Because of abundant nutrition, reproduction is high, with twin fawns being common. A significant number of doe fawns may breed. Mortality

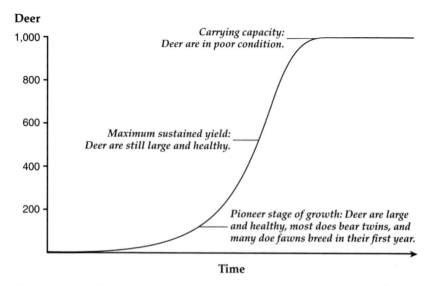

This hypothetical herd can grow rapidly until it reaches the carrying capacity of the habitat–1,000 animals. To maintain the population at carrying capacity, no deer can be harvested; all the deer added are needed to replace those that die naturally. More deer can be harvested when the population is kept at the maximum sustained yield level than at any other.

is low, and the population grows rapidly. As the population increases, nutritional resources are reduced and reproduction declines, so that the number of new animals added to the population (recruitment) each fawning season decreases. Body weights and antler quality begin to decline. As the population continues to increase, nutritional stress increases such that no doe fawns will breed and most older does give birth to single fawns. Where fawn production may have averaged two fawns per mature doe at the pioneer stage, it may be less than 0.5 fawns per doe at carrying capacity. As the population reaches the land's carrying capacity, natural mortality increases until deaths equal births and the population stops growing. At this point body weights and antler quality are low and chronic disease is always present. In years of favorable weather, populations may temporarily exceed the carrying capacity. This can devastate habitats and lower the carrying capacity for subsequent years.

The S curve also can be used to determine how many animals must be harvested to maintain the population at a specified level. When the population has reached carrying capacity (1,000 in the accompanying figure), and if the objective is to maintain the population at that level, no animals can be harvested because the number of births equals the number of deaths. To maintain a population below carrying capacity, the number of animals added to the population must be removed annually. Such harvests are referred to as sustained yields. Note that there are two population sizes that can produce any particular sustained yield (other than the "maximum sustained yield"). In the example given in the figure, we can maintain a postharvest population size of about 90 animals by harvesting 45 deer annually; or at a much higher density, we can maintain a population of 925 deer by harvesting 45 deer annually. At the lower population, nutrition is excellent and a population of 90 deer (assume 45 males and 45 females) produces 45 fawns, whereas at high density, nutrition is so poor that 925 deer are able to produce only 45 more fawns than deer lost to natural mortality.

The maximum sustained yield occurs at the point where the maximum number of fawns are born and survive. Recruitment is affected by the number of breeding females, the rate at which they produce fawns, and the rate of survival of these fawns. The maximum sustained yield for our example is 150 deer per year with a posthunt population size of 500 deer. An important deer management principle is that maximum sustained yield is generally achieved by maintaining deer density at about 50 percent to 60 percent of carrying capacity. The data on growth of the George Reserve deer herd suggest that maximum sustained yield occurred at approximately 60 percent of carrying capacity (McCullough 1979, Downing and Guynn 1985). The greatest individual quality is generally obtained at population levels below the maximum sustained yield level. One indication of this principle is that most Boone and Crockett trophy bucks have come from areas with densities of fewer than 30 deer per square mile.

FACTORS THAT AFFECT POPULATION DYNAMICS

Factors that affect population dynamics include reproduction, mortality, movements, and dispersal. Reproduction is not the same for all deer populations. Reproductive parameters, which include timing of the rut (breeding dates), fertility rates (number of young per doe), conception rates (percentage of does carrying young), age at first breeding, and sex ratios of offspring can be altered by population density, habitat conditions, and, in some cases, genetics.

The influence of nutrition is well known. Does on high-quality diets produce more fawns and may breed earlier in the season. The percentage of fawns that breed also is influenced by nutrition. As many as 85 percent of fawn does on high-quality range in midwestern farm country become pregnant. Conversely, on poor range in the southern coastal plain, some does do not breed until they are 2 ½ years of age.

The age does start breeding can dramatically affect herd growth and the number of deer produced for harvest. It is rare to see fawns breeding at the extremes of the whitetail's range. In northern states, doe fawns do not breed their first year because it is energetically too costly to do so. Near the tropics, poor soil fertility and a wide range in birth dates prevent most doe fawns from becoming large enough to reach puberty and breed in their first year. This occurs at about 80 pounds on northern ranges, though southern deer may breed at lower weights.

Some experiments (Verme 1983) suggest nutrition affects sex ratios of offspring. Deer in poor condition on overpopulated ranges may have a higher percentage of male than female offspring (Verme 1985). Age of the mother also affects sex ratios of offspring. Yearlings characteristically give birth to single fawns that are more likely to be males. Researchers also have found that when deer are raised in captivity on good diets, 2-year-old and older does have a higher percentage of female fawns (Ozoga and Verme 1982; Verme 1983, 1985; Degayner and Jordan 1987; Jacobson 1994*b*). The time at which a doe breeds also may affect sex ratio of offspring. Does that breed late in the estrous period are thought to conceive more males than females (Verme and Ozoga 1981). Obviously, fawn sex ratios can have a major effect on deer population dynamics.

It might be tempting to conclude that the way to produce more bucks is to have overpopulated ranges. Just the opposite is true, because the ultimate factor in population growth is fawn survival. Few fawns, male or female, survive on ranges with high densities.

The final factor in reproduction is the time of the rut. Nutrition, genetics, and availability of males affect the time when breeding occurs. Well-nourished does can be expected to breed earlier. Deer near the equator have less defined breeding peaks than deer in more northerly latitudes because of less distinct photoperiod cues or more subtle selection pressures.

Why would deer have different rutting periods? Probably because reproduction is timed to favor fawn survival. In the North, selection pressures are extreme. Fawns born too early are likely to die from exposure in late-spring storms. Fawns born too late will not have the size and energy to make it through lean winter months. In the South, selection pressures are less predictable. Floods, summer drought, and biting insects may all influence fawn survival. Selection factors have been confounded by extensive movements of deer and mixing of genetic stocks in restoration projects. For example, a January rut of deer in Mississippi and eastern Alabama may arise from the fact that much of Mississippi's deer population was restored with animals from Mexico (Jacobson et al. 1981).

Another factor that affects the time of rut is the ratio of bucks to does. If there are too few bucks, some does may not be bred during their first or second estrous cycle. The importance of sex ratios at rutting time has been demonstrated in areas in Mississippi and South Carolina. In both locations, the peak of breeding occurred much earlier after sex ratios were improved by a balanced either-sex harvest (Jacobson 1992, Guynn et al. 1986). In Mississippi, areas that were changed from a largely bucks-only harvest to antlerless harvest exceeding 40 percent of the total harvest had peak breeding dates ten days earlier than buck-exploited populations (Casscles 1992).

Fawns born later in the year than normal have reduced odds of survival and also are unlikely to reach puberty and breed as soon as an early-born fawn. Also, late breeding can affect an adult doe's productivity. In a study at Mississippi State University where captive does were prevented from breeding until the second or third estrous cycle, a number of the animals failed to have fawns in subsequent breeding seasons (Jacobson 1984). Apparently, the additional strain of producing late fawns and demands of late nursing caused some of these does to fail to conceive.

MORTALITY

Mortality patterns of mammals, including white-tailed deer, suggest a U-shaped relationship between age and mortality rate (Caughley 1966). Natural mortality is high for fawns and old deer and relatively low for other age classes. Very high fawn mortality and late puberty occur in unhunted populations that approach carrying capacity. In a study of an unhunted Texas herd on the Welder Wildlife Refuge, 66 percent of fawns died before they were 32 days old (Cook et al. 1971). On the Aransas National Wildlife Refuge in Texas, 60 percent fawn mortality was estimated during some summers (White 1973). In hunted populations, fawn mortality rates are generally less than half as high as those from unhunted populations (O'Pezio 1978).

Peak breeding dates

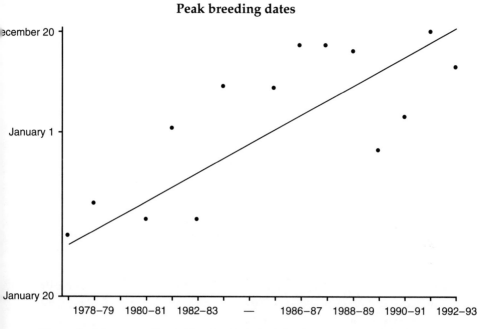

The peak of the rut on Davis Island, Mississippi, has been determined by examination of pregnant does and fetal aging since 1977. In the 1977–78 hunting season, the peak rut was January 14. Before 1977, there was little antlerless deer
harvest on Davis Island and the buck-to-doe ratio highly favored does. A major
population reduction with substantial doe harvest was initiated and in 1983 a
quality deer management program established. Average doe harvest exceeded
buck harvest 1.15 to 1 for this period. The buck-to-doe ratio greatly improved and
by 1992 the peak rut had shifted to December 25. Early breeding in one season
creates a greater likelihood that a doe will be able to conceive again during the following breeding season.

There is a close relationship between maternal nutrition and fawn
mortality (Verme 1962, 1963). When pregnant does were well fed, birth
weights averaged 7.7 pounds and only 7 percent of the fawns were lost.
With poor nutrition, birth weight averaged only 4.2 pounds and 93 percent of these fawns were lost. Most fawns were born alive but died
because they were too weak to nurse. Poorly nourished does suffered
delayed lactation or refused to nurse and abandoned the fawn. Two-
year-old does were poorer mothers than older does. In another study,
Missouri researchers reported a 42 percent loss of fawns by does on a 7
percent protein diet, a 27 percent loss on a 10 percent protein diet, and
no loss of fawns on a 13 percent protein diet (Murphy and Coates 1966).

Mortality of adult males appears higher than for adult does even in unhunted herds. The mortality rate of males may have been twice as high as that for does in an unhunted white-tailed deer population in Washington (Gavin et al. 1984). During a five-year study, the sex ratio of deer more than a year old was a nearly constant three females per male. In a Montana study, average annual mortality rate for males more than a year old was more than twice that of females in a herd where both sexes were hunted (Dusek et al. 1989). Nearly all adult mortality (88 percent) occurred during the fall. Before the hunting season, adult sex ratios ranged from thirty-seven to fifty-eight bucks per one hundred does and averaged about two females per male. A telemetry study in South Texas found that 25 percent to 29 percent of adult males died annually during an unusually dry period (DeYoung 1989). More recent data suggest that 12 percent to 15 percent of adult males died during more normal periods of rainfall. Hunting, poaching, coyotes, and mountain lions were major factors. One explanation for high mortality rates of adult bucks is the additional stress of the rut and resulting poor body condition predisposing animals to disease and predation (Gavin et al. 1984).

Recent radiotelemetry studies (Dusek et al. 1989, Fuller 1990, Nixon et al. 1991) indicate that most adult deer mortality in hunted populations is human related. Its causes include legal harvest, unrecovered kills by hunters, poaching, automobile collisions, and predation by dogs. Fewer

Causes of death for deer other than yearlings

	Central Minnesota		Lower Yellowstone River, Montana		Central Illinois	
	bucks	does	bucks	does	bucks	does
Legal hunting	61%	49%	91%	77%	48%	34%
Unrecovered kills	10	5	—	—	17	25
Poaching	9	18	1	—	13	16
Predation	12	24	9	22	—	—
Other	9	5	—	—	22	25
Total annual mortality rate	0.54	0.31	0.43	0.27	0.61	0.32

In hunted populations, most mortality of deer is caused by humans. "Other" mortality factors include automobile accidents. Data are from radiotelemetry studies by Fuller (1990), Dusek et al. (1989), and Nixon et al. (1991).

than 25 percent of adult mortalities were attributed to natural causes such as diseases, parasites, accidents, and predation.

MOVEMENTS AND DISPERSAL

Two additional factors affecting population dynamics are movements and dispersal. The home range of a deer will determine how much time it spends within the boundaries of the management unit. Home range size and shape depend on several factors: the diversity and condition of the habitat, sex, age, and social composition of the population.

An animal's movements determine, to a large extent, its vulnerability to harvest. If the home range is large, it may cross the boundaries of several landowners, increasing its vulnerability as a result. Habitat structure has a major effect on animal movement. Large home ranges have been reported for deer in bottomland hardwood habitats (Mott et al. 1985), in south Texas brush country, and in midwestern farm country (Sparrowe and Springer 1970). Smaller home ranges are found in mixed hardwood and pine forests of the southeastern United States (Bridges 1968, Lewis 1968, Marshall and Whittington 1968, Cartwright 1975). In the far northern extremes of the white-tailed deer's range, deer congregate during the winter months in limited wintering areas called yards. Movements to and from the yards can involve migrations of 10 miles or more (Carlsen and Farmes 1957, Rongstad and Tester 1969, Sparrowe and Springer 1970, Verme 1973, Hoskinson and Mech 1976). Similarly, migratory movements have been reported in areas with periodic flooding such as the Mississippi Delta and other southern river swamps (Byford 1970, Hood 1971, Morrison 1985). The timing of these movements relative to hunting seasons is obviously important.

Movements to and from food sources also can affect harvest. Harvest rates are higher near food plots compared with areas without food plots (Vanderhoof and Jacobson 1988).

Whitetails commonly disperse from the area where they were born. Though female fawns often remain associated with their mothers, males are rejected from the matriarchal group before the fawning season. Studies have indicated that yearling males often disperse 2 to 6 miles from the maternal home range (Kammermeyer and Marchinton 1976, Swayngham et al. 1988). Why some males disperse and others don't may relate to maternal aggression. Females disperse less frequently. One study reported that 46 percent to 80 percent of yearling males and 13 percent to 20 percent of yearling females can be expected to disperse (Nelson and Mech 1992).

Perhaps the most important movements that affect population dynamics of the white-tailed deer are those associated with the rut. Whitetails increase their activity during the rut. Both males and females have been found to leave their normal ranges at this time. These movements are temporary and not considered dispersal.

DENSITY DEPENDENCE

As discussed earlier, white-tailed deer respond predictably to herd density changes. Deer have a complex social structure; aggression and submission are key components. Michigan researchers reported high fawn mortality due to maternal territoriality at the time of birth in a captive, well-fed whitetail population that was crowded (Ozoga et al. 1982). First-time mothers lost the most fawns because of their low dominance status and their inability to establish or defend a suitable fawning area. Obviously, the higher the population density, the more likely that social interactions will affect the physical and mental well-being of individuals.

Though we still know little of the role of social stress in regulating deer populations, we do know high densities can greatly affect forage production and the availability of cover. These factors indirectly affect growth, survival, and reproduction.

Body growth and antler development are usually related to herd density. With some exceptions, even poor habitats will produce enough high-quality forage so that at least a few deer can reach their potential growth. In some habitats, there may be only enough high-quality forage to produce a deer for every 50 acres or more. Other habitats may produce enough to support a deer for every 10 acres and still meet optimum growth characteristics. As deer density increases, sooner or later consumption of high-quality forage will exceed the ability of the habitat to produce it. When this happens, deer switch to a lower-quality diet, and body weights and antler measurements begin to decline.

These changes do not happen overnight. In fact, research has shown there may be a two-year lag between the time that range conditions change and body weight and antlers are seriously affected. The reason for the lag time is that body weights and antlers reflect forage conditions from the previous growing season. Thus, the effect of density change is not seen on forage until the growing season one year after the change. An example of this can be seen in a deer population at Davis Island, Mississippi. The herd was overpopulated in the late 1970s because of buck-only hunting. This was followed by either-sex harvest and herd reduction. Changing antlerless harvest levels at Davis Island since the

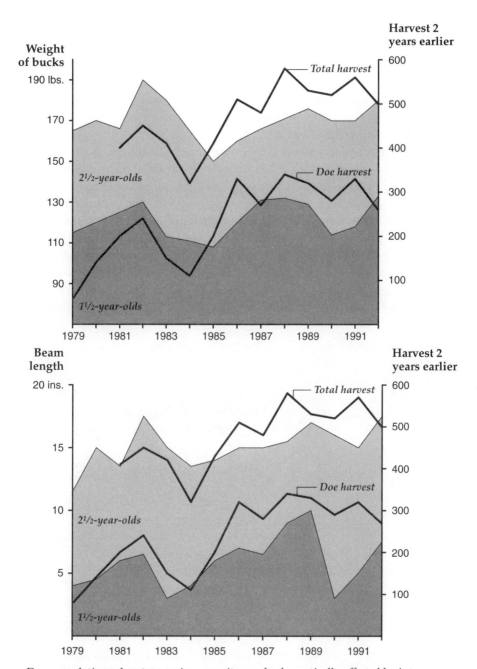

Deer populations close to carrying capacity can be dramatically affected by intensity of doe harvests. Increases in the size of bucks and length of antler beam parallel the increase in harvest two years prior.

initial reduction attempts have resulted in a roller-coaster response in herd condition.

Like body weights and antler measurements, reproduction also responds to changing habitat conditions, although it appears to respond faster than other indicators. The harvest data from Davis Island showed only a one-year lag between a higher doe harvest and an increase in the number of fetuses per doe.

Fawn survival follows a two-year time lag similar to body weight and antler development when density affects habitat. Lactation is an indirect measure of fawn survival, since if a doe is lactating, it means she is still nursing a fawn. The Davis Island lactation data again illustrate the relationship between changing density and fawn survival.

The above relationships should not be confused with carrying capacity. Some habitats can support high numbers of deer well after high-quality forage has disappeared. If we think in terms of a single plant stem, the concept is simple. A single stem may put out 10 inches of annual growth but perhaps only the first ½ inch at the growing tip

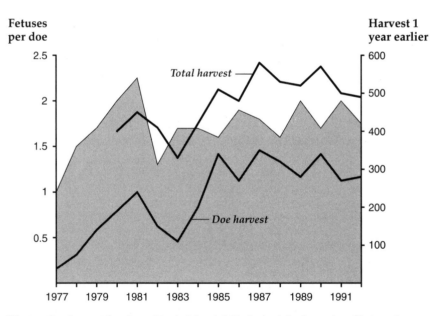

Fluctuating harvest levels on Davis Island, Mississippi, had a major effect on the number of fawns produced per adult doe. Reproduction is more sensitive than body weight and antler measurements to population changes because habitat quality improves the year following herd reduction.

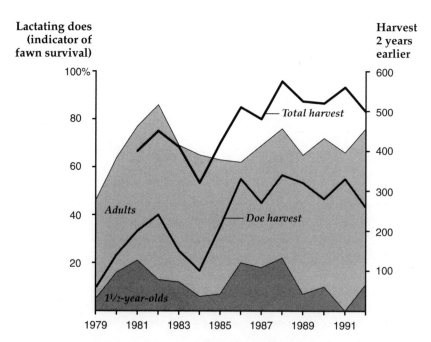

Lactation rates can be used to indirectly measure fawn survival. Like body weights and antler measurements, lactation appears to show a two-year lag relative to density changes. On Davis Island, Mississippi, lactation shows a close relationship to deer harvest two years before, indicating that highest fawn survival follows years of highest doe harvest.

has sufficient nutrients for optimum growth of deer. The remaining growth may provide minimum nutrient requirements for survival or even some growth; however, if a deer eats all of the annual growth, the plant will die and no forage will be available the following year. Most plants that deer eat can withstand about 50 percent consumption of annual growth and still grow the same amount in the following season. Forage quality and quantity are also related to soil fertility. Some habitats, like the lower coastal plain of the southern United States, may have only a few plants with a limited amount of optimum forage. Fertile bottomland hardwood forest and farmland habitats have more plants with high nutrient quality.

When deer begin to reduce the availability of high-quality forage in their habitat, fawn production and survival are affected. When both quality and quantity of preferred deer foods change, fawn production and survival can be greatly impacted.

Overbrowsing affects not only nutritional quality of the range but also escape cover and predation rates. There is no understory in this forest because of over-population of deer. A fawn in such situations is much more vulnerable to coyotes and other predators than when deer populations are in balance with their habitat. PHOTOGRAPH BY HARRY JACOBSON.

Although the effect of deer density on nutrition has perhaps the most serious impact on reproduction and survival, other factors also are involved. At high densities, stress-related hormones produced by the adrenal gland and elsewhere may lower reproductive effort. These hormones also affect the immune system and can lower resistance to diseases. Additionally, because reduced forage availability at high density requires deer to graze close to the ground, some parasitic diseases increase. Stomach and lung worms are likely to increase greatly at high densities, contributing to high mortality of fawns and older adults and lowered condition of prime-age animals (Davidson et al. 1981). Reduced body weights and energy stores contribute to winter mortality, particularly in fawns. Prime-age males that can't overcome both lower nutrition and stress of the rut may be especially vulnerable.

Outbreaks of infectious diseases are more likely at high densities because of increased opportunity for spread from one animal to another, along with lowered immune resistance. Overpopulated deer herds seldom show dramatic die-offs, however. More likely is the insidious condition of high fawn mortality, chronic malnutrition, and chronic infectious and parasitic disease.

One other factor altered by deer density is predation. In some habitats, this can account for mortality of 25 percent to 50 percent of the fawn crop (Cook et al. 1971). When densities are high, escape cover as well as forage can be reduced, increasing the deer's vulnerability to predators.

In arid regions, deer density and fawn survival are linked with annual rainfall and cattle grazing (Teer 1984). Both nutrition and predation likely are involved, as nutritious forage and escape cover are much more plentiful in lightly grazed pastures than in overgrazed areas and in wet years than in dry years.

PRINCIPLES OF HARVESTING

A deer herd should be managed as two separate populations. The females must be managed to maintain productivity. The number of new deer added to the prehunt population is a function of the number of fawns born and their survival. The number of fawns born is determined

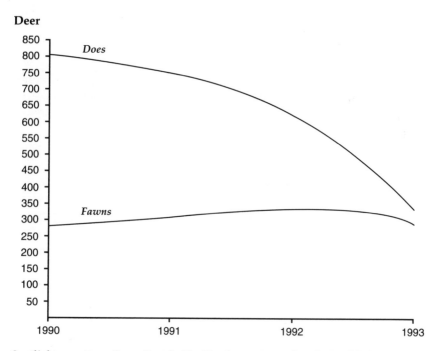

Spotlight counts on Cocoa Ranch, Florida, demonstrate the relationship between doe density and fawn survival. Following reduction of does on the ranch, the number of fawns actually increased.

by the number of does and their condition. Fawn survival depends mostly on the doe's condition, although predation is a factor in some situations. Thus, a large number of does that are nutritionally stressed will not raise as many fawns as a lesser number of healthy does.

Males should be managed to produce the age structure appropriate to management goals. If the objective is to produce mature bucks (age 4 ½ years and older), only 10 percent to 20 percent of the antlered male segment should be harvested. The manager should not be overly concerned about the age of the antlerless harvest. Some button bucks will be mistakenly harvested for does. This is difficult to avoid and, generally, if care is taken to minimize harvest of button bucks, insignificant to overall management.

Questions of how many deer to harvest and what proportion should be bucks or does are seldom answered objectively. Ideally, a manager would know exactly how many deer of each age and sex are present. Accurate information on herd size, the buck-to-doe ratio, reproductive success, rainfall, habitat conditions, and hunting on neighboring properties would allow the manager to easily prescribe what percentage of the herd to harvest. Situations where all pertinent information is available are rare in deer management, however.

Reproduction, mortality, population structure, and population size determine the number of animals that can be harvested from a population on a sustained basis. In the accompanying table, populations have been simulated to illustrate the relationship between carrying capacity and sustained yield. Fawn mortality rates increase from 15 percent to 70 percent as population density increases from 10 percent of carrying capacity to carrying capacity.

For most management situations, maintaining population density at 40 percent to 80 percent of carrying capacity will provide about the same sustainable yields. Assuming that poaching is not a problem, 20 percent to 40 percent of the female segment of the herd should be harvested annually to maintain density within this range. Considerable effort may be required to harvest 35 percent or more of the females. Taking 20 percent to 35 percent of the females annually can provide fair nutritional conditions, assuming the range is not heavily grazed by livestock. Although nutrition will not be as good as when the population density is maintained at or below 50 percent to 60 percent of carrying capacity, hunting may be more enjoyable for many hunters as they will see more deer and deer sign. Maintaining a population at the high-

Carrying capacity	Prehunt population				Sustained yields*				
	Yearling bucks	Mature bucks	Does	Fawns	Yearling bucks	Mature bucks	Does	Fawns	Total
10%	2.0	1.3	6.3	8.2	1.0	0	4.0	2.8	7.8
20	3.9	2.8	12.5	16.3	1.0	1.0	8.0	5.5	15.5
30	6.1	4.1	18.3	22.6	2.0	1.0	10.0	7.1	21.1
40	8.0	5.4	24.5	27.2	2.4	1.6	12.5	8.7	25.2
50	9.7	7.2	30.0	30.3	2.9	2.2	13.1	9.2	27.3
60	11.4	9.0	35.3	32.4	3.4	2.7	12.9	9.1	28.1
70	12.6	10.3	38.9	33.2	3.8	3.1	10.7	7.5	25.1
80	14.0	12.1	43.7	32.7	4.2	3.6	8.6	6.1	22.5
90	11.5	17.3	47.7	18.9	2.2	3.3	0	0	5.5
100	8.0	24.0	52.0	16.0	0	0	0	0	0

*The number of bucks harvested not to exceed 30% of prehunt buck density. Antlerless deer were harvested to stabilize population at specific relative posthunt densities. The number of fawns harvested equals 70% of the number of does harvested.

In theoretical models of sustained yields, the highest harvest rates are achieved at densities of 50 percent to 60 percent of carrying capacity. Modified from Downing and Guynn 1985.

est productivity level (50 percent to 60 percent of carrying capacity) may require a harvest of more than 40 percent of the adult does.

These results are based on the assumption that 30 percent of antlered bucks were harvested each year. Only 19 percent of bucks can be harvested at 90 percent of carrying capacity, however, because a greater buck harvest would cause the population to decline below 90 percent. Harvesting 30 percent of the antlered bucks annually will result in few bucks living to ages greater than 4½ years, and the preseason mature buck-to-doe ratio will generally run about sixty bucks to one hundred does. In our model, the maximum number of mature bucks occurs at a population density of 80 percent of carrying capacity, but bucks will be of much lower quality than those from lower-density populations. If the management objective is to produce mature bucks and a more balanced sex ratio, the harvest rate of antlered bucks should be reduced.

This example must be viewed as a starting point. Proper management requires documentation that a population is responding as expected and that the assumed rates of reproduction and mortality are valid for the area. Nevertheless, the table does establish a most important concept of deer management, that antlerless deer must be harvested to regulate population size and maintain reproductive potential. Assuming that poaching is not a problem, 20 percent to 35 percent of the female segment of most herds should be harvested on an annual basis. There are exceptions; seek guidance from a competent biologist. Managers who cautiously gain experience with their herds may eventually eliminate the need for a standard table. It is hoped that the concepts developed here will make that experience easier to interpret and put into perspective.

MANAGING FOR OLDER BUCK AGE STRUCTURE

A primary goal of most quality deer management programs is to allow bucks to reach maturity and create a more natural age and sex structure. Populations from 40 percent to 70 percent of carrying capacity provide high recruitment and are logical densities on which to base quality deer management. Maintaining the female segment of the herd at maximum sustained yield requires substantial harvest of antlerless animals. If bucks can be protected from harvest until they reach older age classes (3½ to 5½ years), the maximum sustained yield of mature ones would be realized. Some managers may actually choose to manage below the maximum sustained yield level for ease in controlling herd density with fewer hunters, to improve the quality of bucks within age classes, and to reduce chances of bucks dispersing from the managed property.

Many attempts at increasing buck age structure have succeeded and others have been great disappointments. Expectations of abundant old, mature bucks after two to three years of restrained harvest of young bucks sometimes are dashed by unexpected or uncontrollable factors. Harvest strategies that include shooting spike bucks can remove a substantial proportion of the yearling age class in some areas. Bucks that are protected on a managed property may be fair game on adjoining property, killed by poachers, or otherwise lost.

What improvement in age structure of bucks can you expect? Two actual examples of quality deer management are provided below. The accompanying figure shows the age structure of bucks harvested on Kings Point, an 18,000-acre club association near Vicksburg, Mississippi. In 1983, several hunting clubs there voted to voluntarily restrain their harvest of yearling bucks. The association dramatically increased the percentage of 2-year-old bucks while decreasing the harvest of yearling bucks. There also was an increase in 3-year-old bucks and a slight increase in 4-year-olds in the harvest. But, after ten years of substantial restraint in the harvest of yearling bucks, 5-year-olds still are

Buck harvest

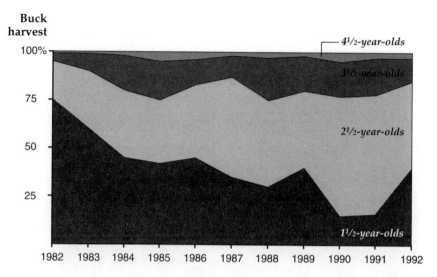

After quality deer management began in 1983, the number of 2-year-old bucks at Kings Point, Mississippi, increased dramatically. After ten years of quality deer management, however, few 4-year-old bucks and no 5-year-olds were in the harvest. Although harvest of yearling bucks was substantially reduced, hunting pressure on 2-year-old and older bucks was so intense that few survived to 4 years.

not being harvested. Essentially, this shows that the intensive harvest pressure placed on bucks has been shifted one age class. Before the quality deer management effort in 1983, 80 percent of the antlered bucks were harvested annually on Kings Point. After 1983, the yearling bucks were protected, but hunting pressure was still intense enough that few bucks made it to 4 years or older.

In 1990, hunting pressure was reduced on antlered bucks and the future harvest on Kings Point likely will show more older bucks. These data illustrate that changes in the mature buck age structure should not be expected overnight. Unless harvest also is restrained on 2½- and 3½-year-old bucks, it may take many years for any 5½-year-olds to be harvested.

A similar example of how quality deer management can affect the age structure of bucks was demonstrated on Longleaf Plantation in southern Mississippi. Beginning in 1984, hunters there began restraining harvest of smaller forked antlered bucks. In 1985, all yearling bucks were protected, although some small spikes were still mistakenly harvested as does. Longleaf Plantation differs from Kings Point in that

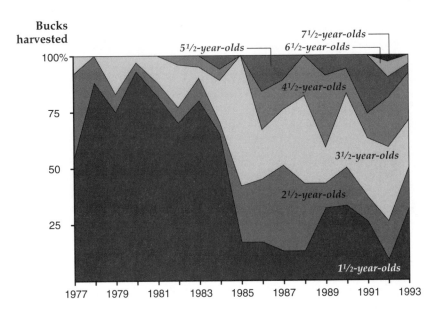

Substantial improvement in the percentage of older bucks harvested can be seen at Longleaf Plantation, Mississippi, shortly after a quality deer management program began in 1984. Since yearling buck harvest was greatly reduced and hunting pressure was also reduced on 2-year-old bucks, harvests of 3-year-old and 4-year-old and older bucks have greatly increased.

hunting pressure was much less intense on 2-year-olds. As a result, a relatively high percentage of 4- and 5-year-old bucks began showing up.

MANAGING FOR A NATURAL HERD STRUCTURE

Tony Bubenik (1988) put forth "An Immodest Proposal" in the *Bugle* quarterly journal defining an appropriate role for man in the long-term welfare of elk. This proposal was adapted for white-tailed deer in the *Sign Post* (Guynn 1991). The proposal was that deer herds should be managed so that the natural structure of populations is maintained. This goal ensures that the behavioral and biological mechanisms that shape deer populations are allowed to function. The density, sex ratio, and age structure of the deer should mimic a population regulated by natural predators and hunting by the Native Americans.

Examinations of deer remains in Native American middens show herd structure during historic and prehistoric times. Elder (1965) reported age composition of prehistoric Native American deer harvest based on mandibles from three sites in Missouri. Age compositions from the sites are remarkably similar and suggest that the Native Americans killed few fawns (8 percent or less of each sample), many deer survived to older ages (20 percent to 26 percent of the population was 6½ years or older), and longevity of deer was great (each sample showed some deer 10 years or older). Parmalee (1965) pointed out that the small percentage of fawns in archaeological remains may be biased because the delicate bones of young animals disintegrate or break more easily than those of adults. Nevertheless, Elder (1965) felt that, even given this consideration,

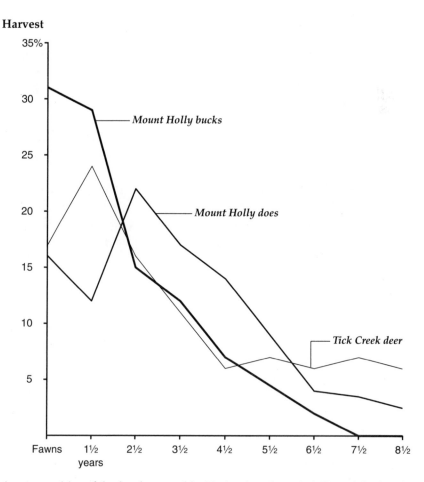

Age composition of the deer harvested by Native Americans in Missouri during the prehistoric period is similar to the age structure of the harvest under quality deer management on the Mount Holly Plantation from 1982 to 1991. The prehistoric data are based on a study of 759 mandibles recovered from the Tick Creek Midden.

the low percentage of fawns in the middens suggests that Native Americans avoided taking them.

Age composition of modern deer harvests in Iowa and Missouri are extremely different from those of the Native American harvests in that nearly one-third of the harvest is fawns, about 2 percent of deer live to 6½ years, and very few deer live as long as 8½ years (Elder 1965).

The sex composition of deer from the Tick Creek midden in Missouri is 23 percent females and 77 percent males (Parmalee 1965). Again, the fact that the frontal area of fawn and doe skulls may disintegrate or shatter more easily into unidentifiable fragments may bias these data. Virtually all of the buck skulls had hardened antlers or no antlers when killed. Thus, it would appear that deer hunting was concentrated in the fall and winter. Interestingly, deer provided an estimated 85 percent of the meat at Tick Creek and more than 90 percent of all bone tools were fashioned from deer (Parmalee 1965). Antler tines were particularly important for flaking flint in the making of arrow points.

Though the middens do not provide specific data on herd structure, they suggest that modern deer management produces herds with age-sex structures that are much younger and more unbalanced in favor of does than herds hunted by the Native Americans. Mature bucks were important components of natural deer populations. Quality deer management strategies are compatible with the goal of maintaining herds in a natural condition. For example, the age composition of deer harvested under a quality deer management strategy on the Mount Holly Plantation from 1982 to 1991 is similar to that from remains at the Tick Creek midden as described by Parmalee.

—Harry A. Jacobson and
David C. Guynn, Jr.

CHAPTER 7

Age and Quality Relationships

The curious naturalist often feels sorry for those of his fellow-men who miss such an experience; and miss it so unnecessarily, because it is there, to be seen, all the time. Nor is reading about it anything more than a poor substitute; direct, active observation is the only real thing.

—N. TINBERGEN

Quality deer are determined by age, nutrition, and genetics. Age, which is perhaps the easiest to manage, often is the most neglected component of the equation. It should seem obvious that age is related to growth, but few sportsmen understand how significant age can be to antler quality and few may realize that age can affect fertility of does and even the sex ratios of female offspring.

Perhaps if more people understood age, we wouldn't hear the inevitable response to "What did you kill this year?" The answer is almost always "I killed an eight-point buck," or whatever. Have you ever heard anyone answer, "I killed a five-year-old buck"? The number of points is perhaps the least important measure of buck quality. Age, however, is a highly predictable measure.

AGE AND BODY GROWTH

The relationship between age and body growth differs little between males and females. At birth, females weigh slightly less than males. Captive deer in the Mississippi State University deer research facilities average 6 pounds, 12 ounces at birth for females, compared with 7 pounds for males. Females reach mature body weights at 4 years of age compared with 5 years of age for males, and females reach a much higher percentage of their mature weight in their first year of growth.

By the time that most females reach 18 months of age they are more than 80 percent of their mature weights, whereas males are only about 60 percent of their mature weights at this age.

AGE AND ANTLERS

The formation of antlers begins in the young buck when he first produces small amounts of the hormone testosterone. Testosterone causes the formation of the pedicle, or the place on the skull where antler growth begins anew each year. The requirement for male sex hormones in antler growth was discovered as long ago as Aristotle's time. It was known even then that if a young buck was castrated before his pedicles were formed, he would never grow antlers (Fennessy and Suttie 1985). If the pedicles were formed and the buck was castrated, though, antlers would grow but would always remain in velvet.

The seasonal release of testosterone causes the antlers to harden into bone and the seasonal regression of the testes causes the antlers to be cast each year. Most males do not produce enough testosterone in their first year to grow hard antlers. Under good nutrition, however, up to 30 percent or more of fawn bucks will develop small calcified buttons at about 8 months of age. Sportsmen often are concerned that hunting regulations that allow the taking of any deer with hardened antlers visible above the hairline will cause high numbers of these button bucks to be taken.

This is not the case because when fawn bucks do develop these first antlers, it is usually after the hunting season. Antler development of more than two hundred fawn bucks has been recorded in the deer research facilities at Mississippi State University. Only about 20 percent of these developed buttons their first year, but not one of these was seen before the fourth week in January and most developed these antlers in February and March. In other words, none could have been classified as legal antlered bucks during the deer hunting season.

Yearling antler growth is related to fawn development in the first year of life. This becomes evident when we look at the month a male fawn is born and his antler quality at 18 months. Antler data from deer raised in captivity show that date of birth is very important for antler quality. Regardless of birth date, all bucks cease antler growth for the year at about the same time. This takes place during September and October, when the antlers mineralize and velvet is shed. Thus, when fawns are born over a six-month period, as they are in some areas of

The button buck is a young (6-month-old) male with his antlers beginning to form. The first outgrowth serves as the point of attachment for all subsequent antlers and is called the pedicle. PHOTOGRAPH BY LISA WHITE.

Most fawns won't develop calcified buttons their first year, but an occasional 8-month-old may develop these barely visible antlers. PHOTOGRAPH BY HARRY JACOBSON.

		Yearlings	
Birth	Number of deer	Average points	Spikes
June	20	7.70	0.0%
July	57	5.91	14.0
August	55	4.25	27.3
September	9	3.00	44.4
October–November	4	2.00	100.0

A male fawn's month of birth can have a direct impact on his first set of antlers at 18 months. Late-born fawns generally have fewer points than early-born ones.

the South, some have had only eleven months of growth to complete yearling antlers while others are as old as 16 months.

Fortunately, how a buck begins life may have little to do with antler qualities in later life. There is often little relationship between a buck's antlers as a yearling and his antlers at age 5. A buck may get a bad start because of a later birth date or poor early nutrition but still can catch up in antler growth if adequate nutrition is available later.

Change in antler quality is dramatic with increasing age through 5½ years. Records from twenty-three bucks maintained until a minimum age of 7½ years in captivity show that the average yearling has about 10 percent of his mature antler weight. There is a geometric progression in antler weight until bucks reach 5½ years of age. Other antler measurements generally follow the same trends. It is interesting that on average, prime-age bucks show little decline in antler quality after the age of 5½ and some bucks don't reach peak antler quality until 8½. Some bucks do show antler decline in later life, but unless disease or injury intervenes, this may not occur until 9½ or older.

Another quality that frequently changes with age is antler conformation. Yearling bucks often lack symmetry and one antler can be considerably shorter or have fewer points than the other. Most bucks raised

The yearling spike buck was born September 9 the previous year; the buck with fourteen points was born July 2. The difference in antler quality is primarily due to birth date. Both bucks have genetic backgrounds with Boone and Crockett lineage on both sides. PHOTOGRAPHS BY HARRY JACOBSON.

That two captive Mississippi bucks that had poor antlers as yearlings became exceptional trophies by 5 years shows the importance of age to quality. Photograph by Harry Jacobson.

in captivity to 2½- and 3½-year age classes typically have eight- to ten-point antlers, however. At 4 to 6 years, these same deer may develop very atypical antler growth. Additionally, it is not unusual for bucks to drop from eight- or ten-point to six- or eight-point conformations.

Although injury, nutrition, and disease can cause some of these changes, some deer show dramatic antler changes because of age alone. These appear to be strictly from genetic makeup.

		Average antler measurements			
Age	Points	Inside spread	Beam length	Boone & Crockett score	Weight
1½ years	4.0	6.9 ins.	8.3 ins.	37	5 oz.
2½	8.3	12.7	15.8	89	20
3½	9.0	15.8	18.4	110	32
4½	10.0	16.5	20.5	130	36
5½	9.7	17.0	21.7	142	45
6½	9.7	17.5	21.6	132	44
7½	10.1	16.3	21.3	132	45

The antlers of 23 yearling bucks in Mississippi averaged about 10 percent of the weight of their mature antlers. Most antler measurements increase until about 5 years of age. The Boone and Crockett scores are not adjusted for asymmetry.

At 3 years this twelve-point buck shows typical antler formation. The same buck at 6 years has atypical antlers with twenty-four points. Antlers of some bucks tend to become more atypical with increasing age, whereas others maintain typical conformation throughout their lives. PHOTOGRAPHS BY HARRY JACOBSON.

AGE AND REPRODUCTION

Like body weight and antler quality, reproductive performance is greatly affected by age. In males, age affects seasonal rutting condition. Fawn males that reach puberty in their first year of life produce sperm only very late in the breeding season. Yearlings also reach peak breeding condition later than adult males, with sex organs not reaching their full development until almost a month after adult males.

Female reproductive capabilities differ primarily among fawns, yearlings, and 2-year-old or older does. On very good range in the Midwest, many fawns (up to 80 percent) may become pregnant in their first year (Haugen 1975). At the northern extremes of the white-tailed deer range, however, it is unlikely for fawns to become pregnant even under very good nutritional conditions. Deep snow and very cold weather make it critical that young deer concentrate on survival. In the South, fawn breeding is influenced by birth date and range conditions. Even under ideal conditions, only 18 percent of fawns became pregnant in the Mississippi State University deer research facilities. In South Carolina, where breeding occurs earlier than in Mississippi, it was estimated that 35 percent of fawns became pregnant (Urbston 1967).

When fawns do become pregnant, they almost always have singletons and usually their fawns are born a month or more later than fawns of older does.

The reproductive rate of yearling does also is greatly influenced by nutrition. On very poor or overcrowded ranges, they may fail to breed at all, but under good conditions, pregnant yearlings can be expected to average about 1.6 fawns. Does 2 years and older generally have twins. Under very good conditions, older does can be expected to produce an average of about 1.8 fawns each. Old age has little effect on productivity and several studies have documented very old does (12 or older) consistently producing twins. Thus, the "old barren doe" is just a myth. A doe can be expected to remain productive up to the year of her death.

Frequently triplets, and occasionally litters of up to four, have been reported; however, as in the younger classes, poor nutrition can dramatically lower fawn production. Even well-managed populations may show low production in nutritionally deficient habitat like the lower coastal plain of the southern Gulf states (Harlow and Jones 1965).

Female age can affect not only the number of young produced but also the sex of the offspring (Verme 1983). We know that when well nourished, fawns give birth to more males and yearlings give birth to more females (Jacobson 1994*a*). The reasons for this have not been fully explained. Regardless, these facts and the difference in fawn production by age class (as discussed in chapter 2) are important considerations when managing a herd.

—HARRY A. JACOBSON

CHAPTER 8

The Spike Question

There are times when we need education in the obvious more than investigations of the obscure.

—OLIVER WENDELL HOLMES

The spike buck issue has grown with the increasing deer population densities throughout the United States. The combination of increased densities and traditionally high buck kills has resulted in poor age structure in bucks, imbalanced sex ratios, and populations exceeding the optimum level for the habitat. This produces an ever-increasing supply of spikes.

One of the most controversial issues concerning quality deer management is whether to harvest spike bucks (Brothers et al. 1990). Each side is entrenched. A few hunters have gotten the mistaken notion that "once a spike, always a spike." This, of course, is not true. But it is also incorrect that all bucks start out as spikes.

Prominent researchers in Texas and Mississippi have concluded that antler development is hereditary to some extent but their findings on spikes are basically opposite. They have done extensive research on spikes and the offspring of spikes through multiple generations and followed body size and antler development until the bucks' deaths at various ages. In Texas, yearlings with spikes usually had poorer antler development in subsequent years than yearlings with forked antlers (Harmel 1982; Williams and Harmel 1988a, 1988b). Bucks that started out as spikes also fathered offspring with lower antler quality. The Mississippi researchers (H. A. Jacobson, Mississippi State University, personal communication) did not find this relationship. They could not predict antler development or that of a buck's offspring from the buck's first set of antlers. It may seem strange, but both studies are correct, based on the experimental herds investigated. The reason for the difference is that many factors can cause a buck's first set of antlers to be of poor quality. Neither study covered all herd conditions affecting antler development.

FACTORS THAT AFFECT YEARLING ANTLER DEVELOPMENT

Yearling bucks in optimum habitat and with good genetics occasionally have ten or even twelve antler points. Six- or eight-point yearlings are the norm in some herds and spikes in others. Why is a spike a spike? Antler development, and particularly the occurrence of spikes, depends upon one or more of four factors: age, nutrition, timing of the fawning season, and genetics. Data from years of field observations and collections indicate that some fawns have little or no chance of developing more than spikes when 1½ years old. Reasons include poor nutrition, late birth, and genetics. When the majority of buck fawns are poorly nourished or late born, spike yearlings are common. Unless the reason for a yearling having spikes is known or can be guessed, there is no method to predict the size of his antlers in subsequent years.

Some habitats (certain areas of Florida, for example) are so deficient in forage quality that even when populations are low, bucks do not receive the nutrition needed for growth of forked antlers as yearlings (Shea et al. 1992). In extremely poor habitats, 2½-year-old or older bucks can have spikes and yearlings no antlers. Conversely, when fawns receive good nutrition and are born early (March through June), most will grow forked antlers the following year. Those that do not grow more than spikes under these conditions are more likely to be genetically inferior.

Even when individuals have good genes and habitat, a buck's first set of antlers can be spikes. This may occur where buck fawns are born to does bred as fawns or those born to any doe with multiple births. Single fawns born to 1-year-olds may receive poor nutrition early in life because of their small, inexperienced mothers. When an older doe has twins or triplets, the fawns also can be deprived early because of competition for milk and postnatal care. In both instances, the does are likely to be superior genetically, since they are very productive, but the fawns may be somewhat deprived nutritionally and not achieve their potential as yearlings.

Fawns that are born late (August to October) have much less chance of developing forked antlers as yearlings (Knox et al. 1991, Shea et al. 1992*b*). The likely reason is that they are still very young and less developed when growth of their first antlers begins. Fawns born in September, for example, would be about 8 months old, and those born in May a full year old. In herds or individuals that breed very late, few of the yearlings can produce more than spikes, but this may not affect the antlers they produce at older ages or those of their offspring.

There is still much to learn about why some herds have breeding and fawning seasons different from others. Nevertheless, in certain regions of the country (particularly the South) breeding seasons are "naturally" late. This is thought to be related to some survival advantage accruing to the fawns. In other words, it is nature's way of increasing their chances of survival. There are other situations where late or long breeding seasons may not be normal or desirable. That is, they are caused by overpopulation or possibly too few mature bucks (see chapter 9). These situations can often be corrected by population management.

FACTORS THAT AFFECT SPIKE HARVEST DECISIONS
There is little debate that antler characteristics are inherited (Williams and Harmel 1988*a*). The question is whether poor yearling antler development is a result of heredity or environmental factors. If a lot of yearlings have spikes, one would suspect environment or late breeding is responsible. In any case, by studying a herd, biologists can usually conclude why most of the spikes are spikes. From this, a rational decision on whether to harvest spikes can be made that takes into consideration the biological facts and goals of the landowner or club.

Usually, the harvest of spikes should not be considered until all problems with herd density and sex and age structure have been corrected. Factors that should be evaluated before a decision is made to shoot spikes include deer density, recruitment rate, the buck-to-doe ratio, control of the buck harvest, and age distribution within the sexes.

Density is often the most important problem. Very dense populations, especially those not within deerproof fences, usually have sex ratios strongly biased toward does, low recruitment, and high percentages of spike yearlings. The most effective way to correct this is to focus harvest on the females. This can not be overemphasized! If males make up a high percentage of a dense population, it may be desirable to remove significant numbers of them, but this is usually not the case. Overpopulated areas generally have far more does than bucks, even when they have not been hunted. Furthermore, bucks tend to occupy separate niches much of the year and may not compete significantly with females for food. This can vary with habitat characteristics. If the bucks do not compete with does, their posthunt numbers would have little effect on fawn recruitment.

Where deer density is low and the habitat is capable of supporting a larger, productive herd, it is usually unwise to harvest spikes. This decision is especially appropriate if deer density is low, combined with a poor buck-to-doe ratio. As a rule, before harvesting spikes, deer density should be adequate but low enough that the deer are in excellent condition. Also, there should be nearly as many bucks as does, an acceptable recruitment rate, and effective control of the buck harvest. The herd should include substantial numbers of bucks in the middle and older age classes.

The higher the recruitment rate, the more flexibility in the harvest decision. When a very high population is reduced, habitat often improves and the high-quality food available for each doe may increase. Does produce many more fawns, and if half of these are males, then the recruitment of males will be much greater. If the recruitment rate is high in a herd that has a good sex ratio and age distribution, and there is good harvest control, then a substantial removal of males may be necessary. Conversely, a low recruitment rate combined with the absence of other desirable herd conditions may preclude a spike harvest.

The buck-to-doe ratio is important. It is generally unwise to harvest spikes when the sex ratio is badly skewed and when most bucks are 1½ or 2½ years old. Control of the buck harvest is essential to quality management. Nevertheless, if bucks of any antler type or age class are to be generally excluded from harvest, there should be a reasonable assurance that many of the excluded animals will not be harvested in another area.

SHOOT OR DON'T SHOOT

No single prescription on whether to shoot spikes is universally applicable and the prescription for what to harvest cannot always be based on biological facts alone. Practical considerations involving the attitudes, desires, and objectives of the hunters are important. It may be politically prudent to allow harvest of some yearlings to satisfy the hunters' desire for a buck. In fact, managers may be justified in making recommendations based on a variety of nonbiological and biological reasons.

Nevertheless, early in a quality deer management program, shooting spikes is usually undesirable biologically. Immediate genetic benefits are probably negligible, so spike harvests should at least be delayed until population density, sex ratio, and age structure problems are corrected. Population density reduction is best achieved by focusing harvest on the does. Leaving all yearling bucks, including spikes, allows herds to achieve sex ratio and buck age structure goals more rapidly. When adequate numbers of bucks have been achieved, however, yearlings can make up some of the buck harvest, since they are present in higher numbers than any other age class. If some yearling bucks are going to be harvested, spikes are often the best ones to take. They are the only bucks that the average hunter can identify in the field for what they are.

In unfenced areas of less than 5,000 acres, where high numbers of bucks are lost to dispersal or harvest on adjoining properties, improvements in age structure will be slow. Shooting spikes is most logical in a quality management program with good controls (e.g., within a high fence), when desirable sex ratio, age structure, and density have already been achieved and the manager seeks long-term genetic improvements. In Texas, spikes are often harvested in fenced, moderate-density herds with low buck harvest rates (less than 30 percent of antlered harvest composed of yearlings) and with a low percentage of spike-antlered yearlings (Brothers and Ray 1975). Under these conditions, harvesting spike bucks has little impact on adult sex ratio or buck age structure, aids in reducing herd density, and removes bucks that may exhibit poor antler quality at maturity. Nevertheless, it has become increasingly common for hunters with the stated intention of improving buck quality to harvest spikes from herds having a poor sex ratio and age structure. Avoid this. Culling spikes or older bucks that exhibit inferior antlers generally is appropriate only if all other problems with herd structure have been corrected and there is an excess of bucks. These situations are rare.

Can the individual hunter or landowner decide whether it is desirable to shoot spikes on a specific area? Generally, no. He should seek advice from an experienced wildlife specialist. Then, with well-defined management objectives and pertinent information on herd condition and habitat, a decision on shooting spikes can be made. Without expert advice to the contrary, the best decision is not to shoot them.

—AL BROTHERS,
DAVID C. GUYNN, JR.,
JOE HAMILTON, AND
R. LARRY MARCHINTON

CHAPTER 9

Deer Sociobiology

It is a matter of surpassing remark . . . what a change in the landscape occurs when you have made a place of your own; how the shape of an oak tree emerges in the darkness to take on that definition which can only be oak; how stars shine brighter . . . how the sound of some running brook . . . chants its quiet cadence; how the smells rush at you . . . the smell of leaves, green leaves dampened by dew, but of other leaves also, old leaves . . . that sweet soft odor of death's decomposition. And then there is that muskiness. There is an animal somewhere.

—Robert Ardrey (1966)
The Territorial Imperative

White-tailed deer evolved in North America several million years ago. Since then, they have been exposed to many pressures that have shaped their physiology, anatomy, and behavior. Predators, diseases, habitat conditions, and hunting by Native Americans have affected the population characteristics. The whitetail social organization or sociobiology originated as an adaptation to these environmental factors. A normal social organization is essential to its healthy existence.

No one knows for sure what sex ratios and age structures were normal in whitetail populations when Europeans began to colonize the New World. Most likely, the demography was quite different than it is now in most of our heavily harvested populations. Densities likely were lower than they are today in many intensively managed herds. Also, original herds probably had a much older age structure, especially among males, and sex ratios were more even.

All mammals have evolved mechanisms that minimize social tensions or strife within a species. According to Bubenik (1972), "The performance of the species-typical patterns of social behavior depend not only on the sex and maturational state of the animal, but also on the demographic conditions of the population." Specific behaviors of individuals depend not only on the age and sex of the individual, but also on the age structure, sex ratio, and density of the population.

Recent studies have shown that heavy harvesting of antlered males can have profound impacts on deer social behavior. These changes often hurt herd productivity, survival rates, and physical condition. So, while proper nutrition is extremely important in producing quality deer, sociobiological factors are also important.

Quality management is the concept of managing deer on an ecological basis to grow quality individuals. This means producing demographic conditions that likely were more typical when herds were "managed" by natural predators and Native Americans. Natural conditions provide not only for a nutritionally healthy herd but for social health as well.

WHITETAIL SOCIAL ORGANIZATION

Whitetails inhabit many environments across the continent, so their adaptive traits vary from one region to the next. For example, some whitetail populations migrate seasonally; some do not. Nevertheless, the basic patterns of social behavior are similar among all populations.

The basic social unit in female whitetails consists of a matriarch doe, several generations of her daughters, and fawns that share an ancestral range. Bucks leave these matriarchal groups during their first or second year and many establish new home ranges. Typically they join all-male groups composed of several compatible, but generally unrelated, bucks.

A strict dominance hierarchy usually is central in the social lives of whitetails. In both sexes, physically and behaviorally mature individuals can suppress the reproductive performance of younger individuals. Among females, dominance is closely related to age. Older matriarchs tend to occupy the best habitat and have the highest fawn-rearing success. Dominance among females also appears to be related to the relative dominance of each doe's mother.

In contrast, a buck's dominance is determined primarily by age, size, and strength. Where they exist, physically superior and behaviorally mature bucks (3½ years old or older) typically dominate younger bucks and do most of the breeding.

Bucks and does tend to have somewhat different seasonal food and cover preferences during the nonbreeding season, so they do not compete equally for the same resources. Therefore, poor growth rates among young deer and reproductive failure among adult does, when associated with food competition and malnutrition, usually are the result of too many females, not too many bucks.

During antler growth, males, especially those older than yearlings, form bachelor groups. They coexist amicably until velvet is shed from their antlers, when they begin testing one another with sparring matches. Bachelor groups break up during the breeding season. PHOTOGRAPH BY KENT KAMMERMEYER.

TODAY'S PROBLEM

To fully understand how demographic changes from a quality management program can help restore a herd's natural sociobiology, first look at the conditions of herds across the country. Many have demographic characteristics unlike those under which deer behavior evolved. Few modern hunters can routinely hunt in a "demographically normal" deer herd. In fact, much of what we know about white-tailed deer behavior came from studies of herds that quite likely had abnormal conditions.

In most areas, a heavy harvest of antlered males is typical. Bucks are taken with few restrictions other than bag limits and season length. Doe harvest, on the other hand, is much more restrictive and generally designed to maintain the population near the carrying capacity of the habitat. Consequently, many herds have a very young male age structure, a sex ratio heavily skewed toward females, and high population densities. Such herds are subject to sociobiological changes that may hurt deer health and vigor. Problems include alterations in the timing and intensity of the rut, reduced growth rates of young males, and changes in the dispersal patterns of young males.

TIMING AND LENGTH OF THE BREEDING SEASON

The initiation of the breeding season in deer is directly related to changes in the photoperiod (Goss 1983). In autumn, as the days grow shorter and the nights longer, physiological changes occur in both sexes. Shortening day length triggers a chain of hormonal events that ensures conception takes place in the fall so that fawns are born in the spring, when forage is prime.

Although the timing is "set" by changing photoperiod, a doe's breeding date may be affected by other factors. Recent studies show that herd demographics and social factors can have pronounced effects on the timing, duration, and intensity of the rut, so photoperiod is not solely responsible for the timing of the breeding season. Changing photoperiod apparently opens a "window" during which breeding can occur, but nutrition and demography can determine exactly when breeding occurs within this window.

When threatened, small bucks usually retreat from older, large deer with large racks, although large "faint-hearted" bucks sometimes are dominated by smaller ones. High testosterone levels have been associated with the ability of one buck to dominate another. PHOTOGRAPH BY BUDDY HERMAN; COURTESY UNIVERSITY OF GEORGIA, WARNELL SCHOOL OF FOREST RESOURCES.

The effects of nutrition and demography on the timing of the breeding season have been demonstrated in a number of recent southeastern studies. Guynn and his coworkers (Guynn et al. 1988) established a long-term research project on the Mount Holly Plantation in South Carolina to study quality management effects on deer populations. Initially, their study herd was typical of many: overharvested bucks, skewed sex ratios, and high densities. The breeding season at the beginning of the study was calculated at 96 days. Selective harvest was used to improve nutrition, balance the sex ratio, and increase the age structure of the bucks. Within five years, these changes resulted in a much shorter breeding season, about forty-three days. Not only did the rut become shorter and much more intense, but the earliest breeding dates and the peak dates came much earlier. Mean conception dates shifted from November 11 in the first year of the study to October 15 during the fifth year. Similar results were obtained by Jacobson (1992) on Davis Island, Mississippi. In response to a decade of quality deer management, the peak of the rut on the 17,800-acre study area moved three weeks earlier.

In these two studies, improved nutrition certainly was fundamental to the changes, but sociobiological factors apparently also were involved. It appears likely that the increased numbers of mature bucks play a direct role in the earlier and shorter breeding season. Another possible factor is a reduction in the number of females remaining unbred during their first or subsequent estrous cycles. The availability of bucks to breed with does on their first heat could account for a shorter breeding season but not an earlier one.

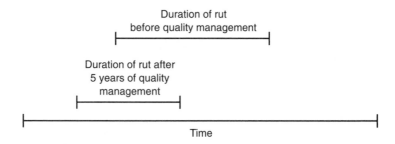

Five years after a quality management program was begun on the Mount Holly Plantation in South Carolina, the range of conception dates was reduced by nearly half. The breeding season became shorter and more intense, and breeding began much earlier.

Studies suggest that the earlier and more synchronized breeding also may be due to increased physiological stimulation of females by mature bucks and their signposts (Miller et al. 1991). There is an inter-action between pheromones from mature males and the females' reproductive physiology. Although there is no definitive proof that priming pheromones exist in whitetails, Verme et al. (1987) found that does penned with bucks experienced estrus earlier than those that were not.

In herding species like domestic ungulates and red deer, visual and chemical communication can be established directly by close contact among animals. In whitetails, this is much less the case because the sexes tend to be socially isolated except during courtship and breeding. In more solitary species, signposts such as rubs and scrapes can be cru-cial in transmitting pheromones between the sexes.

Rubs and scrapes play central roles in deer social life immediately before and during the breeding season. The abundance of rubs on a given area is directly related to the density of mature males. On quality managed areas such as Mount Holly Plantation, rub densities can approach five thousand rubs per square mile. This is in contrast to five hundred to fifteen hundred rubs per square mile on areas where bucks are heavily harvested and few reach maturity (Miller et al. 1987). Simi-larly, Ozoga and Verme (1985) found that yearling bucks lacked the ritualized courtship and scent-marking behavior characteristic of older males. In their study, mature bucks began making scrapes two months before any doe bred, whereas yearlings made only 15 percent as many scrapes, and none until one week before the first doe bred. Yearlings made only 50 percent as many rubs as mature bucks during the breed-ing season.

We believe that these signposts have a strong priming effect on the does' estrous cycles and that they may be a significant factor in the shorter and earlier breeding seasons observed on quality managed areas in the Southeast.

In the northern portions of the whitetail's range, photoperiod changes much more abruptly than in southern latitudes; therefore, the window during which breeding can occur is shorter. Social factors likely have less impact on the timing of the rut. Ozoga and Verme (1985) demonstrated this by altering the sex ratio and age structure of an enclosed herd in the Upper Peninsula of Michigan. Regardless of the age structure of the bucks in the study area, average breeding date of the does stayed near the middle of November.

WHY IS THE TIMING OF THE BREEDING SEASON IMPORTANT?

Nature has designed the whitetail to breed in the fall. On northern ranges, this timing is rigidly enforced by the climate. If a doe breeds too early, she will give birth before vegetation begins to green up in the spring or possibly even before the snow melts. Fawns born under such conditions may die from exposure or malnutrition. Conversely, a late-born fawn may not have time to reach its full growth potential and also store sufficient fat to carry it through its first winter. Natural selection has minimized poorly timed births in northern environments, where a properly timed and brief breeding season is most conducive to reproductive success.

The situation differs in the South. Fawns born outside of the normal period have a much greater chance of survival. Although these late-born fawns sometimes achieve respectable physical proportions at maturity, they tend to be small, poor-quality animals during their first few years of life.

We have already seen in chapter 7 that in a Mississippi study, the antler development of yearling bucks was directly related to a buck's birth date. Similar results were obtained in studies in South Carolina and Florida. They suggest that on southern ranges, the quality of a deer's first antlers may be more closely related to his birth date than to his genetic background. What are the effects of late fawning on a buck's antlers in subsequent years? In controlled situations or in areas with high-quality forage, late-born bucks likely can catch up to earlier-born buck fawns in a few years. In situations of high density and poor forage, late-born male deer may never achieve large body and antler size, regardless of their age.

Fawning date affects doe fawns also. Late-born fawns have a shorter growing season and lower growth rates than earlier-born fawns (Zwank and Zeno 1986), and body weights during their first breeding season are significantly lower. Since the ability of a female to breed as a fawn is related to her size and nutrition, early-born fawns may be more likely to undergo puberty and breed during their first fall.

An adult doe's birth date may also affect the timing of her breeding response to changing photoperiod. In the Southeast, there is considerable variation in the timing of the breeding season. In Georgia, breeding may commence as early as late September or early October, though most occurs in mid-November. In Alabama and Mississippi, breeding may begin in mid-November but most conceptions occur during late December and January. The specific timing of breeding can be affected by several factors, but timing of the window depends on the doe's response to changes in photoperiod.

It is not known whether the opening of the window is under genetic control or is "set" after conception or birth. If the photoperiod cues are set after conception, the later breeding in some regions of the Southeast may be self-perpetuating. For instance, a fawn's timing would have been affected by when its mother's cues were set, and her mother's, and so on. Research at Mississippi State University and the University of Georgia may shed some light on this.

WHY IS THE LENGTH OF THE RUT IMPORTANT?

An abnormally long breeding season can have other serious consequences, ranging from reduced survival of bucks to an overall deterioration of the genetic quality of the herd. With a lengthy rut, bucks will display rutting behaviors as long as estrous females are available. Since rutting bucks eat very little and lose considerable weight, an extended fast exposes them to higher-than-normal winter mortality rates (in the North) or to reduced physical condition (in the South).

A lengthy rut resulting from skewed sex ratios endangers breeding males. In herds under quality deer management guidelines that emphasize normal demographic conditions, the breeding period is intense and brief. Bucks do not use all of their winter reserves and can replenish some of what they have lost before harsh weather arrives.

A long breeding season that results in a prolonged fawning season also can harm fawn survival. To reduce fawn predation, natural selection has developed a mechanism in deer called prey saturation. When most fawns are born during a very short time in the spring, any potential predators become overwhelmed by the sheer number of prey. This ensures that many fawns will survive until they can elude most predators. If the fawning season is prolonged, however, highly vulnerable newborns will be available for predation for a long time, and predators can have a much greater impact on fawn recruitment.

Clearly, prolonged and delayed breeding seasons can harm the sociobiology and health of the herd. Management systems, such as quality deer management, that emphasize socially and demographically normal populations often can return the timing and duration of the breeding season to appropriate normal limits in a short time.

AGE STRUCTURE IS IMPORTANT, TOO

Although few northern deer herds exhibit delayed breeding seasons, young age structures and skewed sex ratios result in other problems that are shared between northern and southern deer herds. Under normal conditions, mature bucks maintain a ritualized breeding system. They dominate younger males and a relatively few dominant bucks in an area have preferential breeding rights. This is nature's way of maintaining genetic health. The best-adapted bucks will contribute more to the genetic makeup of the next generation.

In populations where few, if any, mature bucks remain, this system breaks down. Instead, breeding becomes a frenzied scramble competition among the young bucks to breed any estrous doe in the area. The behavioral patterns that helped to mold the genetic makeup of the herd are discarded in exchange for a system that results in little if any selectivity for adaptive traits.

Mature bucks also tend to suppress aggression and breeding competition among young bucks (Marchinton et al. 1990). This effect caused by the presence of mature bucks and their signposts results in lowered testosterone levels in the younger bucks. These physiological changes generally minimize weight loss and allow young bucks to grow to greater size before assuming breeding duties. Without mature bucks, younger males can compete effectively for breeding opportunities, but they cannot afford such energy expenditure if they are to reach their maximum potential.

MANY DEER, MANY PROBLEMS

Many herds across the country are managed for densities that are at or near the land's carrying capacity. Other herds exceed the capacity of the land to sustain a healthy population. Quality deer management strives to hold deer densities well within the land's inherent carrying capacity. As a result, the herd is maintained on a good diet and lives a healthy life. Crowding and social stress, however, can retard the physical development of young deer, increase fawn mortality, and lower reproductive rates.

Ozoga and Verme (1982) conducted a long-term study at the 1-square-mile Cusino Research Area in Michigan that clearly demonstrated the effects of density stress on deer, independent of nutrition. The population of their supplementally fed herd grew from 23 deer in spring 1972 to 159 by autumn 1976. Peak population densities reached 1 deer per 4 acres. Researchers detected a number of subtle changes in the deer. Young does began breeding later and had lower fawning rates; first-time mothers had very high rates of newborn fawn losses. Since does with newborn fawns defend territories during the fawn's first month, high densities likely limited fawn-rearing space and disrupted maternal behavior. Adequate nutrition was not a factor, so the high fawn mortality resulted either from imprinting failure or outright abandonment of offspring by socially stressed, inexperienced mothers. Other studies also present evidence that high deer densities can reduce newborn survival rates (Miller 1988).

Almost a fourth of the yearling bucks in the Michigan study grew very short (less than 3-inch) antlers, despite being fed high-quality feed. The researchers suggested that stress created by high density caused a serious physiological setback that impaired antler development.

Clearly, the whitetail's social environment is a potent force in its well-being. In many respects, the consequences of social stress are similar to those of poor nutrition, as both factors can hurt deer physical and reproductive performance.

BUCK DISPERSAL

There is a dispersal phase in the life cycle of every species (Mayr 1947) and whitetails are no exception. Most studies have found that yearling bucks disperse at a much higher rate than other age classes of bucks and than does of any age. The highest incidence of dispersal (as much as 90 percent in some populations) is by yearling bucks during or just before the breeding season.

Early studies suggested that dispersal by yearlings was influenced by antagonism from larger males and competition with them for breeding privileges. Recent findings suggest that antagonism from closely related does, particularly their mothers, just before the breeding season may be the most important factor. In fact, dispersing yearling males generally seek association with bachelor groups of other similar aged or older males.

Holzenbein and Marchinton (1992) radio-tracked fifteen male fawns orphaned shortly after weaning and nineteen that grew up with their dams. By 30 months of age, 87 percent of the bucks with surviving mothers had dispersed from their birth ranges, but only 9 percent of the orphans had left theirs. Survival was also much higher among the orphans than among bucks with their mothers. Other studies have demonstrated that buck dispersal can affect the sex ratio in hunted as well as protected populations. These tendencies are most pronounced in herds maintained at high densities (Urbston 1967).

The tendency for young males to disperse in response to social pressures has several important implications for quality deer management, especially in localized situations. Most important is that restraint in harvesting young bucks without adequate doe harvest may not significantly increase recruitment into the older age classes, since many potential recruits may be lost through dispersal. Maintenance of moderate densities through antlerless harvest is paramount if quality deer management is to be acheived.

Since dispersal of yearling males is induced more by pressures from adult females, increases in the density and age structure of males should not affect it. Rather, young bucks simply will be forced into subordinate roles and will benefit as outlined above.

DEER SOCIETY BENEFITS FROM QUALITY MANAGEMENT

In summary, social imbalances in deer populations that often result from traditional management can threaten their social well-being. These problems can be solved by changing the attitudes of hunters regarding how deer should be selected for harvest. Bubenik (1988) said, "It won't be easy. To achieve such a worthwhile goal will require management practices more scientific, flexible and progressive than those traditionally and currently in use—practices that may never be accepted and implemented without the encouragement and support of a great many selfless, farsighted hunters." Quality deer management strives to promote these changes. When hunters overcome their urge to fill their tags with the first legal buck that comes along, they will truly become responsible sportsmen.

Few people have the opportunity to experience hunting on a regular basis in an area having a demographically and socially normal deer herd. Those that do know the benefits that accrue. In a survey of quality management participants (Woods et al. 1992), hunters from Louisiana and South Carolina emphatically described a better hunting experience and improved herd quality, hunter ethics, and image to non-hunters. They said that a quality management program increased their knowledge of deer biology, improved herd quality, and overall was preferable to traditional management. Harvesting a buck was not the true measure of success for them; it was their satisfaction with the opportunity to simply hunt on an area having mature bucks.

—Karl V. Miller,
R. Larry Marchinton, and
John J. Ozoga

CHAPTER 10

Habitat Management
and Supplemental Feeding

Wildlife is never destroyed except as the soil is destroyed; it is simply converted from one form to another. You cannot prevent soil from growing plants, nor can you prevent plants from feeding animals. The only question is: What kind of plants? What kind of animals? How many?

—ALDO LEOPOLD (1945)
The Outlook for Farm Wildlife

In his classic 1933 book, *Game Management*, Aldo Leopold said, "There is a remarkable correlation between game supply and soil fertility throughout North America." As usual, he was right. Since that time, research has shown that the abundance and condition of wildlife can be related directly to soil fertility. This is especially true for deer, since they feed on plants and therefore are only one step removed from the soil itself.

Some of the most fertile soils in North America are in the prairie states. It is no coincidence that this region has produced many Boone and Crockett bucks. Nevertheless, zones of high and low soil fertility occur in all regions.

Soils in the valleys of mountainous regions and along river bottoms in all areas tend to be more fertile than sandy or rocky upland sites. In fact, many record bucks have been taken close to major waterways (80 percent of those harvested in Georgia, for example).

Among different areas of the country, soil fertility and productivity may be the most important factors affecting deer populations. Soil determines the potential for transfer of nutrition through vegetation to a deer herd. Since soil fertility cannot be altered over broad regions, maximizing this potential in any area depends on vegetation management in relation to deer numbers.

129

CARRYING CAPACITY

Just as pastures can support only a limited number of cattle, deer range can support a limited number of deer. One definition of optimum carrying capacity is the maximum number of deer that an area can sustain over the long run without damage to the vegetation. Habitat management involves identifying components that limit a deer population, then manipulating the components to increase the carrying capacity.

Carrying capacities vary greatly and can cause a wide range of deer populations within and among regions. Carrying capacity also is a measure of habitat quality. It is largely determined by soil fertility, age and arrangement of timber types, and agricultural management. It is also influenced by depth and duration of snow cover (in the North), rainfall (in the West), and hard mast (acorns and other nuts) crops. Areas with high carrying capacities can produce not only more deer, but higher-quality deer, than areas with low carrying capacities.

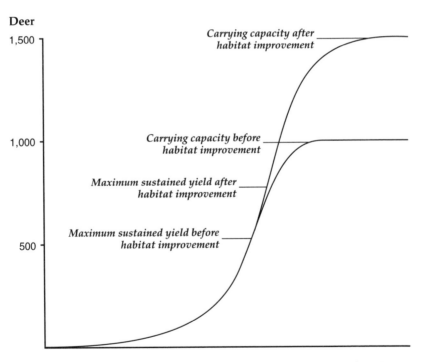

Habitats can be improved so that they support more or better quality deer. Compare this hypothetical herd with the one on page 83. Because the land's carrying capacity has increased, the maximum sustained yield is higher and the quality of the animals is improved.

LIMITING FACTORS

In most of North America, the most limiting season for deer is winter, when the quantity and quality of forage are at their lowest. Although deer adapt somewhat to this, it still is a time of nutritional stress. Good spring nutrition is important to help deer recover and improves fawning success. Consequently, management aimed at producing more or better deer should provide nutrition during the critical periods from late fall through early spring. Forage supplementation involves timber management practices, food plots, artificial feeding, and fertilization.

Where they occur, oaks are an important but unreliable food source. In the southern Appalachians, deer reproduction, weights, and antler characteristics are related to variations in acorn production (Wentworth et al. 1992). When acorns are not available, deer switch to deciduous leaves and evergreen browse, which are often of lower quality in these areas. The double-edged blow of a mast failure followed by a hard winter can devastate deer herds in both northern and southern climates.

In areas of the Deep South (especially the Atlantic and Gulf coastal plains) and the Southwest, there is a secondary stress period in late summer caused by poor vegetation quality. Abundant forage may be available to deer in late summer, but its quality often is low (Short 1971). The length and severity of this stress period is caused by plant maturity, high temperatures, and less soil moisture. In most habitats, the period ends when hard mast begins to fall. Nutritional stresses during this time may reduce lactation, fawn growth, body weights, and antler development. In other regions, there does not appear to be a significant summer nutritional stress period, except under extreme drought.

DIVERSITY AND EDGE

Edge, related to wildlife populations, is the junction of different habitats. Whenever two habitats come together, the edge will be more favorable for many species than either type alone. Leopold stated, "The density of game is directly proportional to the amount of edge for all species of low mobility that require more than one vegetation type." To take this one step farther, edge is directly related to diversity and the more edge that is available, the more diverse the habitat, even within a single-type timber stand.

Why is diversity necessary? Wildlife must have food, cover, and water close together during all seasons to survive and reproduce. Often, it's not the quantity of any component that limits the number and dispersion of animals, but rather how they are distributed.

Generally, areas with a lot of well-interspersed edge have a high habitat diversity and greater deer carrying capacity. This helps overcome a lot of other mortality factors and provides buffers against population fluctuations. Edge makes food, cover, and water available in a much smaller area, reducing the need for long movements. If just one ingredient is missing, such as winter forage, the system can fail. Some northern deer herds, for example, traditionally migrate long distances between summer and winter ranges. If everything needed is available to a deer within a half-mile radius, however, then there is usually no reason for the animal to move.

Deer can move great distances if necessary (movements exceeding 50 miles have been reported) but typically choose small areas in which to live. Even when food drops drastically, southern whitetails rarely shift outside their home range (Carlock et al. 1993). Northern whitetail herds are often locked by tradition into a migratory pattern controlled by winter food and cover. Home ranges of nonmigratory whitetails cover only 146 to 1,285 acres, as determined by radiotelemetry studies (Marchinton and Hirth 1984). Whitetails, like many other species, range less where diversity and edge are highest.

It is rare for a single forest or agricultural type to provide all of a deer's needs. The best habitat contains the largest varieties of plant life and as many stages of succession as possible. Deer managers enhance diversity by splitting woodlands or agriculture into smaller units and use timber harvest and thinning, prescribed burning, and food plots.

FOREST MANAGEMENT

Silviculture is the practice of altering plant succession to guide the development of timber stands. This can help or hinder wildlife. Planning that considers deer habitat as well as timber management will prevent costly mistakes.

There are two methods of timber management: all-aged and even-aged. In all-aged management, only some of a stand is harvested by selecting individual or small groups of trees. Therefore, the stand will be composed of trees of all ages. This is best suited for species such as oak and spruce-fir. All-aged management may be the only choice for managing small (less than 100 acres) deer-wintering areas of spruce-fir in Vermont (Weber 1986).

Even-aged management involves the harvest and regeneration of entire stands. This creates a new stand of trees all of the same age. When properly applied, even-aged management can produce plants with high wildlife value. It is suited for shade intolerant (trees that require full sunlight to grow) species like southern yellow pine, certain northern conifers, and light-seeded hardwoods. It is recommended for maintaining nonwinter range in northern hardwoods and for winter range management in hemlock, white pine, and northern white cedar. Regardless of management, habitat quality depends on the variety of vegetation that occurs within timber stands. Within a stand, habitat quality is determined by regeneration, thinning, prescribed burning, rotation age, and herbicide use. The variety of vegetation is determined by the size, shape, distribution, and species composition of the timber stands.

Plant Succession

Plant succession is the gradual replacement of one plant community by another. When forests are cleared, plants quickly occupy the site, beginning the process of succession. The rate of succession depends on soil fertility, rainfall, length of growing season, and intensity of site preparation. Annuals and grasses dominate early stages and provide deer with spring and summer forage. As succession progresses, these are replaced by shrubs, vines, and shade-intolerant trees that provide browse (leaves and twigs) and soft mast (fruits and berries), especially during spring through early autumn. During midsuccessional stages, tree crowns overlap and shade out many browse and soft mast producers. Stands in this condition primarily provide cover for deer. Late successional stages provide hard mast (nuts), cover, and limited browse.

Management for Browse and Soft Mast

Browse and soft mast are important to a deer's diet. In the spring and summer, they meet the nutritional demands associated with birth and lactation and boost antler development in males. During spring, rapidly growing twigs and leaves provide quality food, but their value and use declines during late summer (Short et al. 1975). When available, evergreen browse is used throughout the year, but it is particularly important during winter, when growth is dormant and mast is not available (Wentworth et al. 1990).

In the South, some evergreens retain quality and digestibility in winter. Where they occur, some broadleaf evergreens can be a crucial source of protein for deer (Blair et al. 1983). Japanese honeysuckle, a high-quality exotic evergreen vine, is one of the most important producers of winter forage in the Southeast (Cushwa et al. 1970). When

Japanese honeysuckle is an exotic, shade-tolerant evergreen vine that grows throughout much of the Southeast. In some areas of the South, it makes up more than 40 percent of the deer's winter diet. PHOTOGRAPH BY REGGIE THACKSTON.

acorn production is low in the southern Appalachians, broadleaf evergreens, such as rhododendron and mountain laurel, replace acorns in the diet (Wentworth et al. 1990). Their quality is low, however, and they do not add much to the overall carrying capacity of the range. The scarcity of even poor evergreen browse, particularly in the winter, limits deer populations in areas such as the Ouachita Mountains of Oklahoma and Arkansas (Segelquist and Pennington 1968).

Grapes, blackberries, wild cherries, persimmons, blackgum, viburnum, crab apples, and other fruits also are important in the diet of deer but are available for a relatively short duration. Since species produce fruit at different times, however, collectively they are available throughout much of the year. As with browse, soft mast is affected by overstory removal. Plants growing in open areas tend to produce more fruit than those under a forest canopy. In young clear-cuts, fruit yields may average 100 or more pounds per acre (Stransky and Halls 1980).

Stand Regeneration

Clear-cutting aspen and jack pine stands on short rotations in Wisconsin produces large quantities of both summer and winter browse

(McCaffery and Creed 1969). Young aspen and jack pine support higher deer densities than mature northern hardwood stands. In an east Texas study, total forage yield in pine-hardwood forests averaged 314 pounds per acre before cutting and 1,558 after cutting (Stransky 1980). Similarly, in a south Alabama study, total deer food was greater in 2- to 8-year-old pine plantations than in a mature longleaf pine forest (Hurst 1979). Similar results can be obtained by timber harvesting over a wide variety of sites throughout the whitetail's range.

Soil disturbance associated with timber harvest and site preparation also affects deer foods. In one study in the flatwoods of Mississippi, food was more abundant during the first summer after preparation on sites where trees were crushed and burned than on bedded sites (Hurst and Warren 1981). Mechanical site preparation retards woody plants but encourages herbaceous growth. Berry and fruit production tends to decrease as the intensity of mechanical site preparation increases (Stransky and Halls 1980). To improve deer habitat in the Pineywoods of east Texas, less intensive methods of mechanical site preparation that preserve the root systems of preferred foods are recommended (Spencer 1981).

With artificial regeneration, seedling spacing is important. Wide spacings, 8 by 10 feet or greater, extend the period of browse and soft mast production. Wide spacings also extend the time to first thinning, until trees reach commercial age.

Importance of Thinning

As the stand grows, tree crowns overlap and shade understory plants. Timber thinnings can open canopies and rejuvenate understory deer food plants. The effects of thinnings vary; heavy thinnings on fertile sites may cause dense, woody growth that shades out desirable plants. Light thinnings on low-quality sites result in limited browse improvement. The use of thinning for deer management should be based on knowledge of local habitat and herd needs.

Thinnings must be applied with caution to northeastern conifer stands that provide critical winter cover for deer. These guidelines are recommended for thinnings in even-aged management of conifer stands on winter deer range in Vermont (Weber 1987):

1. Spruce-fir: Thin to 150 square feet of basal area per acre before age 30 and do not thin beyond age 30.

2. Hemlock: Thin at the same time regeneration cuts are made, provided half the area is left untreated and the area thinned is capable of recovering to 90 percent softwood crown closure in 10 years.

3. White pine: Thin half of stands to about 130 square feet of basal area per acre on a five-year cycle, beginning at age 40, and maintain a crown closure of 90 percent.

In southern pine stands, thinnings increase deer forage production and also may improve quality. Light intensities in the medium to high range result in the most palatable and nutritious browse (Blair et al. 1983). Stands should be thinned when the crowns of the trees begin to touch and with an intensity necessary to create a patchy stand. A good rule of thumb is to thin so that 30 percent of the ground is in direct sunlight at noon. Prescribed fire also should be used to control the growth of dense, woody vegetation that shades out deer foods.

Hardwood stands also can be thinned to increase browse and mast production. In sawtimber or veneer-grade hardwoods, thinnings should be light to prevent branching from the trunk, which can reduce timber quality. On fertile hardwood sites, patchy thinning is even more important than in pine stands to prevent understories from becoming too thick for hunters or deer. Patchy conditions also allow for tree crown expansion, improving mast production. Heavy thinning generally is not recommended, since this often results in prolific woody growth that reduces desirable deer browse. Prescribed fire normally is not recommended for hardwood.

Use of Fire
In certain timber types, fire can improve habitat and is one of the most beneficial and cheapest tools available. In southern pine forests, fire increases legume abundance (Cushwa et al. 1966), browse production and palatability (Lay 1967), soft mast production (Johnson and Landers 1978), and protein content of selected plants (Stransky and Halls 1976). To improve deer habitat, pine stands should be burned from January to March every three to five years (Buckner and Landers 1980). In other words, one-third to one-fifth of the burnable pine stands are burned each year. Burning should be done under moisture, temperature, and wind conditions that will create a patchwork effect. Typically, best results are achieved by burning two or three days after a rain of 1 inch or more, with 30- to 60-degree temperatures, steady winds of 5 to 10 miles per hour, and relative humidities of 30 percent to 50 percent (Jackson et al. 1984). Summer burns sometimes may be used to control dense hardwood competition in pine stands, but they should be avoided in deer management, since summer fire tends to kill root systems of desirable browse plants (Stransky and Harlow 1981).

Burning also is used in other habitats. In Minnesota, burning dete-

Prescribed fire increases legume abundance, browse production and palatability, soft mast production, and protein content of selected forage. Fire, however, is not suited to all habitat cover types and must be applied under the right moisture, temperature, and wind conditions. Landowners should seek professional assistance. PHOTOGRAPH BY REGGIE THACKSTON.

riorating aspen stands is recommended to ensure browse production and prevent them from converting to balsam fir (Rutske 1969). Winter burning is used in the Post Oak Belt of Texas on a six-year cycle to improve deer and cattle range (Yantis et al. 1983). Prescribed burning is not suited for all habitats, however. In general, mast-producing hardwood stands should not be burned, as this can result in tree injury or insect and disease damage that may kill or lower the vitality of the trees. Controlled burning has been used rarely in the northeast because of disastrous wildfires in the past and high accumulations of fuel (Crawford 1984). Prescribed fire, like many other practices, should be applied by professionals who know the techniques and the effect on local habitats.

Forest Openings

Permanent, naturally vegetated forest openings such as old fields are valuable deer habitat. Long, narrow (less than 330 feet) openings ½ to 5 acres in size seem to be preferred by deer. In the Post Oak Belt of Texas, a well-interspersed pattern of openings is recommended with 50 percent woods (Yantis et al. 1983). Further recommendations include separating openings with wooded travel corridors at least 200 yards wide. In southern pine forests, 3- to 5-acre permanent openings should be well distributed over the forest (Spencer 1981).

Productive openings can be maintained by periodically burning or mowing during late winter or early spring. A two- to three-year cycle, where one-half to one-third of an opening is treated each year, will encourage browse and soft mast production and increase diversity.

Rotation Age (Cutting Interval)

In the Northeast, rotations of 70 to 100 years for spruce-fir, 100 to 150 years for hemlock, 100 years for white pine, 160 years for northern white cedar, and 40 years for hardwood browse-producing stands that surround wintering areas are recommended (Weber 1986).

In southern pine forests, long rotations can also benefit deer by allowing hardwoods to reach mast-producing age, and by accommodating the use of thinning and prescribed burning to enhance natural browse and soft mast production. Rotations of 60 to 80 years for pines and 100 to 150 years for mast-producing hardwoods produce good saw-timber and deer habitat. When short rotations are used, certain hardwood stands should be identified and managed as key hard mast-producing areas.

Timber Stand Size, Shape, and Distribution

Size, shape, and distribution of forest stands determine plant and animal diversity. Deer make greatest use of the first 300 feet inside a clear-cut. The U.S. Forest Service (1981) recommends pine stands of 10 to 80 acres and hardwood stands of 10 to 40 acres for deer in national forests in the South. They also suggest that hardwood stands be at least 25 to 30 acres in size in areas with high deer populations, to ensure the establishment of hardwood regeneration. Stand sizes of 10 to 25 acres are recommended for nonwinter deer range in Vermont (Weber 1986). For winter range, stand size should be 10 to 20 acres for spruce-fir, hemlock, and northern white cedar; 5 to 10 acres for white pine; and 1 to 5 acres for hardwood buffer strips along the perimeter of conifer stands.

Stand shape is more important than size in providing edge. Long, narrow stands with irregular boundaries provide more edge than stands of the same size that are square or circular. Stand widths of 600 to 800 feet are good and lengths up to a quarter mile are reasonable (McGinnis 1969). Stands should be arranged to provide a variety of timber and age classes within a deer's home range (300 to 500 acres). In the Southeast, the following guidelines can be used: Distribute stands so that no more than one-third of a square mile is occupied by age classes under 20 years; separate regeneration areas with older stands, buffer strips, or streamside management zones of mature timber; and if young stands must join, maintain a minimum age difference of 5 to 7 years.

For summer range in the North, it may be desirable to maintain at least 10 percent of an area in the 0 to 10-year age class and 30 percent in mast-producing age classes of 50 years or more (Weber 1986). Quality winter range is a combination of conifer shelter mixed with high-quality browse.

Management for Hard Mast

Hard mast (acorns, beechnuts, chestnuts, pecans, and so forth) is critical to the whitetail's diet. Because of their abundance, distribution, and high preference by deer, acorns are by far the most important. They are high in energy, which is important for body growth, maintenance, and reproduction. A Missouri study found acorns from eleven species of oaks to constitute 38 percent of the total foods eaten by deer (Korschgen 1962). In the Southeast, when acorns are abundant, they may compose up to 76 percent of the diet during November and December (Harlow et al. 1975).

It's best to have at least 20 percent of an area in mast-producing hardwoods, of which oaks predominate. It's also desirable to maintain a variety of oak species of acorn-producing age.

Most oaks do not produce acorns until they are 20 years or older and do not produce substantial amounts until they are at least 40 (Goodrum et al. 1971). A mixture of red and white oaks improves consistency in production. The white oak group flowers and produces acorns in the same year, whereas red oaks take two years from flower to mature acorn. Climatic factors, such as late-spring freezes, that hurt acorn production in one group may not affect the other in the same year. A twelve-year study in the southern Appalachians found that maintaining a mixture of red and white oaks tended to prevent the complete production failures that would have occurred had only one of the groups been present (Beck 1977).

Acorns and other hard mast are important parts of the whitetail's diet in most areas. For quality deer habitat, it is desirable to have a minimum of 20 percent of the area in hardwoods, predominantly oaks (if suited to your area). Photograph by Kent Kammermeyer.

Acorn yield increases along with tree crown size and trunk diameter. Yields also vary among trees. Periodic thinnings can enhance crown size and increase acorn production. Thinnings should liberate oaks that are good producers while removing those that consistently fail.

Acorns are especially important in certain habitats with infertile soils and poor winter browse. Portions of the Ouachita, Ozark, and Appalachian mountains, the Sandhills region of the upper coastal plain, and certain river flood plains have acorn-dependent deer herds. Extensive clear-cutting in these types often does not improve winter deer range, but replaces mast-producing hardwoods with low-quality woody browse (Johnson et al. 1986, Wentworth et al. 1990). In these areas, maintain mature hardwood stands for mast production and increase habitat diversity by any means possible, including food plots.

AGRICULTURAL MANAGEMENT

Some of the most exciting and significant deer research in the past ten years has dealt with the value of food plots. Although they are not a cure for poor population management, they do provide high-quality food where habitat is poor or deer do not have access to existing agriculture. Even in good habitat, food plots can increase deer numbers, condition, or reproduction. Food plots have been used since 1935 but their benefit to deer was questioned and debated among biologists for years (Larsen 1969). Recent research overwhelmingly supports food plots as a valuable tool. Intensively managed agricultural openings produce higher harvest and better deer condition (Johnson et al. 1987, Vanderhoof and Jacobson 1989, Kammermeyer and Moser 1990). One study demonstrated that food plots can nearly double the fall deer population (Rogers 1980). Consequently, in recent years sentiment that food plots are eyewash and do not benefit the herd has diminished. Deer sometimes adjust movement, core areas, and home ranges to conform to food plots and high-quality openings (Scanlon and Vaughan 1985).

Today, hunters are willing to pay for more intensive deer management, which often includes establishment of food plots. Deer hunting has been raised from being a secondary product of other land uses to a

Food plots provide a high-quality food source that can raise deer population, improve condition, or increase reproduction. They also can help with selective or increased harvests. A good management program includes at least 1 percent of the land in high-quality agricultural food plots. PHOTOGRAPH BY KENT KAMMERMEYER.

multimillion-dollar recreation. The primary questions are what, where, and how much to plant; the distribution of acreage; and cost versus benefit.

How Many Acres to Plant

Deer certainly benefit from food plots encompassing 5 percent to 10 percent of the land in a heavily forested area. This means four or five plots averaging 2 to 10 acres per square mile (Osborne 1990). This may be unrealistic for some land managers because of the cost. But even 1 percent or less of an area in high-quality plots improves deer diets and enhances reproduction, growth, and antler development (Johnson et al. 1987). In Arkansas, 2 percent of a 600-acre enclosure planted in high-quality food plots doubled the size of the deer herd and stopped drastic fluctuations caused by hard mast failure (Rogers 1980). In northern Wisconsin, biologists suggest no more than 1 percent of the forest be converted into openings (McCaffery et al. 1981). A realistic goal for deer managers could be to develop 6.4 acres of food plots per square mile. Even half of this acreage has produced positive results in antler development (Vanderhoof and Jacobson 1989) and harvest (Kammermeyer and Moser 1990). With grass-legume mixtures producing 5,000 to 12,000 pounds of dry forage per acre annually (Hoveland et al. 1986, Ball et al. 1991) and deer eating more than 5,000 pounds (Kammermeyer et al. 1992), it doesn't take many high-quality acres to help a deer herd where native forages are low in quantity or quality.

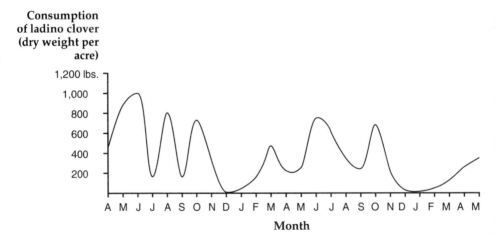

Consumption of ladino clover (dry weight per acre)

In a two-year study in northeastern Georgia, annual use of ladino clover totaled more than 5,000 pounds per acre per year (dry weight). This is in comparison to 50 pounds or less of available forage in mature woodlands.

Size and Location of Plots

In moderate to high deer populations, grazing pressure can be intense on new plantings. To prevent overgrazing, most managers recommend plots of 2 to 5 acres, though successful plots have been established on less than ½ acre.

Plots should be on the most fertile soil available because of fertilizer costs; however, the cost of clearing often dictates food plot location. Many managers use powerlines, log landings, and skid roads for food plots because such sites are convenient and economical. But though some of these openings require less initial bulldozer work, they may cost more in the long run because of shade, poor soil, soil compaction, rocks, weed competition, or excessive slope. If plots are limed and fertilized according to soil tests and maintained or replanted over several years, carefully chosen fertile sites may be more successful and cheaper in the long run.

What to Plant

There is no single plant suited for every situation. Avoid any variety that is promoted to grow under all possible conditions or solve all of your deer nutrition problems. A recent survey of southeastern states identified sixty-two species commonly planted for deer (Jacobson et al. 1985). Wheat, rye, ladino clover, corn, oats, ryegrass, milo, soybeans, crimson clover, and Japanese honeysuckle were planted in the greatest acreage. Wheat, corn, ryegrass, ladino clover, rye, and oats were given the highest preference for winter plantings. Soybeans, peas, alfalfa, reseeding cowpeas, and ladino clover were given the highest preference as summer plantings.

The manager must know when native forage is most limited and select plants or mixtures that fill this void. In most of the whitetail's range, winter is the most limiting season and cool-season forage is the best supplement. In parts of the arid Southwest and the Atlantic and Gulf coastal plains, however, late summer is also a stress period for deer, especially in drought years. Effective plantings require warm-season forage when native range quality is poor in late summer (Kroll 1991). Annuals and perennials are available for both warm- and cool-season plantings and species selection depends upon adaptability, soil type, costs, and objectives.

Cool-season plots improve herds if they are of higher quality than native forages. On some southern ranges, native forage is low in energy and minerals for seven months of the year (Dobson and Beaty 1980). In midwinter, deer do not eat much, even when provided with an abun-

Region	Type	Species	Suggested variety
North, South	Fall perennial mixture	Ladino clover Red clover	Regal or Osceola Kenland or Redland
		Ryegrass Rye (or oats) Wheat	Marshall or Tetraploid Wrens Abruzzi or Elbon Stacy
North	Fall perennial mixture	Orchardgrass, timothy, bluegrass Ladino clover Red clover	Shiloh or Potomac Regal or Osceola Kenland or Redland
North, West	Fall perennial	Alfalfa	Alfagrazer Varies by region
North, South	Fall annual mixture	Austrian winter peas Rye (or oats) Wheat	 Wrens Abruzzi or Elbon Stacy
South	Fall annual mixture (reseeding)	Crimson or arrowleaf clover	Dixie Reseeding or Tibbee; Amclo, Yucci, or Chief
North, South, West	Fall annual mixture (reseeding)	Crimson clover Rye Wheat	Dixie Reseeding or Tibbee Wrens Abruzzi or Elbon Stacy
North, South,West	Fall annual (reseeding)	Ryegrass	Marshall or Tetraploid
North, South	Early spring or fall perennial mixture	Ladino clover Ryegrass	Regal or Osceola Marshall or Tetraploid
North, South, West	Late spring annual	Grain sorghum	Savannah 5 or WGF (bird resistant)
North, South	Late spring annual	Corn	Varies by region
South	Late spring annual	Aeschenemone (jointvetch)	

Get soil test. In lieu of soil test use 800 lbs. per acre 10-10-10 fertilizer at planting. Add 150 lbs. per acre ammonium nitrate for plantings with no legumes. All plantings need a pH of 6.0 or higher for establishment or optimum yield.

lanting dates	Seeding rate	Comments
ugust to November	10 lbs. per acre 10 10 30 30	Mow as needed to control weed competition. Fertilize as needed in early September. This mixture should remain in clover and ryegrass for 3 to 5 years.
ugust to November	20 lbs. per acre 5 5	Mow as needed to control weed competition. Fertilize as needed in early September.
ugust to November	30 lbs. per acre	High maintenance: Needs annual weevil and weed control.
ugust to November	30 lbs. per acre 30 30	Stand can be reestablished by disking lightly in August.
ugust to November	20 lbs. per acre	Stand can be reestablished by disking lightly in August.
ugust to November	20 lbs. per acre 30 40	Clover stand can be reestablished by disking lightly in August. Wheat and rye can be over-seeded at this time, if desired.
eptember & October	40 lbs. per acre	Ryegrass usually reseeds without disking. Without clover, stand quality is diminished.
arch 1 to April 1	10 lbs. per acre 25	Mow as needed to control weed competition. Fertilize as needed in early September. This mixture should remain in clover and ryegrass for 3 or more years until weeds, drought, or grubs destroy the stand.
ay to July	5–10 lbs. per acre	Let stand through following winter and deer will eat seedheads.
pril to June	10 lbs. per acre	Excellent deer forage but difficult and expensive to grow.
ay to July	20 lbs. per acre	Stand is killed by first frost. Can be successfully mixed with sorghum.

There are a variety of cool- and warm-season deer food plot mixtures. Mixtures should be chosen by region and season of use.

dance of good ration. Consequently, in most parts of the country, plots should produce forage in late fall and early spring. Good spring nutrition is important for recovery of deer after winter and to improve fawning. Deer use food plots heavily in early spring before native woodlands green up.

Many deer biologists and managers recommend clover-grass mixtures for cool-season planting. Clover is nutritious and fixes nitrogen for better growth of the grasses. Grasses protect the clover seedlings from drought and overgrazing and use the nitrogen that might otherwise be taken by weeds. As with any planting, the species selected must be adapted to the soil type and region. Also, soil should be tested and fertilizer requirements followed precisely. If the soil fertility is inadequate, you won't get good results.

There are annual and perennial mixes of clover and grass; careful mixing is important. A perennial mixture will come back year after year. The perennials generally have higher production, lower maintenance, and lower cost per year; however, many perennial grasses eventually overtake the clovers. One popular grass (Kentucky 31 fescue) is of relatively low quality and can even be mildly toxic if infested with a certain fungus (Hoveland et al. 1986), though there have been some major advancements in recent years in identifying and developing fungusfree varieties that are productive and palatable. Unfortunately, the fungusfree varieties are proving difficult to establish and maintain.

A major objective in cool-season clover-grass mixtures is to maintain a rich clover component or even allow the stand to revert to pure clover. A mix of ladino and red clover with ryegrass, rye, and wheat accomplishes this in many soil types and regions. The ladino is perennial, the red is a weak perennial, and the grasses are annuals, with ryegrass being a good reseeder. The result after the first year is usually ladino, red clover, and ryegrass with the red clover fading out after the second year. The ladino and ryegrass (or pure ladino) can be maintained indefinitely as long as weeds, insects, and disease can be controlled as needed. The mix may have to be mowed once or twice per summer and fertilized each September. Managed correctly, ladino clover may persist for up to ten years. Typically, replanting is required at three- to five-year intervals. White grubs can be controlled with an application of various pesticides, and weedy grasses can be controlled with an application of a selective herbicide, such as Poast (or Vantage) at 2 pints per acre.

In acidic or excessively drained soils, crimson clover, arrowleaf clover, or hairy vetch can be substituted. In some areas, crimson clover, vetch, and ryegrass will reseed without disking; in others, it will require a light disking between August and October. A local biologist or county agent can provide advice.

Annual cool-season mixtures also can be grown in many combinations. Choose high-quality legumes and noncompetitive grasses, preferably reseeding varieties. Legumes may include almost any of the clovers, vetches, or Austrian winter peas with any of the annual grasses, including oats.

Pure grasses are not as palatable or productive as the grass-clover mixes and require more nitrogen fertilizer. The advantage of clover is its high protein (20 percent to 30 percent) and calcium content (Dobson and Beaty 1980). Clovers may be difficult to establish and maintain compared with grasses, however. They require inoculation, soil pH above 6, high fertility, and good rainfall.

This browse exclosure dramatically illustrates the impact of grazing on ladino clover during a one-month period in March. By clipping and weighing the clover inside and outside the cage, researchers can calculate clover consumption by deer. Differences such as that shown here represent consumption exceeding 400 pounds per acre per month (dry weight). PHOTOGRAPH BY KENT KAMMERMEYER.

Perennial grasses may be better for clover mixes in northern deer ranges, especially if they are managed by heavy grazing or mowing to keep grasses from outcompeting the clover. Possible perennial grasses include fungusfree fescue (several varieties are available, including Kentucky 31 and A.U. Triumph), orchardgrass, bluegrass, perennial ryegrass, timothy, and velvetgrass. Mixed with perennial ladino clovers, these grasses produce an abundance of high-quality forage, though they may outcompete the clover and form a pure stand of grass within three to five years. Although pure grass is not a bad deer food plot, a clover mix is better.

There are a couple of annuals that qualify as combination winter-summer deer foods. These are corn and grain sorghum (milo). Both are high in fats and carbohydrates and make ideal late summer–early fall energy foods for deer. Larger cornfields and bird-resistant grain sorghum often provide food well into winter if they are not eaten up early. Corn is a highly preferred planting for deer, especially in the Midwest and Northeast. It is best incorporated in a deer management system in which agreements can be made with farmers to leave 10 percent to 20 percent of the crop unharvested. The farmer usually pays all planting expenses. Corn has some disadvantages when planted specifically for deer in small fields. It requires high fertility, herbicides, pest control, and cultivation. Planted in small fields, corn is depleted by birds, squirrels, raccoons, opossums, and other wildlife.

Grain sorghum almost duplicates the food value of corn without some of the disadvantages. Early-maturing or light-headed varieties (yellow endosperm) provide early food for deer in August before hard mast drops. Late-planted or dark-headed varieties (bird-resistant) mature later and resist early browsing because they are high in tannic acid. As the mature seed stands in the weather, it gradually becomes more palatable, though deer may not eat it until after acorns are depleted in winter. Grain sorghum is much easier to grow than corn and is subject to less depredation and insect damage but still requires a heavy application of nitrogen for proper growth. Food plots composed of one-half grain sorghum and one-half clover-grass mixture make an excellent year-round food supply for deer.

Warm-Season Food Plots
Warm-season food plots are recommended only where late-summer vegetation is poor enough to cause nutritional stress for deer. In the

Grain sorghum almost duplicates the food value of corn without some of the disadvantages. It is much easier to grow, is more drought resistant, and resists insects better. It still requires a heavy application of nitrogen for proper growth and seed production. Photograph by Kent Kammermeyer.

Deep South, including the Atlantic and Gulf coastal plains and Texas, late-summer stress may justify summer deer plots. The best summer plots are made up of legumes, including alfalfa, Alyce clover, sweet clover, red clover, or jointvetch. A mix of jointvetch (15 pounds per acre) and grain sorghum (5 pounds per acre) may be ideal in the South.

Late-summer stress periods are often caused by drought or deep sandy soils. Almost any food plot planted as a summer supplement is subject to the same drought stress as native plants. There may be one exception. Alfalfa may be the best plant for deer in arid regions for a combination cool- and warm-season forage. It has a deep root system that withstands droughts and can maintain very high production (4 to 6 tons of hay per year) and quality (about 30 percent protein) (Sell 1976). Alfalfa also has its drawbacks. It does not do well in the Deep South, it is expensive, it requires high maintenance, and it is subject to overgrazing, weevil damage and weed encroachment. Contact your local extension agent for advice about alfalfa.

Supplemental Feeding for Deer
Supplemental feeding of deer with corn, pelleted ration, or hay not grown on the area always has been controversial among American wildlife managers. Europeans have done this successfully on game preserves for years. Properly done, feed must be put out for a long enough time and in enough quantity to increase deer carrying capacity during the most stressful period of the year (usually winter). A winter feeding program can theoretically result in more deer (or healthier ones) carried through the year. This clearly separates supplemental feeding from baiting, which is conducted during hunting season to attract deer.

Supplemental feeding, however, is very expensive, is a stopgap, and can cause herd health problems and habitat damage when it is discontinued. There is certainly some merit to these arguments, but studies show supplemental feeding works if you are willing to pay for it (Ozoga 1972, Zaiglin 1977, Ruth 1990).

Supplemental feeding has been conducted in the North and West for years. It is routinely practiced on large ranches in Texas. Recent studies found that emergency feeding in severe winters could reduce mortality in mule deer and whitetail populations (Ludwig 1980, Baker and Hobbs 1985). A report from Washington stated that the success of a winter feeding program is measured in greater animal production for recreational hunting (Moreland 1969).

Supplemental feeding of 5,000 pounds of whole corn per week for nine months of the year significantly raised deer harvests and condition on a commercial hunting operation in South Carolina (Simmons and Ruth 1990). Feeding increased deer harvest from eight per square mile in 1984 to more than fifty per square mile from 1988 through 1990 (Simmons et al. 1991). In addition to increases in population and harvest, antler development, reproduction, and body weight also improved.

There is debate over the relative value of corn versus pelleted ration for feeding deer. A Georgia study found nearly equal preference for corn and pellets by wild deer when presented together (Murphy et al. 1992). In a Minnesota study, pellets proved superior in food shortages but wild deer preferred corn during usual winter conditions (Ludwig 1980). Corn may be an adequate (and inexpensive) supplement when deer have access to native browse. Although low in protein, corn is high in energy and is highly digestible. Since it is also low in fiber, vitamins, and minerals, deer supplemented with corn need access to these from other sources. Although supplemental feeding can artificially raise carrying

Feeding deer corn or pelleted ration has always been controversial among American wildlife managers. If used, feed should be available long enough and in enough quantity to increase deer carrying capacity during the most stressful period of the year. PHOTOGRAPH BY KENT KAMMERMEYER.

capacity, there is still a limit to the number of deer the land can support without damaging its basic productivity.

Baiting for Deer
Baiting and hunting over bait are even more controversial than supplemental feeding. Baiting normally is discontinued after hunting season and thus does not provide supplemental feed during winter shortages. It facilitates harvest but may do little to improve the herd. Proponents claim the practice accomplishes harvest goals more easily with fewer hunters. This may not always be the case, since most bait use by deer occurs at night (Jacobson and Darrow 1992). We feel that baiting rarely has a place as a management tool. Doe harvest can probably be done more effectively with food plots and other habitat improvements. In this way, the herd benefits at the same time harvest efficiency improves.

Another concern is that many believe baiting is not ethical and it therefore lends ammunition to antihunting groups. Baiting is legal in twenty-six states in the United States and appears to remain controversial with about half of hunters on each side of the issue (Smith 1991).

Fertilization of Existing Plants
Deer production is tied to soil fertility because it directly influences quality and quantity of browse plants, so another management technique is to increase soil fertility. Japanese honeysuckle is an excellent introduced deer browse plant that grows extensively in the Southeast. It responds well to ammonium nitrate (150 pounds per acre) and superphosphate (50 pounds per acre) applied in March and September (Seqelquist and Rogers 1975). Fertilization and daylighting of Japanese honeysuckle is a cheap and effective way of increasing high-quality deer browse. Although unproven by research, fertilizer may improve production of native fruit- and nut-bearing species like crab apples, persimmons, grapes, plums, viburnums, and even oaks. A complete fertilizer like 10-10-10 applied in early spring at a rate of about 1 pound per every inch of trunk diameter is recommended (Kammermeyer et al. 1988). Contact your local biologist or county agent for details.

Economics of Food Plots and Artificial Feed
The cost of food plots will depend on the site and cost of materials and labor. If land must be cleared, creating and maintaining openings for agricultural plantings can be expensive. In Alabama, costs of establish-

ing wildlife openings in 1986 dollars were $347 per acre, including clearing, planting, seed, and fertilizer (Carver 1989). If open land is available, budgeting a per-acre cost for establishment of $60 to $100 may be sufficient, depending on the species. Maintenance costs $15 to $45 per acre annually. In one study, reseeding annual clovers cost only $5 per ton of forage over an eleven-year period (Kroll 1991). In a Louisiana study, costs for establishing fourteen plots (7 acres) were about $350 (Johnson et al. 1987).

In a Georgia study, costs were higher. Clearing costs in 1989 dollars varied between $500 and $600 per acre. Soils were acidic and required 4 tons of lime per acre at $30 per ton. Fertilizer costs were about $36. Seed (ladino clover, red clover, ryegrass, rye and wheat) was about $50 per acre. Thus cost of materials for initial establishment alone was $206 per acre. Counting clearing ($500 per acre) and labor ($150 per acre), costs would easily be $850 per acre for a high-quality clover-grass food plot. Obviously, the use of existing clearings would be considerably cheaper. Estimating a maintenance cost of $100 per acre for mowing and fertilizing each year for five years, the cost per ton of forage consumed by deer was $70 in the first year and $12 every year thereafter (Kammermeyer et al. 1992). This still looks good compared with the price of whole shelled corn, which ranges from $100 to $200 per ton, or pellets, which range from $170 to $225 per ton.

A South Carolina study estimated a consumption of 1 pound of corn per deer per day for about nine months of the year (Simmons and Ruth 1990). Their costs ran about $13.50 per deer per year for bulk corn at $100 per ton. This represents low-cost supplementation, assuming native forages are capable of withstanding extra browsing pressure, the program is consistent, and the problems of feed quality and distribution are solved along with the problem of nontarget consumers, such as hogs, birds, foxes, raccoons, skunks, or opossums.

Ozoga and Verme (1982) reported a cost of $83 per deer to supplement a Michigan herd for one year with a commercial feed. In Texas, deer response to pellets was rapid and deer with access to this feed had significantly more fawns. The cost of supplementing deer year-round was considered excessive but supplementation for short stress periods was feasible.

In summary, there is no substitute for good integrated timber and deer management programs that include at least 0.5 percent to 1 percent in high-quality food plots. Forest management for deer must include a thinning or final cut that considers production of browse and soft and hard mast supplies. Agricultural management includes identifying the most stressful season and planting productive, high-quality crops that fill the void left by native vegetation. Carrying capacity may be increased during winter stress with a consistent supplemental feeding program or use of commercial fertilizers on key browse or fruit- and nut-bearing plants. An integrated system has great potential to increase deer numbers or condition (or both) and create a sound quality deer management program.

—KENT E. KAMMERMEYER AND
REGGIE THACKSTON

CHAPTER 11

Mineral Supplementation for Antler Production

Biologists, and most of all, wildlife biologists, know that any thought of man that he is apart from the rest of the living world is a perilous delusion.

—C. H. D. CLARKE (1958)

It is appropriate that a chapter on deer antlers begin with an ancient quote. William Twiti said in 1327, "The head grows according to the pasture; good or otherwise" (Geist 1986). This tenet still is ultimately true; the best lands generally produce the largest deer and best antlers. Several other factors also influence antler growth. Despite the obvious interest in the nutritional requirements for antler growth, much remains to be learned. This void is an impediment to active nutritional management and challenges professional research biologists. It also makes providing a meaningful synopsis especially difficult!

The ultimate goal of mineral supplementation is to increase antler size in a wild population of deer. Achievement of this goal is not straightforward, because the size of a deer's antlers depends not only on mineral nutrition but also on the age, genetic makeup, and non-mineral nutritional status. In addition, many complex interactions among these factors affect antler production. Considering one without reference to the others is folly.

Before considering this topic, realize the limitations in the present database. Almost all of the experiments done to examine antler growth have been with captive animals. There are several problems in studying large animals in captivity, such as the following:

1. The sample size usually is small. In many cases, only one or two animals receive a certain treatment.

2. Research animals usually are fed a complete ration at times other than during experimentation. During an experiment, the animals often are supplied the same ration except with a regulated (generally decreased) amount of the nutrient in question. Consequently, the interacting effects of concurrent deficiencies often experienced in the wild are not addressed; neither are the roles of nontested micro- and macronutrients.

3. Most animals used are either wild trapped or the offspring of wild-trapped animals, and therefore their genetics are virtually unknown.

4. Captivity itself can stress individuals. Density often is much greater in captive situations than in the wild. High density and stress can hinder body mass and antler size in the wild and may likewise affect captive animals.

In spite of these shortcomings, studies of captive deer provide most of the information available for evaluating effects of specific nutrients on antler size. Virtually no studies in the wild adequately address these questions. Many reports are anecdotal or unsubstantiated manufacturers' claims. At best, we must rely on comparing naturally varying nutrient levels with body and antler characteristics.

ANTLER GROWTH IN DEER

Antler growth in most species of deer is an annual cycle governed largely by photoperiod. In North America, whitetail antlers typically begin to grow in April, harden off with shedding of velvet in August to September, and drop in January or February. The process begins in the spring, when increasing day length causes the pineal gland to secrete less melatonin. Production of hormones such as prolactin and growth hormone from the pituitary gland increases. Pituitary hormones evidently do not stimulate antler growth directly, but inhibit testosterone production. This prevents premature cessation of antler growth and stimulates production of possible growth-promoting hormones like the somatomedins (Bubenik 1990*a*). The growth process is still not fully understood. Nevertheless, it is well known that calcium-regulating hormones (calcitonin and parathyroid hormone) are important in antler mineralization, which involves both release of calcium and phosphorus from bone (Banks 1974, Brown et al. 1978) and increased absorption from the gut (Eiben et al. 1984, Stephenson and Brown 1984).

Throughout the summer, antlers grow through deposition of materials from the velvet, which has a rich blood supply. Growing antler is composed principally of a protein matrix (80 percent by weight) combined with various minerals. The growing tips of antlers are only about 8 percent minerals. Mineralization occurs some distance behind the growing tip. Most of the minerals are deposited in the last third of the velvet phase (Kay et al. 1981). As fall approaches, testosterone levels rise dramatically and stimulate final maturation of the antler and shedding of the velvet. The hardened antler is 50 percent to 60 percent mineral, with the rest mostly protein.

Hormones are important in antler growth and maturation, but the central nervous system also plays a direct role. The velvet of the growing antler is well supplied with nerves. Severing the nerves early in growth does not prevent antler growth but results in malformed beams and points. Injury during velvet results in deformity of antlers, such as spurious tines characteristic of nontypical racks (Bubenik 1990b). When only one antler is denervated, it undergoes shape changes and reduced growth, suggesting that the changes are caused by loss of nervous stimulation rather than subsequent injury to the desensitized velvet antler (Suttie and Fennessy 1985). One of the most important aspects of this phenomenon involves "trophic memory" by the nervous system. If a growing antler is injured in one year, which is not uncommon, the resulting malformation may be "remembered" by the nervous system and often will recur in the same spot on antlers produced in subsequent years (Bubenik and Bubenik 1986).

Chemical Composition

It would appear easy to determine the nutrients needed to produce antlers simply by analyzing their mineral content; however, it is not that simple because of the dynamics of antler growth and the variety and magnitude of minerals involved in antler formation. Even the hardened antler contains 40 percent to 50 percent organic material, principally protein. Calcium and phosphorus are the most abundant minerals, followed by much lower levels of magnesium and sodium. The calcium-to-phosphorus ratio averages about 2. These large quantities of minerals must be deposited in only a few months and are irreversibly lost when deposited in antler. The demands of antler production on the buck's mineral balance can be significant, requiring a net accumulation of 0.5 to 1 gram of calcium and 0.25 to 0.5 gram of phosphorus per day (Ullrey 1982).

Species	Source	Calcium	Phosphorus	Magnesium	Sodium	Ca
White-tailed deer	Miller et al. (1985)	19.01%	10.13%	1.09%	.50%	1:
White-tailed deer	Ullrey (1982)	24.52	11.12	—	—	2:
White-tailed deer	Ullrey et al. (1975)	23.02	12.46	.46	—	1:
White-tailed deer	Magruder et al. (1957)	21.90	9.95	—	—	2:
Red deer	Kay et al. (1981)	—	—	—	—	2:
Red deer	Hyvarinen et al. (1977)	22.62	10.62	.31	—	2:

A number of studies have shown remarkable similarities in the chemical composi-tion of deer antlers. Antlers are mostly calcium and phosphorus. These elements invariably occur in a 2:1 ratio.

In whitetails, the levels required for antler growth are low compared with the expected dietary intake (Brown 1990). In larger species such as red deer or elk, however, the amount of calcium in a set of antlers is only slightly less than that produced by a lactating female. The amount of phosphorus in antlers is about half that lost during lactation (Arman et al. 1974, Brown 1990). The calcium content of deer milk is not known. The mineral content of moose and white-tailed deer milk is similar and is about twice that of the domestic cow (Robbins 1983, Silver 1961). If the calcium and phosphorus percentages in whitetail milk are similar to those in moose milk (22.4 percent of mineral matter is calcium and 17.3 percent phosphorus, Cook et al. 1970), a doe producing milk for two fawns (1,500 to 2,000 milliliters; Robbins and Moen 1975) would lose 7.6 grams of calcium and 5.9 grams of phosphorus per day. If the average production is similar to that of black-tailed deer (1 kilogram of milk per day over a sixty-day period, Sadleir 1980), total loss would be 215 grams of calcium and 166 grams of phosphorus for the first 60 days. Milk pro-duction is a significant mineral drain on the doe, so contrasting this loss to minerals incorporated into antlers helps us understand how much stress antler production is on the maintenance of mineral balance in bucks.

Antler weights vary widely, even within age groups, so the calcula-tion of mineral loss is a rough approximation at best. A pair of antlers from yearling deer generally weighs 70 to 300 grams (Weeks 1974, McCullough 1982). An average yearling rack should weigh about 200 grams. Weights of adult antlers range up to 1 kilogram (2.2 pounds), although some deer never reach this level. An occasional set of antlers may weigh more than 1.2 kilograms.

A yearling with a small rack (70 grams) would contribute about 15.5 grams of calcium and 7.6 grams of phosphorus to antler growth; a yearling with a more substantial rack (200 grams) would contribute 44.2 grams of calcium and 21.8 grams of phosphorus. Amounts needed for antler growth increase with age, with large antlers (900 grams) containing 198.9 grams of calcium and 98.1 grams of phosphorus. Deer with antlers weighing more than 1,200 grams would need to net more than 265 grams of calcium and 130 grams of phosphorus (amounts that equal well over half the calcium and about half the phosphorus lost during the entire lactation of a female) to accomplish growth.

There are many other minerals found in antlers that could limit their maximum growth. Essentially the only source of data on mineral content of white-tailed deer antlers other than calcium and phosphorus is a study at the University of Georgia (Miller et al. 1985). Researchers analyzed eighteen antler sets from seven captive deer receiving good nutrition and found levels of magnesium and sodium to be 1.09 percent and 0.50 percent, respectively. In addition, the following levels of lesser minerals were found (in ppm): potassium, 900; iron, 55; manganese, 6.6; zinc, 116; aluminum, 128; strontium, 92; and barium, 129.

The amount of sodium lost in antler material (average of 3.6 grams) is much less than is lost during a full lactation period of females (72 grams) (Pletscher 1987).

Dietary Requirements
The classic study of dietary mineral needs for antler growth was in Pennsylvania in the 1950s (French et al. 1956, Magruder et al. 1957). Based on the few animals studied, the researchers concluded that a dietary level of 0.64 percent calcium and 0.56 percent phosphorus was needed for best antler growth. Other recent research suggests that 0.40 percent calcium is sufficient for proper growth of male and female fawns, and that 0.30 percent phosphorus (Ullrey et al. 1975) or even 0.14 percent to 0.29 percent phosphorus (Jacobson 1984a, Grasman and Hellgren 1993) might be adequate for antler growth. Grasman and Hellgren (1993) predicted that dietary phosphorus levels for adult bucks was at or below 0.12 percent. Growing deer and lactating does undoubtedly require more. All these studies were on captive deer where diets were otherwise adequate in all components, including protein and other minerals. Also, physiological changes related to season affect the

amount of a given nutrient that can be absorbed from food.

The calcium-phosphorus ratio is important in livestock nutrition and likely in that of deer as well; however, if levels of both are sufficient, an animal's performance is not affected by ratios between 0.6:1 and 6:1. Most natural diets probably fall within this range (Jones and Weeks 1985).

White-tailed deer mineral requirements other than calcium and phosphorus have not been determined. Although magnesium requirements of deer are unknown, domestic livestock generally need 0.20 percent in the diet (Jones and Weeks 1985). Even the exact requirements for sodium are not well established.

Source of Mineral Nutrients and Seasonal Need

All nutrients needed for antler growth must come from the deer's diet. Exactly when those minerals are consumed is important because that may suggest when mineral supplementation may be beneficial. Just as some animals store fat for winter, limited storage of minerals may be possible.

Because antler growth is highly seasonal, constructing annual budgets or even stating requirements as a percentage of the diet is suspect. Diets of wild deer vary dramatically during

Calcium (g/kg)

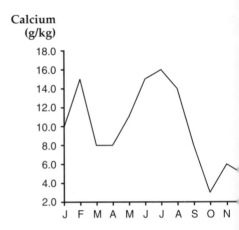

Potassium (g/kg)

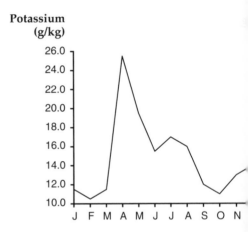

Phosphorus (g/kg)

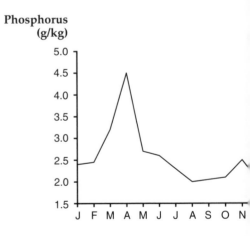

Sodium
(ppm)

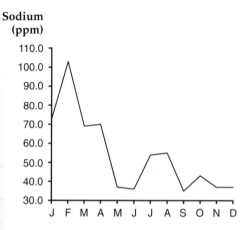

gnesium
(g/kg)

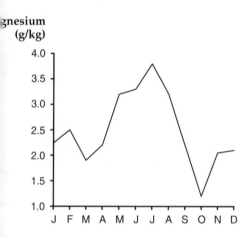

The content of calcium, phosphorus, magnesium, potassium, and sodium in the diet of white-tailed deer varies greatly from month to month. Calcium and phosphorus are at their lowest levels in late summer and early fall; sodium levels are lowest during late spring. Calcium, phosphorus, and magnesium data were taken from Jones and Weeks (1985) and potassium and sodium from Weeks and Kirkpatrick (1976).

the year. There also are seasonally different absorption rates of the various nutrients (Stephenson and Brown 1984, Muir et al. 1987). Thus, the questions of where materials come from and how efficiently they are used are important when attempting to maximize antler production.

Absorption of calcium from the gut increases during antler growth; part of it moves to bone and part to antler (Stephenson and Brown 1984). Deer deposit both calcium and phosphorus in their skeletons before antler growth and then transfer these minerals to antlers during active growth (Banks 1974, Stephenson and Brown 1984). Although normal dietary intake might supply sufficient phosphorus and calcium for antler growth in whitetails (Ullrey 1982), it is inadequate for large-antlered species (Bubenik and Bubenik 1986) and may be inadequate for large white-tailed deer as well. In a study of calcium metabolism in red deer, deer on one forage obtained 25 percent to 40 percent of the calcium requirement for antler growth from the diet, whereas on another forage 60 percent to 80 percent came from the diet (Muir et al. 1987).

In summary, although the mechanisms are still largely unknown, absorption of minerals (at least calcium) from the gut becomes more efficient during antler growth. Calcium and phosphorus from both the diet and skeletal bone are used for antler growth. These skeletal components are replaced immediately after antler maturation. In addition, calcium and phosphorus are accumulated in bone during the months immediately preceding antlerogenesis, presumably as a "stockpile" in anticipation of antler growth. Therefore calcium and phosphorus levels in the diet before and during antler growth may be important in determining their size.

Magnesium is an important component in antlers, but since little information exists on its behavior during antler growth, we can only assume that most requirements are met from the diet. Based on findings with calcium and phosphorus, it is not unreasonable to assume that some movement between bone and antler may occur also. The situation is somewhat different with sodium, which is often supplied as common salt. Sodium is the major extracellular cation in the mammalian body but is a minor component of bone tissue. Only a small portion of bone sodium is available during times of stress (Forbes 1962). In addition, the rumen fluid (from saliva) may be a reservoir for sodium during times of high availability. It could be used in times of stress by substituting potassium for sodium in saliva (Denton 1957). This has been proposed as a storage mechanism for moose (Botkin et al. 1973, Jordan et al. 1973). Such storage meets only short-term (days or weeks) and not long-term needs, however. In most habitats, soils and plants are very low in sodium. Therefore, such storage may be a moot point, since there is no period of abundance that allows accumulation. We have to assume that most sodium for antlers comes from the diet during the period of growth. This includes materials from salt licks as well as other sources.

SUPPLEMENTATION WITH MINERALS

The desire for quality deer is increasing rapidly. In response, intensive management of many herds will be more common. While major supplemental feeding is often controversial, ecologically questionable, and expensive, mineral supplementation may be effective in increasing antler size and could circumvent some of the problems generally associated with supplemental feeding.

Mineral Availability—Regional Variations and Deficiencies

Forage must supply the nutrients for growth, maintenance, and the production of antlers. A plant's nutrient content reflects soil content,

Mineral content of deer foods

Species	Location	Season	Parts per million				
			Calcium	Phosphorus	Magnesium	Sodium	Potassium
Acer	New Hampshire	Late summer	6,000	1,800	1,200	16.3	10,100
saccharum	Indiana	Spring	8,845	4,389	1,905	41.4	14,166
(Sugar maple)	Indiana	Summer	12,157	1,496	2,470	34.1	8,415
Smilax spp.	Louisiana	Spring	8,200	1,600	—	—	—
(Greenbrier)	Louisiana	Summer	13,000	900	—	—	—
	Indiana	Spring	4,010	5,414	1,889	63.8	23,334
	Indiana	Summer	9,065	1,286	2,246	44.7	14,684
Cornus florida	Indiana	Spring	24,200	3,329	4,608	38.2	12,776
(Flowering	Indiana	Summer	23,933	1,433	4,515	44.9	12,117
dogwood)							
Nyssa	Louisiana	Spring	5,100	1,500	—	—	—
ylvatica	Louisiana	Summer	8,000	900	—	—	—
(Black gum)							
Solidago spp.	New Hampshire	Summer	9,800	3,100	4,100	25.5	53,800
(Goldenrod)	Indiana	Spring	7,051	4,329	1,877	27.2	37,983
	Indiana	Summer	8,677	3,006	2,354	16.1	30,881
Quercus spp.	Illinois	Fall	663	1,000	713	30.0	9,303
(Oak)	Indiana	Fall	1,045	1,127	643	14.3	8,425

The mineral levels in plant species eaten by white-tailed deer—all leaves, except
Quercus, *which are acorns—vary by region and season. Data came from Likens
and Bormann (1970), Jones and Weeks (1985), Weeks (1978), Blair and Epps
(1969), and Havera and Smith (1979).*

but also is influenced by the plant's ability to absorb and retain various
minerals, which varies seasonally. It is not surprising, therefore, that
varying levels of minerals are recorded for forage species, with some
above the levels required for adequate body and antler growth and
some below.

In a state-by-state consideration of deer size relative to soil characteristics, one study found a direct relationship between the amount of
available minerals, especially calcium and magnesium, in the soil and
deer weight and productivity (Jones and Hanson 1985). This study
reported that in the upper Mississippi Valley, "calcareous rocks; lime-
stones; dolomites and shales; and the more recent, thick deposits of

loess—which tend to be base-rich" produced large deer with record-size antlers and a high reproductive capacity. Many areas of the eastern United States have low soil fertility, characterized by low levels of calcium and magnesium, and have not produced trophy antlers.

In Mississippi, Jacobson (1984*b*) also found a strong correlation between soil mineral content and deer size, although no correlation with adult antler size was found. He concluded that soil phosphorus levels were the best indicator of body size. Other minerals also were important but were highly correlated with phosphorus levels. Phosphorus levels in many soils are low, especially in the Southeast, and its availability to plants varies.

Several studies have calculated mineral contents of diets by month or estimated annual nutrient budgets. On one area in Indiana with low soil fertility, calcium and magnesium levels during antler growth were reported to be adequate (Jones and Weeks 1985). Except during early spring, however, monthly intake of phosphorus was at or below that considered desirable for growth and antler production. In fact, in many regions of the United States, the amount of phosphorus required for peak body and antler growth is rarely reached. Phosphorus may even limit antler growth (Vogt 1948). Vogt produced world-class antlers in red deer by feeding sesame seed after they had been pressed for oil. Phosphorus content of pressed sesame seed is 1 percent to 1.13 percent and calcium content is 1.4 percent to 1.56 percent (Lennerts 1989). Such phosphorus levels far exceed those in natural forage.

Sodium exists in very small amounts in most soils. Since it is not required for growth of most plants, these soils are rarely termed deficient. Almost all soils greater than 25 to 50 miles from a seacoast are low in sodium. In Indiana, sodium varies from 37.0 to 69.5 ppm in whitetail diets during the period of active antler growth (Weeks and Kirkpatrick 1976), reflecting the very low sodium content of most forage plants (Weeks 1978*a*), except fungi and some aquatic plants (Botkin et al. 1973). This is well below the dietary requirement. Sodium needs to be obtained from sources other than forage.

Most other micronutrients vary widely in soils. Although occasional deficiencies are noted, their importance in herbivore nutrition is not well known.

Other Mineral Sources and Supplementation
Deer generally must make up deficiencies by seeking out concentrations in nature. Such concentrations may be certain plants, such as

Natural mineral licks, such as this one in an old bottomland field in south-central Indiana, form when runoff water collects in low spots and cannot percolate through the clay subsoil and subsequently evaporates. Natural licks are uncommon, so supplementation may be useful in management programs. PHOTOGRAPH BY HARMON P. WEEKS, JR.

fungi (Weeks and Kirkpatrick 1976) or aquatics (Botkin et al. 1973); bones, antlers, or salted roads (Weeks and Kirkpatrick 1978, Fraser 1979); and mineral licks. Natural mineral licks are high in minerals, usually produced by high-mineral springs or evaporation. Such licks are used by many species of wildlife but there is not agreement as to the elements that attract animals to licks. Sodium is common to almost all licks (Weeks 1978*a*) and is the most frequently identified attraction (Weeks 1978*b*). Magnesium also is significant; phosphorus evidently plays no role in lick use (Jones and Hanson 1985). Spring lick use by deer evidently is driven by a sodium deficiency brought about by high potassium and water content of the spring forage that interferes with efficient sodium conservation in the deer's body (Weeks and Kirkpatrick 1976).

The attraction of large ungulates to mineral licks has fascinated man for centuries. The use of minerals, especially sodium, to attract deer for harvesting was quickly seized upon by pioneers and has continued until this day. Because minerals may be inadequate for maximum growth and fecundity, supplementation has become a management strategy for deer in many regions of the United States, especially the South. This is also true for red and roe deer in Eastern Europe, where nutrient supplementation has been used for decades (Geist 1986).

Current Management Practices
Clearly there are times when minerals are limiting to deer in natural habitats and supplementation might improve deer and antler quality. It is not clear, however, what minerals are needed and when and how they should be supplied. One study (Thackston 1991) surveyed sixteen southeastern U.S. wildlife agencies relative to their attitude toward mineral supplementation as a management practice. Most states do not use mineral supplementation on public lands nor endorse its use on private lands. However, a corresponding survey of thirty Georgia hunting clubs revealed that 70 percent used mineral supplements (some only salt) and 85 percent felt they helped increase antler size.

Unfortunately, there are few controlled studies of effects of mineral supplementation on wild deer. A study in south-central Louisiana (Schultz 1990) investigated the impact of mineral supplementation on body and antler size in both captive deer and wild populations on areas of low fertility. It found no differences in growth rate, body size, and antler quality. Although supplementing the wild populations was complicated by small experimental areas and deer movement, these results raise concerns regarding the actual benefits of mineral supplementation.

INTEGRATING IT ALL
Drawing all of this information together into a synopsis and recommendation is difficult. It is like prescribing a treatment for a disease we know little about and for which the effects on the patient have not been determined. There is enough evidence that mineral availability can raise body and antler size in whitetails that mineral supplementation, as a management tool, deserves further study. Until that time, I hope you will be satisfied with recommendations liberally laced with personal (and what I hope is expert) opinion!

What to Use as a Supplement
Most supplementation efforts are based on the assumptions that common salt is sought at natural licks and therefore must be limiting, or if mineral mixes contain everything, they are bound to supply whatever might be limiting.

Mixtures high in calcium and phosphorus make intuitive sense, given their importance in antler material, their proven impact on antler growth, and the frequent environmental deficiency of phosphorus. A problem with interpretation of almost all studies of calcium and phosphorus, however, is the role of sodium in deer nutrition. Experimental diets that include calcium and phosphorus always contain large quantities of sodium, a total deviation from the content of natural forages. Therefore, it is difficult to assess the effects of sodium deficiencies in natural situations on antler growth or to identify any interaction sodium levels might have with those of other minerals.

Similarly, all commercial mineral mixes have salt as their most common ingredient, usually about one-third by weight. This inclusion is probably to increase the palatability of the mix. Several "cafeteria" experiments have found that compounds of calcium, phosphorus, magnesium, and potassium mixed with soil are used little, if any, by white-tailed deer (Weeks 1974) and other ungulates (Stockstad et al. 1953). Given that deer can identify and ingest materials that they lack (Robbins 1983), it is interesting that only sodium is selected.

Thus, it appears that any mineral supplementation should include salt. Though added advantages of other minerals have not been proven, it makes sense that inclusion of phosphorus and calcium would help in regions where soils are deficient. Much research must be done before we can draw definite conclusions regarding the value of mineral supplementation other than as an attractant.

How, When, and Where to Supplement

An effective method of supplementing minerals is to mimic natural licks. Pour the mineral mix either into a depression or just onto the soil in a 1-square-meter area (Schultz 1990, Thackston 1991). Natural licks are very attractive to deer when concentrations of sodium in the soil are only 200 to 300 parts per million, suggesting heavy concentrations are not necessary. Indeed, I have observed that wild deer have an aversion to licking a mineral mix or salt block, preferring instead to eat and lick surrounding soil into which the minerals have leached. Therefore, minerals spread on the ground and mixed with soil may be more effective and attractive. Of course, a granular mix would leach into the soil more quickly.

It appears that supplementation is not needed year-round. Peak use of natural licks is in April and May (Weeks and Kirkpatrick 1976, Thackston 1991), closely following the major spring green-up period.

Some use continues during the summer and fall. There is little or no use during the winter. Annual "recharging" of licks may help, especially when established on porous soils. This should occur in late winter. Furnishing minerals to wild populations before antler growth begins in April is impossible, since wild deer do not use licks before this. If the soil type on which the lick is established is selected carefully, one recharge per year should suffice. Availability of mineral concentrations in midsummer, when deposition of minerals in the antler is at its peak, may be important for bucks.

Natural licks are found in many soil types, but most commonly in silt-loam. The clay in the soil is often of illite and kaolin (Jones and Hanson 1985). Clay is important because it decreases leaching and increases evaporative concentration of the minerals. When establishing supplemental licks, choose a site with fine soil texture. Also, a soil high in clay or a clayey subsoil is desirable (Weeks 1978*b*). Although it is easier to establish licks close to roads, visual obstructions between the road and lick will minimize disturbance and the potential for poaching.

CONCLUSIONS

There is no proof that mineral supplementation assists in producing quality antlers in wild deer, but some studies suggest possible benefits. Even if it ultimately proves beneficial, mineral supplementation is only one of several factors (including age structure, genetic quality, population density, and food quality) that must be managed to produce a quality deer herd. Assuming all of these variables are optimized, mineral supplementation may be the final factor that boosts antler quality from good to superior.

—Harmon P. Weeks, Jr.

CHAPTER 12

Genetics

To the natural philosopher . . . as well as to the common observer, the most important to cultivate, and, at the same time, hardest to acquire, is that of seeing what is before him.

—GEORGE PERKINS MARSH
Man and Nature

In this chapter, deer quality is defined primarily in terms of antler size, though many other characteristics could be included, such as body size, condition, general health, fitness, and so forth. Within a given herd or region, however, most such characteristics likely are related to antler size.

Boone and Crockett records (Nesbitt and Reneau 1988) are a convenient measure of an animal's ultimate antler quality. This is not the only or maybe even the best reflection of antler quality, but it certainly is the most widely used system in North America. Because of the Boone and Crockett system's popularity, it is likely that most antlers that are large enough to qualify have, in fact, made it into the record books. Thus Boone and Crockett records probably provide the least-biased sample of actual genetic potential by region.

By focusing on Boone and Crockett records, we are not demeaning the fine whitetails in many parts of North America that basically do not have the genetic or environmental potential to achieve that particular record book. Quality is represented by the best that a given herd can achieve. When hunters can manage for, produce, and ultimately harvest the finest animals in their area, they can be just as proud as hunters in other parts of the country whose finest are world records.

ENVIRONMENT VERSUS GENETICS

What are the effects of environment on the quality of a deer? The environment can be loosely defined as everything that affects an animal. It is easy to identify certain factors that are likely to directly or indirectly influence physical characteristics. Many can be lumped into what we call habitat. Certainly diet is an important environmental factor. To produce large deer with large antlers, their food must be of high quality and quantity. For this to be true, soils must be fertile and numbers of deer (or other herbivores) cannot be so great as to limit quantity.

There are many other factors. The other deer in the area represent a social environment that unquestionably influences the animal's development. These effects are poorly understood, but some of our ideas are discussed in the chapter on sociobiology.

The physical environment includes things like climate and weather. These probably have some direct as well as indirect effects on physical characteristics. The direct effects include deep snows and severe cold that limit forage and deplete energy. Drought and high temperatures also can reduce the quantity and quality of forage. Indirect effects include genetic changes that can influence the physical characteristics of deer in different climates. These changes occur through natural selection over long periods of time.

Photoperiod (the amount of daylight in relation to dark during a twenty-four-hour period) is also a part of an animal's environment. It changes with the seasons and latitude and has been proven to be an environmental trigger for inherited mechanisms governing the antler growth and reproduction cycles. But now we are discussing environmental triggers to *genetic* mechanisms. Environment and genetics are beginning to get tangled up, so it is important that we take a look at the other side of the quality coin, namely, genetics.

What is genetics? In this case, we are primarily referring to the characteristics that are inherited from parents. These may be expressed as obvious physical characteristics, such as large antlers, or "hidden" and passed on as recessive or nonexpressed genes to the next generation. Generally speaking, an animal's genetic makeup is a result of natural selection. Through processes such as "survival of the fittest," animals with the best combination of genes for survival in a certain environment are the ones that live long enough to pass on their genes. These genes are the ones that are in the present-day animals. This becomes a little complicated today, when we realize how white-tailed deer have been moved around in this country. Many deer are not in the same environments where their ancestors evolved and may not be ideally equipped for survival where they now are. Nevertheless, most seem to be doing fairly well and apparently populations are capable of rapidly adapting to new environments. One reason for this adaptability is the whitetail's very high levels of genetic variability.

Environment and genetics are both involved in the quality of deer. Separating them or assigning a relative importance is difficult, maybe impossible. In fact, one of science's most persistent debates centers on the relative importance of environment and genetics in shaping the characteristics of living things. The overwhelming conclusion that is always eventually reached is that they both are important. In deer, as in all animals, excellence in both is essential for achievement of the ultimate expression of any of their biological potentials.

BODY AND ANTLER SIZE RELATIONSHIPS

Every wildlife biology student learns about the biological rule that relates to the body size of warm-blooded animals. Bergmann's Rule states in part that warm-blooded animals from colder climates tend to be larger in size than their counterparts in warm climates (Allee et al. 1949). This is thought to be a survival advantage, since large bodies result in less surface area relative to body size and therefore relatively less heat loss. This phenomenon occurs widely, but certainly not universally, among birds and mammals. It does seem to hold for white-tailed deer. The average body sizes of white-tailed deer from the northern tier of states and southern Canada are larger than those from farther south, unless severe overpopulation or other factors restrict food quantity or quality. Key deer (a subspecies of whitetails found in the Florida Keys) are the smallest in the United States and are the most southern. It is interesting, however, that some whitetails in South and Central America are much larger than the Key deer. Nevertheless, although many exceptions can be found, the general trend of larger, more compact bodies in their northern range seems to hold true.

It also is probable that the trend in body size identified by Bergmann is not entirely (although may be partly) the result of direct environmental effects on an individual but rather has been incorporated into the genetics of the animals over generations. We know of no particular study documenting this but it is suggested by our observations of the relationships of stocking source to body size in areas of Georgia, where native populations of deer were extirpated and restocked with northern animals. There seems to be a tendency for larger deer to occur in the areas stocked from northern sources, other things being equal. Nevertheless, these animals only rarely reach the sizes attained by northern deer in their native habitats. Also, it is clear that overpopulation or poor soils can eliminate any size advantage the northern stock may have. This suggests that environment and genetics play a direct role in Bergmann's Rule.

Soil fertility also is an important environmental factor for deer body size and antler growth. Organic content in soils, an important component of fertility, tends to decrease in warmer, wetter climates because of greater oxidation and leaching. Some of the best soils are in the upper Midwest, where topsoil was deposited by glaciers.

So, body size usually gets larger as you go north. What is the relationship between body size and antlers? Once again, there are exceptions, but they usually get larger, too. Possibly antlers increase proportionately more than body size. This means large deer would have very large antlers. This does seem to be true when you compare among species (Allee et al. 1949). Many large species (elk, moose, and caribou) have proportionately much larger antlers than small species (whitetails, brockets [*Mazama* spp.], and so forth). The great Irish elk *(Megaloceros giganteus)*, now extinct, carried the greatest antler mass of any species. Some reached 11 feet from tip to tip.

It is less clear whether the proportionately greater increase in antler size for a given increase in body size holds true within a species, but larger whitetails tend to have larger antlers. This means that antlers should tend to be larger as one goes north. Although there are exceptions, some of which are easily explained and some not, whitetails do tend to get larger and in many instances have larger antlers in northern regions.

The Westward Trend

There seems to be another antler size trend. Larger antlers are found as one goes west, at least until the center of the continent is reached. For example, if one starts in South Carolina or Florida and moves into Texas and even Mexico (where the "muy grandes" live), antlers seem to get larger in proportion to body size. There are exceptions. If one continues farther west into the Coues' deer *(O. v. couesi)* range, the deer and their antlers get smaller. In areas of the South where deer were extirpated and restocked from northern and western sources, the bucks

The "muy grande" bucks of the Texas and Mexican brush country are exceptions to the rule of large antlers being associated with large body size. Their large antlers and relatively small bodies make them truly spectacular animals. Photograph by Mike Biggs.

sometimes grow larger-than-expected antlers. But generally, the trend of large antlers as one goes west into the Great Plains seems to hold and also occurs if one moves west across the northern tier of states.

Why? One possible explanation is that the habitat opens up as one goes west. Large antlers are an advantage in terms of display. Their size is intimidating to other bucks and possibly attractive to does. Large antlers help a buck maintain the right to breed and pass his genes on. They also have disadvantages, especially in dense vegetation. They can hinder the buck's movement and escape from predators as well as making it more difficult to browse. Large antlers should be less of a disadvantage in more open habitat because they would not hinder the animal as much as in the forests. Woody vegetation does seem to have been historically and prehistorically less dense in the center of the continent, because of sparser rainfall. Low rainfall itself may also have an indirect effect on antler size through the reduced leaching of minerals from the soil.

In summary, there is a general trend for larger body sizes with an associated increase in antler development as one goes north. There is also somewhat of a trend, for whichever reason, for larger antlers as one goes west toward the heartland. If we put the trends together, where should the record antlers come from? You guessed it. The upper Midwest and south-central Canada. This generally seems to be true.

There is another idea that could just as easily account for this. That is the effect of glaciers and soils in this upper Great Lakes region. Rich soil scraped off of the areas to the north was deposited there by glaciers. Good soils tend to produce big antlers. This possible relationship should be studied. So, while we can identify by the Boone and Crockett records where large numbers of world-class whitetails have been found, we are not sure why, and several factors probably are involved.

RESTOCKING AND SUBSPECIES

So far, we have dealt mainly with where native deer have the largest antlers. But white-tailed deer were once virtually extinct from most of their range in North America. It is difficult to imagine a time when there were so few deer that they had to be imported, but this was exactly the situation from the late 1800s until organized restocking began in the 1930s and '40s. Decades of market hunting and overharvest had decimated the whitetails.

Several laws were passed to protect deer and other wildlife, but they often were unenforceable or ignored. In many cases, deer were

The Jordan buck held the Boone & Crockett world record for typical antlers for many years with a score of 206⅛. It was taken in Wisconsin, in an area of rich soils deposited by glaciers. PHOTOGRAPH COURTESY OF LARRY HUFFMAN.

	Low population	Restocked	Estimated 1990 population
Alabama	1,000 in 1915	3,755+ in 1926–1992	1,300,000
Arkansas	<500 in 1930	3,112+ in 1915–1991	700,000
Colorado	Almost extirpated in 1920–1930	100 in 1965	5,000
Florida	— 1935	2,922 in 1941–1978	750,000
Georgia	Almost extirpated early in 1900s	4,067 in 1928–1992	1,200,000
Idaho	Almost extirpated —	166 in 1985–1989	75,000
Illinois	Extirpated in 1878–1893	624 in 1903–1953	—
Indiana	Extirpated in 1893	407 in 1934–1955	230,000
Iowa	Almost extirpated in 1898	97+ in 1884–1940s	200,000
Kentucky	— 1927	9,164 in 1919–1992	425,000
Louisiana	15,000 to 20,000 in 1920	2,988+ in 1949–1980s	650,000
Maryland	Almost extirpated —	2,023 in 1914–1963	180,000
Mississippi	Almost extirpated in 1900–1925	3,339 in 1931–1980	1,500,000
Missouri	Almost extirpated in 1900s	2,648 in 1925–1957	800,000
Montana	Almost extirpated in 1941	424 in 1945–1951	400,000
Nebraska	Almost extirpated in 1930s	19 in 1959–1960	140,000
New Jersey	Almost extirpated in 1900	1,992 in 1903–1968	153,000
New York	Almost extirpated in 1880–1890	159 in 1889–1976	800,000
North Carolina	Almost extirpated in 1900–1925	3,493+ in 1890–1987	650,000
Ohio	Extirpated in 1904	863 in 1919–1932	270,000
Oklahoma	500 in 1917	8,956 in 1942–1972	325,000
Pennsylvania	Almost extirpated —	5,055 in 1906–1968	1,000,000
Rhode Island	— —	16 in 1967–1971	5,000
South Carolina	Almost extirpated in 1915–1920	642 in 1950–1989	500,000+
Tennessee	Almost extirpated in 1900	9,120 in 1932–1985	750,000
Texas	Almost extirpated in 1890s	30,000+ in 1938–1991	3,200,000
Vermont	Extirpated in 1870s	17 in 1878	125,000
Virginia	— 1925	4,268 in 1926–1992	600,000
West Virginia	Almost extirpated in 1900s	2,864 in 1921–1992	800,000
Wyoming	Almost extirpated in 1890s	306 in 1949–1953	47,000

In the early 1900s, deer populations had reached extremely low levels across the country. Restocking in at least thirty states helped restore the whitetail to its former range.

completely absent from areas where they had been abundant. Small, scattered populations of deer remained only in the most remote and inaccessible places. In 1890, it was estimated that there were only 300,000 white-tailed deer in the entire United States. That doesn't sound too bad until you consider that today, some *states* annually harvest more than 300,000 deer.

Initial deer restoration efforts began as early as the late 1800s. These efforts were relatively small and usually consisted of a single restocking or relocating of deer. The public, aware of the potential extirpation of many species of wildlife, became increasingly interested in the return of deer. These first efforts at restoration were financed in part by private individuals (usually sportsmen and large landholders) and state game agencies. In 1937, the passage of the Pittman-Robertson Act created a source of funds to help pay for the restoration of wildlife in the United States. These funds allowed larger, more organized efforts during the 1930s, '40s, and '50s that continue in some states. Most efforts to restore white-tailed deer to their former range were completed by the late 1960s and early 1970s. Protection through enforced regulations, the creation of wildlife refuges and management areas, and aggressive restocking programs all have contributed significantly.

At first it was hard to locate a source of deer. In many cases where there were remnant populations, local people opposed trapping and transferring deer to other areas. Many states stocked refuges with deer from other states and then used these herds to repopulate other areas. Of the thirty states that restocked or relocated deer, at least twenty-one obtained some of them from outside sources. The states contributing the most deer were Michigan, North Carolina, Texas, and Wisconsin. Deer from seven or more states were imported into Alabama, Florida, and Pennsylvania. West Virginia received deer from at least nine states, and Virginia was restocked with deer from at least eleven. So, much of the whitetail's present range is populated with animals whose ancestors evolved somewhere else.

Most deer texts list thirty-eight subspecies of whitetails in the Americas. Seventeen of these occur in the United States. What all the mixing and shuffling has done to the genetics is unknown, but to some extent the idea of seventeen distinct subspecies in North America is impractical.

A subspecies is a geographically adapted population that is statistically different from other populations. The statistical difference refers

Source of restocked deer	State and number of deer received				
	Alabama	Arkansas	Colorado	Florida	Georgia
Alabama	3176				
Arkansas	9	2702			
Florida				1409	
Georgia	43				2204
Idaho					
Illinois					
Indiana					
Iowa					
Kentucky		45			35
Louisiana		23		356	
Maine					
Maryland				10	9
Massachusetts					
Michigan	122				
Minnesota					
Mississippi					
Missouri					
Montana					
Nebraska					
New Hampshire					
New Jersey					
New York					
North Carolina	178	35		17	186
Ohio	2				
Oklahoma			100		
Pennsylvania				49	
Rhode Island					
South Carolina				28	
Tennessee					
Texas	26	?		437	1,058
Vermont					
Virginia					1
West Virginia					
Wisconsin	20	309		616	439
Wyoming					
Mexico					
Unknown					135

State and number of deer received

Idaho	Illinois	Indiana	Iowa	Kentucky	Louisiana
					2,429
166					
	618				
		11			
			95+		
				8,710	
	5				
			2		
				7	
				24	
				123	
					196+
	1			300	363
		396			

Source of restocked deer	State and number of deer received				
	Maryland	Mississippi	Missouri	Montana	Nebraska
Alabama		?			
Arkansas					
Florida					
Georgia					
Idaho					
Illinois					
Indiana					
Iowa					
Kentucky		225			
Louisiana		35+			
Maine					
Maryland	1,773				
Massachusetts					
Michigan	13		253		
Minnesota			12		
Mississippi		2,491			
Missouri			2,292		
Montana				424	
Nebraska					19
New Hampshire					
New Jersey					
New York					
North Carolina		35			
Ohio					
Oklahoma					
Pennsylvania	10				
Rhode Island					
South Carolina					
Tennessee					
Texas					
Vermont					
Virginia					
West Virginia					
Wisconsin	(71)	358			
Wyoming					
Mexico		495+			
Unknown	156		91+		

State and number of deer received					
New Jersey	New York	North Carolina	Ohio	Oklahoma	Pennsylvania
		?			
			26		
					16
					21
8					
97					417
					84
1,887+					64
	59	?			
		3,319			50
			426		16
				8,956	
			56		3,719
				?	
		167+			
	100	7	1,355		

Source of restocked deer	State and number of deer received				
	Rhode Island	South Carolina	Tennessee	Texas	Vermont
Alabama					
Arkansas					
Florida					
Georgia					
Idaho					
Illinois					
Indiana					
Iowa					
Kentucky			111		
Louisiana					
Maine					
Maryland			76		
Massachusetts					
Michigan			50		
Minnesota					
Mississippi					
Missouri					
Montana					
Nebraska					
New Hampshire					
New Jersey					
New York					10
North Carolina			370		
Ohio					
Oklahoma					
Pennsylvania					
Rhode Island	16				
South Carolina		642			
Tennessee			7,679		
Texas				30,000+	
Vermont					
Virginia					
West Virginia					
Wisconsin			662		
Wyoming					
Mexico					
Unknown					7

| State and number of deer received | | |
Virginia	West Virginia	Wyoming
15		
	5	
19		
	121	
6		
	6	
210	80	
	?	
	?	
4		
310		
9	5	
446	29	
16		
1,601		
13	1,665	
369	447	
		306
1,250	506	

Of the thirty states that restocked or relocated deer, at least two-thirds received deer from other states or Mexico.

to differences in physical measurements. In fact, whitetail subspecies have all been distinguished by comparing characteristics such as coat color, dimensions, cranial details, and antler tine size and spread. Most were described before the 1940s, before restocking peaked in the mid-1950s.

Movements from state to state often introduced subspecies from diverse regions of North America. This raises questions about the original concept of seventeen subspecies and the possibility that distribution maps may be outdated. Some subspecies were introduced into areas where they had not occurred before. If new studies were undertaken, perhaps entirely new intergrades or hybrids of subspecies would be described.

Stocking source seems to be an important factor in producing Boone and Crockett bucks in areas where deer have been restored. The genetic potential of any herd is important when trying to manage for quality; however, with few exceptions, in most areas, poor genetics is not a problem. The key word is *potential*. Any given location may have the genetic potential to produce a quality buck, but without all the ingredients working together at the same time, that potential will never be met.

		Subspecies	Date
Alabama	400	*O. v. virginianus*[A]	1926–1992
	144+	*O. v. borealis*	
	26	*O. v. texanus*	
	9	*O. v. macrourus*	
Arkansas	307+	*O. v. borealis*	1915–1991
	80	*O. v. virginianus*[A]	
	23	*O. v. macrourus*[B]	
	—	*O. v. texanus*	
Colorado	100	*O. v. macrourus*[C]	1965
Florida	675	*O. v. borealis*	1941–1978
	437	*O. v. texanus*	
	356	*O. v. macrourus*[B]	
	45	*O. v. virginianus*[A]	
Georgia	1,058	*O. v. texanus*	1928–1992
	439	*O. v. borealis*	
	221	*O. v. virginianus*[A,D]	
	115	*O. v. nigribarbis*[E]	
	30	Unknown	
Illinois	6	*O. v. borealis*	1903–1953
Indiana	—	*O. v. borealis*	1934–1955
	—	*O. v. virginianus*[A]	
	396	Unknown	
Iowa	2	*O. v. borealis*[F]	1884–1940s
Kentucky	324	*O. v. borealis*	1919–1992
	123	*O. v. virginianus*	
	7	*O. v. macrourus*	
Louisiana	363	*O. v. borealis*	1949–1980s
	196+	*O. v. texanus*	
	—	Unknown	
Maryland	94	*O. v. borealis*	1914–1963
	156	Unknown	
Mississippi	358	*O. v. borealis*	1931–1980
	248	*O. v. virginianus*[A]	
	196	*O. v. texanus*[G]	
	46	Unknown	
Missouri	265	*O. v. borealis*[F]	1925–1957
	91	Unknown	
New Jersey	105	*O. v. borealis*	1903–1968

White-tailed deer restoration often introduced one or more subspecies into a region in which they were not native. This mixing calls into question the validity of the seventeen distinct subspecies recognized in North America.

		Subspecies	Date
North Carolina	167+	*O. v. borealis*	1890–1987
	—	*O. v. seminolus*[H]	
	7	Unknown	
Ohio	261	*O. v. borealis*	1919–1932
	176	Unknown	
Oklahoma	—	*O. v. texanus*	1942–1972
Pennsylvania	602	*O. v. borealis*	1906–1968
	66	*O. v. virginianus*[A]	
Tennessee	788	*O. v. borealis*	1932–1985
	722	*O. v. virginianus*[A]	
	6	*O. v. texanus*	
Vermont	10	*O. v. borealis*	1878
	7	Unknown	
Virginia	1,073	*O. v. borealis*	1926–1992
	338	*O. v. virginianus*[A]	
	6	*O. v. macrourus*	
	1,250	Unknown	
West Virginia	682	*O. v. borealis*	1921–1992
	—	*O. v. macrourus*	
	5	*O. v. seminolus*	
	6	*O. v. virginianus*	
	506	Unknown	

[A] Includes at least some deer from NC that were originally stocked with deer from NC, FL, and NY, and may include *O. v. seminolus* or *O. v. osceola* and *O. v. borealis*.
[B] May include *O. v. mcilhennyi*.
[C] May include *O. v. texanus*.
[D] Includes 516 deer from coastal islands that include *O. v. nigribarbis*.
[E] Although these deer are from within the state, they represent a subspecies, *O. v. nigribarbis*, that occurs only on Blackbeard Island and not on the mainland.
[F] May include *O. v. dakotensis*.
[G] From Mexico; may also include either *O. v. carminis* or *O. v. miquihuanensis*.

STOCKING SOURCE AND RECORD BUCKS

Recently, we examined the relationships between where deer were obtained and the production of Boone and Crockett–class antlers for certain stocked areas (Marchinton et al. 1991). The study was done in 1987 and the projected numbers of records were based on official and unofficial scores of bucks harvested then. Alabama, Georgia, South Carolina, and Florida were chosen for the study. Dates and locations of restockings as well as deer numbers and sources were determined from previously compiled records (Allen 1965, Blackard 1971, Jefferies 1975).

The number of animals from each state that met Boone and Crockett standards, as well as time and place taken, were based on published records (Nesbitt and Wright 1981, Dobie 1986) and from communications with local biologists.

Of the four states, Florida and South Carolina had produced no more than one record buck each. Florida was stocked from a variety of sources, including Louisiana, Texas, and Wisconsin, as well as with native deer, yet at the time of our study did not have a record buck. Florida deer were not reduced to the extent they were in other southern states. With the small native subspecies *(O. v. osceola* and *O. v. seminolus)* still present, these outside stockings may have had little effect on Florida's gene pool. Also, Florida is farther south than the other three states and has a more subtropical environment (remember Bergmann's Rule) along with inherently poor soils.

To the credit of its wildlife agency at the time, South Carolina was able to restock entirely with local animals *(O. v. virginianus)* from the lower coastal plain, and also has recorded only one record, a nontypical. Alabama had produced more than a dozen record bucks, perhaps more than 20. Most were taken on or near the rich soils of the Black Belt region and were apparently derived from Alabama stocking sources *(O. v. virginianus* and *O. v. osceola)*. Small numbers of northern deer were stocked in Alabama, 132 from Michigan and 20 from Wisconsin, but apparently deer descending from these sources have produced few record antlers.

Georgia was emphasized in our research because it had produced more than forty-two record bucks, a greater number than any other southern state with the exception of Texas (a state four times larger), and because the deer herd was derived from a variety of stocking sources. One thousand fifty-eight deer from Texas *(O. v. texanus)* were stocked primarily in the northern third of Georgia because biologists thought they might carry the screwworm fly *(Cochliomyia hominivorax)*. It was believed that the colder winters in north Georgia would prevent the fly's survival. Four hundred thirty-nine deer from Wisconsin were stocked in the Piedmont and coastal plain and smaller numbers from several other out-of-state sources were released around the state. Two thousand two hundred four deer also were captured from several locations in Georgia and stocked in various areas of the state.

The Wisconsin deer *(O. v. borealis)* are of particular interest as a stocking source. Based on Bergmann's Rule and the other antler size predictors, they should produce some of the largest antlers. They are, in fact, one of the largest-bodied and largest-antlered subspecies.

Importance of Soils

The Atlantic Coast flatwoods region in southeastern Georgia has produced no record bucks, irrespective of stocking sources. The habitat is relatively poor; soils are sandy and of low fertility. Likewise, the southern Appalachian ridges and valleys and the Blue Ridge area in north Georgia have produced no records. Again, the habitat in these regions is relatively poor. Soils are shallow, rocky, and of low fertility, so environment is clearly a limiting factor. The southern Piedmont and southern coastal plain regions have produced all of the Georgia records. This clearly indicates that without adequate nutrition, a buck is unlikely to reach record size.

Also of interest is the fact that of the forty-one Georgia records with known kill locations, thirty-four (83 percent) were taken close to major river systems (Dobie 1986). Dense cover associated with these waterways provides areas in which to escape hunters, allowing bucks to mature enough to develop large antlers. Bottomland also provides better browse and tends to have greater mast production than most other habitats.

Importance of Stocking Source

Stocking histories for all counties in Georgia (Jefferies 1975) were compared with record buck harvest by county (Dobie 1986). Counties that are predominantly urban or in the Atlantic Coast Flatwoods, Appalachian ridges and valleys, and the Blue Ridge regions, where no records have occurred, were excluded. We assumed that most deer reaching record size would be harvested. This allowed us to work with only one basic variable, that being genetics as dictated by stocking source.

The harvest of a record buck was not independent of stocking source. Counties stocked with a combination of Wisconsin and Georgia deer stood out. Eight of the eleven counties stocked with both types produced records. This was greater than the three expected if production of records is independent of stocking source. Twenty-five counties were stocked with only Wisconsin deer. At least one record was taken in thirteen of these, significantly more than would be expected by chance.

Twenty-one counties were stocked with Texas deer. Record bucks were killed in only four of these, less than expected by chance. These results suggest that Texas stockings were not as conducive to the production of record antlers as are other stocking sources.

There were twenty-seven counties stocked with only Georgia deer, twelve of which produced record bucks. Our analyses also indicate that there is a relationship between deer descending from Georgia sources and record antler production. At first this seemed surprising, since many of the deer stocked were coastal island animals. On studying histories of the islands, however, it becomes evident that, except on Blackbeard Island, the deer are not entirely derived from native stock (Johnson et al. 1974). Apparently, northern deer were placed on the islands by their owners in the late 1800s or early 1900s. Only about 150 of the relatively pure *O. v. nigribarbis* occurring on Blackbeard were used for restocking the mainland.

It could be argued that the wide variety of stocking sources in Georgia results in a "hybrid vigor" effect and this influenced antler size. Smith et al. (1982) demonstrated a relationship between heterozygosity (genetic variability) levels and number of antler points among yearlings. Nevertheless, high heterozygosity levels are evidently not the cause of Georgia's success, since a separate study found that all restocked populations studied there and in surrounding states had lower levels of heterozygosity than populations that had never been extirpated. This is presumed to be due to the "bottleneck" effect resulting from the relatively small numbers of animals used to reestablish populations.

Other Factors
The number of new records in Georgia seems to be increasing, but the areas producing them have changed. This may be in part because record antlers are more likely to be recognized and scored than in the past. Also, more rich farming areas now support deer than in the past. Until 1975, fourteen of the seventeen records taken were from the central Piedmont. From 1976 to 1985, there were twenty-four records and only three of these came from that region while the western Piedmont yielded seven and the coastal plain, fourteen. The shift seems to follow a pattern. When deer first become established, either by stocking or immigration, the potential for producing records is high. With the population low, nutrition is not a limiting factor. Because hunting pressure is light, bucks can reach the age of maximum antler development. As populations increase, nutrition becomes limiting and the higher densities result in increased hunting. A dramatic reduction in the buck age structure follows. Much of the western upper coastal plain region,

now producing most of Georgia's records, apparently has not reached this stage. With quality management, this area should be able to break the cycle and continue to produce quality animals. If this happens, quality management will have achieved the ultimate success we all believe it can.

Evidence from this study clearly indicates that good soils and habitat are absolutely required for records. Within areas capable of producing large animals, those restocked from certain sources are more likely to produce record antlers. This study did not solve the nature-nurture debate but, as expected, the evidence suggested that both genetics and environment play a role.

SHOULD WE BRING IN BETTER STOCK?

There is very little good deer habitat left in the United States that does not support a population, so few areas need to be restocked. Based on what we have discussed so far in this chapter, one might conclude that antler quality could be enhanced by releasing deer from a region known to produce large antlers, like the upper Midwest or Canada.

Generally, this is not the case, however, because there is an enormous difference in the genetic impact that, say, fifty deer released into an established herd would have compared with the same number released into good but unpopulated habitat. In the case of the established herd, genes from new animals likely would be swamped. Also, it would be tough for the new animals to compete with the established animals. This would decrease their chances of survival and of passing on genes.

Scientists can rarely say "never" when discussing biological phenomena. Considering this, it is worth pointing out that in special situations (such as deer populations isolated by high fences), some benefits from the addition of new stock may be identified in the future. New research also could reveal ways to maximize genetic impacts while adding only a few new animals; however, we know of no published reports of measurable genetic enhancement resulting from adding animals to any established herd. On the other side of the coin, scientific evidence clearly supports the value of better habitat as well as sex and age structure in improving deer quality.

—R. LARRY MARCHINTON,
KARL V. MILLER, AND
J. SCOTT MCDONALD

PART III

Regional Issues

CHAPTER 13

Poor-Quality Habitats

The notion espoused by so many nonprofessional ecologists—that the living world is "marvelously" and "delicately" attuned to its environment—is not so much scientifically reasonable theory as a mystically satisfying dogma. Its abandonment might lead to a useful fresh start . . .

—Pielou (1991)

Quality management in poor habitats may sound like a hopeless proposition. Poor habitats present unique problems and challenges, but quality management can work. Many clubs and public hunting areas in the Southeast have implemented quality deer management on low-quality habitats. The QDM efforts in these areas are similar to those for any habitat; however, there are several differences. Hunter expectations must be based on local range conditions and strategies must be adjusted to deal with the limitations of poor range conditions.

HABITAT QUALITY

Soil fertility and moisture, cover, and deer density are what limit the quality of whitetail habitat. Forage quality and quantity may have the greatest impact on QDM. These factors also may be the most difficult to manage. Although habitat and harvest management can ease problems caused by lack of cover or excessive densities, not much can be done to improve infertile range.

Soil Fertility and Moisture

Productivity is the ability of a soil to produce plants under a certain management system (Millar et al. 1966). For a soil to be productive, it must be fertile; however, not every fertile soil is productive. Moisture greatly influences fertility. Heavy rainfall on permeable soils can rapidly leach nutrients plants need. On the other hand, dryness can trap nutrients and prevent their absorption by plants.

Soils in arid regions tend to be more fertile than those in humid regions. Essential nutrients such as calcium and potassium often accumulate as soluble salts in these regions. These salts dissolve in moisture and become available to plants. Rainfall rarely leaches nutrients from the soil, but the soil may be unproductive if it does not receive enough precipitation to release adequate plant nutrients.

In contrast, soils in humid regions generally have lower fertility and are highly leached. Many soils of the Southeast also are poorly drained. Poorly drained soils of flatwood and pocosin (dense "bay" thickets) habitats are strongly acidic and have little oxygen, limiting the availability of nutrients (Abrahamson and Harnett 1990). These soils often are low in organic matter and minerals; they are unproductive and their vegetation is not very nutritious.

Soil fertility and moisture also affect the quantity of deer forage. Herd health, productivity, and density are directly affected by food abundance. The effects of forage quality and quantity are related, however. Nutrition is not always directly linked to forage quantity. The nutrition of deer on an area with abundant poor-quality food may be less than that of an area with much less food of higher quality.

Although soil fertility and moisture may limit an area's plant production, it has an even more profound effect on plant composition. Plants that can tolerate poorer soil conditions predominate in these areas and often offer low nutrition. There is a lot of vegetation on some poor soils in the Southeast but most forage is of low quality (Harlow 1959, Short 1975, Tanner and Terry 1982a). This affects herd condition even when other forage is abundant. Compare this with many habitats in the northern United States and Canada. The glaciated soils in these areas often produce high-quality foods, but the quantity and availability of winter forage may be low.

Cover

Many land managers underestimate the value of cover for deer. Deer must have shelter to survive. Thickets, young forest stands, windrows, and other dense vegetation provide places of escape, bedding sites, and fawning areas. Mature conifer stands provide cover for winter yarding areas, which assists in temperature regulation during extreme cold in northern whitetail range.

Most of the poor habitats of the southern range have abundant evergreen shrubs and young forest plantations to provide cover; however, in many northern areas, insufficient size and distribution of deer yards often limit distribution and carrying capacity. Poor forest management in these areas can further compromise habitat. Cover also may be limiting in many prairie habitats. Although cover can limit carrying capacity, some habitats that lack it produce very high-quality deer. Many areas of Iowa lack cover, but good forage is abundant; subsequently, Iowa produces many Boone and Crockett bucks, although total deer density may be limited by cover.

Proper forestry and agriculture often improve habitat. Land use changes may be detrimental, however, depending on their extent and type. For example, in North Carolina the extensive drainage and clearing of pocosins and their conversion to fields of soybean, corn, and wheat has dramatically improved the quality of deer food. Cover has declined, though, and many areas now support fewer deer.

Stocking Rate

When population density remains too high for several years, deer can actually lower the carrying capacity of their habitat. This happens when they deplete the vegetation to the extent that new plant growth is retarded or overbrowsing changes the species composition of the remaining plants to those that are less palatable. This is most common in upland habitats or in northern areas of deer range where food quantity is limited. The effects of overpopulation on poorer habitats are less pronounced, especially in the southeastern states. A major problem of deer management in much of the South is identifying optimum levels of stocking (Lay 1956). Any attempts at improving habitat and herd condition should be considered carefully with knowledge of local carrying capacity and the deer density relative to the carrying capacity.

SUBOPTIMAL WHITE-TAILED DEER RANGE

We conducted a survey of wildlife agencies of state and provincial governments in the United States and Canada to determine the distribution of suboptimal habitats. The agencies were asked to identify populations that were within carrying capacity but had condition indicators and productivity values lower than those of populations in other habitats in their state or region. In other words, the participants identified range where poor forage quality or quantity was causing these problems. Participants were asked not to include areas where overpopulation had decreased range quality. Areas where populations were limited only by winter severity and lack of cover also were not included; however, some areas that were identified as being deficient in forage quantity and quality also were limited by cover, winter severity, or both.

All agencies responded. Colorado, Idaho, and New Mexico were the only states that did not have sufficient information on white-tailed deer habitat conditions to interpret quality. Most states and provinces identified certain portions of their deer range as suboptimal. Some pockets of good habitat may be located within these areas and small, isolated areas of poor habitat were not delineated.

Although the habitats identified were considered suboptimal for particular regions, the standards of quality were quite different. A habitat identified as suboptimal in the Midwest may be better than good habitat in the Southeast. The management philosophy and opinions of deer biologists also varied. A few habitats common to several states in the same physiographic region were considered suboptimal by some but not by others. Not all of the habitats identified as suboptimal were considered poor. Some were considered suboptimal because they were not as productive as other habitats in the same region. Some of these areas support relatively high deer populations, whereas others have few but high-quality animals.

All Canadian provinces within white-tailed deer range identified suboptimal habitats except Manitoba. Habitats identified as suboptimal included the boreal uplands of northeastern British Columbia and the dry and moist mountains, plateaus, and valleys of the southeastern part of the province; alpine, subalpine, boreal foothills, and short-grass and mixed grass habitats of Alberta; jack pine, black spruce, tamarack, and poplar boreal forests of Saskatchewan; boreal forests and sandhills in central and southwestern Saskatchewan; boreal forests and poor-quality deciduous forests in the Great Lakes region of Ontario; Anticosti Island and the balsam fir–spruce forests in southeastern Quebec; black spruce, peat bogs and swamps, and jack pine forests of the Northumberland coast, and the balsam fir–spruce forests of New Brunswick; and the Granite Barrens in Nova Scotia. Most of the northern portions of these provinces were outside normal whitetail range.

Only a few habitats were identified as suboptimal in the northeastern United States. They included the Green and White mountains of Vermont and New Hampshire; the spruce-fir forests of Vermont's Northeast Kingdom; the northern Berkshire Mountains and the pitch

A survey of state and provincial wildlife agencies shows that there are many areas of poor-quality deer range across the United States and Canada. They may require considerably different management prescriptions.

pine–scrub oak habitats of Cape Cod, Martha's Vineyard, and Nantucket Island in Massachusetts; the Tug Hill Plateau east of Lake Ontario, the Adirondack High Peaks in the north, and the Mongaup Hills in the south and the oak-pine barrens of Long Island in New York; the Pine Barrens of New Jersey; western Maryland; and the estuarine and palustrine wetlands of Delaware and Maryland.

The Midwest and Plains states have some of the most fertile soils in North America, so few suboptimal habitats were identified there, although some occur in Michigan, Minnesota, and Missouri. In Michigan, the spruce-hardwood forests of the northern Upper Peninsula and areas lacking agriculture and abundance of tolerant shrub and tree species in the Lower Peninsula were identified. The Canadian Shield–Border Lakes area and the Agassiz Lowlands of Minnesota also were considered suboptimal. The oak-pine forests of southern and mixed bottomland forests and tupelo swamps of southeastern Missouri also were recognized.

The Dakotas and Wyoming were the only Plains states to report suboptimal habitats. The short-grass prairies of southwestern North Dakota and the sandhills in the north-central and southeastern portions of the state were identified, as were the ponderosa pine forests and short-grass prairies of western South Dakota. Suboptimal habitats in Wyoming were the montane lodgepole–spruce-fir forests in the northeastern portion of the state, the sagebrush-saltbush-greasewood cold desert shrub habitats, and the sagebrush grasslands.

Many states in the western whitetail range reported that populations were small and management emphasis was on other big-game species. Some herds in these states also were expanding, making habitat quality determinations difficult. Subsequently, Montana was the only western state to identify suboptimal range, in its northwestern coniferous forests.

Much of the suboptimal range in the United States was in the Southeast. Mountain ranges have steep slopes with shallow and infertile soils, making these regions suboptimal for whitetails. Subsequently, habitats in the Appalachian Mountains of Pennsylvania, West Virginia, Virginia, Kentucky, Tennessee, the Carolinas, Georgia, and Alabama were considered suboptimal. The shortleaf pine forests in the Ozark and Ouachita mountains of Arkansas and Oklahoma also were identified, as were the Trans-Pecos Mountains of Texas.

Many coastal plain habitats were considered suboptimal in the Southeast. Pine flatwoods in Georgia, Florida, Alabama, Mississippi, and Louisiana were identified, as were the pocosins and Carolina bays of Virginia and the Carolinas. The dry and wet prairies of Florida and most freshwater, brackish, and salt marshes of the Gulf and Atlantic coasts also were considered suboptimal.

Another habitat type commonly identified in the Southeast was dry pine-oak uplands. These areas included the Sandhills of the Carolinas, Georgia, Tennessee, and Florida and the scrub oak ridges of central Florida. The remaining suboptimal habitats identified were the High Plains and the Blackland Prairies of Texas.

EFFECTS OF POOR-QUALITY HABITAT

Although versatile foragers, whitetails must receive proper nutrition for optimal growth and antler development. Fawns require more protein than older deer (Ullrey et al. 1967, Smith et al. 1975, Holter et al. 1979). Though studies show that 6 percent to 10 percent protein is adequate to maintain adults, the requirements for body growth, antler development, and reproduction are probably much higher (French et al. 1956, McEwen et al. 1957). The amount of digestible energy in a deer's diet also is important (Ullrey et al. 1970, Ammann et al. 1973, Thompson et al. 1973). Deficiencies in digestible energy harm herds more in northern regions, where winter severity is a limiting factor.

White-tailed deer also require the proper balance of nutrients and vitamins. The daily calcium requirements (dry-matter basis) for adult and fawn deer are 0.25 percent and 0.45 percent, respectively (Ullrey et al. 1973). Daily requirements for phosphorus and nitrogen (dry-matter basis) are 0.28 percent and 1.2 percent, respectively (Ullrey et al. 1975).

The vegetation on poor range may lack one or several of these components. Deer diets in coastal plain habitats of the Southeast typically are deficient in energy, protein, and minerals (Short 1975). For example, browse in some flatwood habitats of Florida has a mean protein content of 7.7 percent (Tanner and Terry 1982*b*). The nutritive value of vegetation commonly eaten by deer in some areas of Florida is suboptimal for body growth and antler development and meets only basal energy requirements (Wood and Tanner 1985). The quality of some browse is insufficient to supply adequate digestible energy for growth, reproduction, or body maintenance (Ammann et al. 1973). Phosphorus concentrations also are well below optimum levels.

Physical Condition

Though deer can live on poor range, their condition often is poorer than that of deer on better habitats. Antler development and weight may be below average. The percentage of spikes frequently is high, especially for yearlings. It is not unusual for 70 percent to 90 percent of yearling bucks to have spikes on poor range (Harlow and Jones 1965, Shea et al. 1992*a*). Although body size and antler development increase with age, they are still limited by nutritional deficiencies in poor habitats. Subsequently, few record bucks are produced on poor range, even under intensive management.

	Habitat quality	Live weight	Antler points	Spikes	Inside spread
Southern Piedmont	Good	114.6 lbs.	4.1	32%	7.9 ins.
Roanoke	↑	110.2	3.8	36	6.9
Cape Fear		104.2	2.9	64	5.8
Northern Pisgah	↓	95.2	2.6	70	5.4
Nantahala	Poor	93.6	2.4	80	4.6

The average characteristics of yearling bucks differed markedly among management zones of differing habitat quality in North Carolina from 1986 to 1989.

We compared the characteristics of yearling bucks from several areas in North Carolina. The lowest weights and poorest antler development were in zones with the poorest habitats. For example, the Nantahala area has poor, thin soils with little good deer browse. Forage is limited during winter, especially in years of poor mast crops. On this area, the vast majority of yearlings are spikes and they weigh less than 100 pounds. In contrast, the southern Piedmont has much better soils and good forage is more abundant. Only a third of the yearlings in this area are spikes, and weights average 20 pounds more than in the Nantahala area.

Although deer on poor range almost never attain the size or antler development of those on good range, they are well adapted to their environment. Genetics probably has played a role in the development of their physical characteristics. Small size and low productivity may enhance survival in some areas. Weight and antler dimensions should not be judged by the standard of deer from better habitats. They are just as wild, elusive, and enjoyable to hunt as any deer. Producing and harvesting a 100-point Boone and Crockett buck on poor range may require more management effort than a 150-point buck from good range. There is no difference in satisfaction or pride in producing and harvesting these deer. It's like growing tangerines or oranges; size may vary, but the taste is still sweet.

Productivity

Like physical characteristics, reproductive performance is related to forage quality. One study found that productivity was three times greater for does on good nutrition compared with those on poor nutrition (Verme 1967). An average of less than one fetus per doe is not uncommon on poor-quality habitats. Few fawns reproduce, twinning

Poor habitats can produce quality bucks. These were photographed at the same location on a Florida public wildlife management area under quality managment. Although habitat was poor, bucks attained good body and antler size. The nine-point buck was later harvested and aged at 3½ years. PHOTOGRAPHS BY STEVE SHEA.

Nutrition	Fawns per doe			
Low	0.05	0.50	1.31	0.54
Moderate	0.84	1.40	1.85	1.43
High	1.18	1.53	1.78	1.50
Age when bred:	1 year	2	3 and up	All does

The productivity of white-tailed deer herds is related to the previous autumn's nutrition. Adapted from Verme (1967).

in adults is not common, and triplets are scarce. Low productivity of deer in areas of the Northeast and Southeast has been attributed to poor forage and range quality (Harlow and Jones 1965, Hesselton and Jackson 1974, Osborne et al. 1992, Shea et al. 1992a).

Such low productivity requires special management. Though some of these areas can support relatively high populations, population growth usually is slow. With this inherent low recruitment, these herds are not very resilient and excessive hunting should be avoided. In fact, some herds have such naturally low productivity that even a light antlerless harvest may hinder them.

Carrying Capacity

It may be difficult to identify when populations approach or exceed carrying capacity in poor habitats. Recent studies on poor range found that textbook style management may not produce the results expected on good range. For example, on good habitats, reduction of density results in an increase in physical condition and productivity. This may not be the case in poor habitats. One Florida study found that the condition of deer in a poor habitat was not affected by changes in density from forty-five to twelve deer per square mile over a ten-year period (Shea et al. 1992a). Another Florida study found that productivity did not differ among populations of different densities (Petrick et al. 1994). Deer in other poor habitats of the southern Appalachians and coastal islands of Georgia also indicate weak relationships between physical condition and population density (Osborne et al. 1992).

Why are weight, antler development, and productivity not sensitive to changes in population density on poor habitats but very sensitive on good habitats? This phenomenon is related to forage quality, quantity, and competition. There must be competition among deer to identify the inverse relationship between condition and population density (Eve 1981). The effects of competition are most noticeable in habitats where some good forage is available. In these areas, nutrition is high when deer populations are low, but herd growth may deplete the top-quality forage. If populations are reduced, more forage becomes available for each deer, and condition and reproduction respond. The effects of competition are much less dramatic on ranges where forage is abundant but all is low quality. There is little good forage, so in these areas nutrition is relatively low, even when populations are small. In areas where there are large amounts of poor forage, competition is less and populations grow slowly but still can reach high levels.

The growing season is long and forage is abundant in many poor habitats of the Southeast. Even at relatively high population levels, forage abundance and diversity remain high. The poor relationship between physical condition and population density in Florida flatwoods is related to the low level of competition. The nutritional level of deer in these areas does not improve after herd reduction. Therefore, physical condition and productivity of deer may not respond as well to herd reduction as in better habitats.

QUALITY MANAGEMENT RECOMMENDATIONS
Most of the recommendations and guidelines needed to produce quality deer in poor habitats are similar to those in better habitats. There are, however, some notable exceptions.

Habitat and Harvest Data Evaluations
The deer manager must know the land's potential for producing quality animals before proceeding. If he embarks on a quality management program in a poor habitat expecting to produce record bucks, the program is doomed. Success must be measured against realistic expectations.

Contact a wildlife professional to interpret and evaluate habitat and harvest information before developing a quality deer management program. In most instances, wildlife agencies and private consultants know the problems of habitats in your area. They can provide information on habitat and harvest strategies and can help you determine realistic goals.

The deer manager must examine harvest data and evaluate the body size and antler dimensions of each age class to determine harvest criteria. If young bucks predominate, consult with a biologist or neighboring manager to determine the antler size of mature bucks. Try hard to compare local herds with others of similar habitat and density. Habitat potential may vary greatly, even among nearby lands.

The age that bucks must reach to achieve desirable antler size must be determined. Do not set your sights too high. Since productivity and recruitment are usually low in poor habitats, it may take several years to produce significant numbers of bucks in these older classes. Usually the harvest of 3 ½-year-old bucks is reasonable. This goal can be changed if the herd responds well to harvest and habitat management.

Harvest Management

Traditional management involves interpreting changes in weight, condition, antler measurements, and age structure to identify trends in population density relative to nutrition. Changes in the condition of the herd indicate whether the habitat is carrying too many deer to meet management objectives. Harvest rates can then be adjusted based on these characteristics. In poor habitats, however, traditional evaluations may not provide an accurate assessment of herd and habitat condition. This is especially true when trying to determine the population level in relation to carrying capacity. Because the physical condition of deer generally is less sensitive to changes in density on poor range, weight and antlers may be poor regardless of population levels.

Although the condition of yearlings often is used to evaluate herds, older deer may provide a better index on poor range. The nutritional stress of body growth in yearlings reduces the amount of nutrients available for antler growth. In portions of the Southeast, deer also are born late, which lowers the effectiveness of using yearlings to assess herd condition. The condition of adults more likely reflects population levels in relation to carrying capacity because most skeletal and body growth is complete (Shea at al. 1992*b*).

Where the condition of deer is insensitive to changes in density, track counts (Tyson 1952) and spotlight surveys (Cook and Harwell 1979) can be used to assess population trends. Management decisions should not be based on these techniques alone, but they do provide useful information on whether the herd is increasing or decreasing.

Antlerless Harvest

Hunter success and the weight, fat levels, reproduction, antler development, and harvest age structure of deer in some poor habitats in the Southeast may not accurately reflect density in relation to carrying capacity (Wentworth et al. 1990, 1992; Shea et al. 1992*a*; Osborne et al. 1992). Some studies have found that populations are influenced more by mast crops than by density, so if weight and antler development on your area are poor, do not assume that there are too many deer and that increased antlerless harvests are necessary. Insufficient data could lead to erroneous conclusions about the benefits of herd reduction on poor range (Gross 1972, Shea et al. 1992*a*). If improvements do occur, they may be delayed or attained at much lower densities than on good habitats.

Though physical condition may not be sensitive to population changes, antlerless harvests usually become necessary. Where deer reproductive rates are low because of poor soils or mineral deficiencies, herds still can reach high densities, but herd increases occur at much slower rates (Harlow and Jones 1965). Harvest rates of does should be conservative. For example, on good habitats where herd density and sex ratios are at desired levels, doe harvests of 40 percent to 60 percent of the total harvest may be appropriate (Osborne 1981), whereas only 20 percent or less may be required to maintain density on poor range. In fact, low- or no-antlerless harvests are known to maintain population levels on a few habitats in the South.

Though antlerless harvests must keep up with increases in productivity after herd reduction on good range, reproduction does not appear to respond as well on poor range. Too few does harvested is often better than too many on poor range because the chances of physical condition or range quality deterioration are lower. Harvesting too many does may set a program back several years because of low recruitment.

One advantage of low productivity and recruitment on poor range is that the doe harvest recommended by biologists is more easily attained. Low harvest levels often are more palatable to hunters concerned about shooting too many does.

Some states in the Southeast have early hunting seasons, when does may have dependent fawns. Harvest of these does may hurt the survival of fawns in poor habitats where nutrition already is deficient. Delay the harvest of does in these areas until later in the hunting season. Avoid harvest of button bucks late in the season. During this time, they are more likely to be separated from the doe and often are mistaken for does.

Buck Harvest

Harvest strategies for bucks also need to be altered on poor range. Fewer bucks can be harvested from areas where productivity and recruitment are low. Excessive harvest of bucks has a greater impact on age structure in these areas. Carefully monitor the relationship between harvest rate and age structure on any poor habitat. As discussed earlier, it may take several years for a quality deer management program to recover from overharvesting, because of low recruitment.

The key to growing bucks with large antlers and bodies on poor range is the same as on good range. Deer must be allowed to mature. Contrary to popular belief, many poor habitats consistently produce large bucks. Deer in these areas reach older ages more often than on better range. Several factors contribute to this. Many yearling bucks have very short spike antlers, and they often are mistaken by hunters for does; therefore, more bucks survive to the next season. There also tends to be less hunting pressure on poor range because of the lower deer densities and dense, rugged, inaccessible terrain. For example, many of the largest deer harvested in the Northeast come from low-quality habitats in the mountains.

Some of these factors may be why the average weight and antler measurements of all bucks harvested in poor habitats of North Carolina are sometimes better than in good habitats. Although the physical condition of yearling bucks declines with habitat quality, the sizes of the average bucks taken are comparable among management zones. This is because of age structure. Sixty percent of the harvest on the poorest habitat zone is composed of bucks 2½ years old or older.

The important point is that landowners using quality management guidelines on poor sites can expect to see better deer if they allow more bucks to mature. Passing young bucks is the most common strategy for improving age structure. This works the same on poor habitats as it does on good range, although depending upon the harvest criteria of a club, a buck may need to be older on poor habitats in order to reach the desired size.

Selective Harvest

Selective harvest (culling) based on antler shape and size sometimes is used to remove bucks that are considered inferior. Harvest strategies for quality deer management sometimes involve selective harvest of spikes. High incidence of spikes is common in herds on poor or overstocked range (Brothers and Ray 1975, Shea et al. 1992*a*). Spikes are not considered inferior in areas where habitat is poor. Excessive culling of spikes in poor habitats can reduce buck age structure without substantially improving antler characteristics of the herd; therefore, we do not recommend culling young bucks on most poor range. Hunters also must be careful not to mistake bucks with small spikes for does.

In portions of northwestern Florida, 80 percent of yearling bucks have spikes. Protection of spikes is one strategy used in this area to limit the harvest of yearling bucks. Although the protection of spikes allows most yearlings to survive, it also allows spikes 2½ years old or older to survive. Some herds in the Appalachian Mountains and the coastal plain of North Carolina have from 20 percent to 40 percent spikes in the 2½-year-old age class. In areas of northwestern Florida, 18 percent of 2½-year-old and 10 percent of 3½-year-old or older bucks have spikes (Shea and Breault 1989). Regardless of habitat, some managers may recommend removal of these older spikes.

Developing guidelines that allow harvest of 2½-year-old spikes, while protecting as many yearlings as possible, is similar to the development of harvest criteria on good habitat. First, age-specific antler data must be gathered. Then a criterion is selected that protects most yearlings but not older bucks. For example, on one area in Florida, 70 percent of all spike-antlered bucks with main beams as long as or

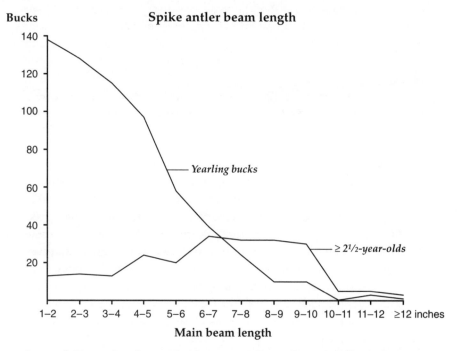

In poor habitats of northwest Florida, most yearling spike-antlered bucks have beam lengths of 6 inches or less, whereas 2½-year-old or older spikes have antlers greater than 6 inches.

longer than their ears (7 inches) were at least 2½ years old (Shea and Breault 1989). Using ear length to estimate main beam length, hunters can selectively harvest older spike-antlered bucks. Only 30 percent of the yearlings had equivalent-length antlers. With the development of one simple rule, we were able to protect most yearlings. As always, beam length or other criteria comparisons must be determined on a site-by-site basis.

Depending on herd management objectives, the benefits of culling adult spikes may be limited. This strategy, however, allows hunters to supplement the harvest with bucks that most likely would not develop into quality animals. These bucks can be a welcome bonus and meat on the table for hunters who, because of low recruitment and age structure objectives, harvest fewer bucks on poor range.

HABITAT MANAGEMENT

Habitat management strategies often can be the most effective way to improve physical condition, productivity, and carrying capacity for deer on poor habitats. Most of the strategies discussed in chapter 10 are appropriate in poor habitats. Management often is harder and more expensive in these areas, however, so land managers should evaluate the strategies before deciding to spend a lot of time and money on poor range.

Although inferior habitats may have a lack of food, it is more likely that the forage is of poor quality. Mast often determines the physical condition, productivity, and harvest rate of deer in these habitats. Mast includes nuts (acorns or beechnuts) and fruits (apples, palmetto berries, and blueberries) that are preferred and nutritious for deer. The quality of habitats actually may vary from year to year because of availability of mast. Although mast is readily consumed in good habitats, it may not be a critical part of a deer's diet. Often in these habitats, other good foods are available; however, mast is the only high-quality forage available in some poor habitats of the Southeast. Although alternatives often exist, they generally are of poor quality, so timber management and harvest practices should emphasize mast production.

Site preparation for pine regeneration should be designed to reduce damage to oaks. Prescribed fire should be excluded from oak ridges because most oaks are susceptible to fire. Thinning of mixed pine-oak and oak stands promotes crown development and increases mast yields. Shelter wood cuts should be used instead of clear-cuts in mixed hardwood forests.

Food Plots and Supplemental Feeding

Although expensive and labor intensive, agricultural plantings and supplemental feeding can be important options in poor habitat. Because so little good food is available, planting even small areas may improve deer condition. One study showed that planting as little as 1 percent of an area in some poor habitats of Mississippi improved antler development (Vanderhoof and Jacobson 1991).

Agricultural plantings where soil fertility is low may be more expensive because of lime and fertilization requirements. Many of the soils in these areas will be acidic. Soil treatment is especially important when trying to establish clover and other legumes. Soil tests should be used to identify areas that should be planted and how much lime and fertilizer are required. By locating food plots on the most fertile portions of a property, fertilizer costs can be greatly reduced. Local wildlife biologists and extension agents can determine which crops are best suited for deer in the local area.

Regardless of their impact on deer condition and physical parameters, food plots do concentrate deer for harvest and improve hunter success. Plantings may be important especially in poor habitats that are dominated by excessive cover. Openings in these areas may facilitate attainment of quotas, selective harvest of antlered bucks, and reduction in the harvest of button bucks.

—Stephen M. Shea and
J. Scott Osborne

CHAPTER 14

The North-Central States

There are two kinds of conservationists. . . . One kind feels a primary interest in some one aspect of land . . . with an incidental interest in the land as a whole. The other feels a primary interest in the land as a whole, with incidental interest in its component resources. The two approaches lead to quite different conclusions as to what constitutes conservative land-use, and how such use is to be achieved.

—ALDO LEOPOLD (1944)

Quality deer management originated in a comparatively mild (southern) climate where the idea has been favorably accepted and widely practiced. Aside from the recent involvement of Wisconsin hunters (Wegner 1991), we know of no other instance in which it has been implemented on a large scale in the Great Lakes region; however, aspects of quality deer management have been researched in southern Michigan's George Reserve (McCullough 1979, 1984), Upper Michigan's Cusino enclosure (Ozoga and Verme 1982, 1984, 1985) and Wisconsin's fenced-in Sandhill area (see sidebar).

This does not imply that there is less need for quality deer management in northern regions. There are numerous examples of deer overabundance and skewed herd sex-age composition, resulting from inadequate antlerless deer harvest, in conjunction with unregulated buck harvest, throughout northern deer range. In some areas, where human-deer conflicts abound, the whitetail has been relegated to pest status; in other areas, periodic heavy winter kills lead to waste of a valuable resource.

White-tailed deer living at the northern edge of their geographic range have evolved different traits from those of their southern cousins. Management also has usually differed because herd characteristics vary according to climate, vegetation, and human factors. Therefore, latitudinal constraints must be carefully considered to effectively implement quality deer management, sometimes even within the same state.

In this chapter, we discuss the life cycle of deer in Michigan to demonstrate important aspects of its biology, as well as complex human dimensions that often determine management strategies in the Great Lakes region. Our purpose is to evaluate the opportunities and obstacles for implementing quality deer management in Michigan. It is hoped that our discussion will apply to other northern regions.

ECOLOGICAL CONCERNS
Michigan is almost 400 miles from north to south, yielding variable conditions and a wide array of plants and animals. Throughout the region is a natural division of deer habitat between forest and farmland. In Michigan, Wisconsin, Minnesota, and Ontario, this line conforms closely to the southern edge of the coniferous–northern hardwood forest type (Blouch 1984).

Michigan is divided into three administrative regions that generally correspond to four broad ecological zones (Albert et al. 1986). Upper Michigan (Region 1) and northern Lower Michigan (Region 2) are primarily forested. Southern Lower Michigan (Region 3) has a milder climate, more people, more farmland, and much less forest cover. The regions vary greatly in their capacities to produce deer.

Upper Peninsula
The Upper Peninsula (UP) of Michigan contains two distinct ecosystems. The eastern half is a relatively low, flat glacial lake plain where soils are primarily derived from sandstone and are calcareous. The western UP is a high plateau underlain by Precambrian igneous and metamorphic rock.

About 84 percent of the UP is forested, of which 38 percent is managed by the state and federal governments; 34 percent is owned by private corporations; and the rest is in small parcels of private property. Slightly more than half of the commercial forest land is in hardwoods. Lowland conifer forest, composed mainly of northern white cedar, represents 24 percent and 10 percent, respectively, of the forest cover in the eastern and western UP.

Deer live at relatively low densities along Lake Superior, where there is abundant lake-effect snowfall and severe winter conditions. In

Wisconsin's
Sandhill Wildlife Area

The Sandhill State Wildlife Area in Wisconsin is a 9,150-acre tract surrounded by a 9-foot deerproof fence. It is one of the largest enclosed areas in North America that is open to public whitetail hunting. Sandhill is in central Wisconsin, a region of flat topography with sandy ridges and irregular upland blocks interspersed with extensive marshes.

Controlled either-sex public hunts were initiated in 1963 and continued annually during most years. Deer were completely removed by hunting in 1972, but deer reentered the area through a temporary hole in the fence in late 1973. Hunting resumed in 1977 after the herd had reached desired levels.

The quality deer strategy (QDS) grew out of muzzle-loader hunts in 1977–78, during which some exceptional bucks were taken. The highest Boone and Crockett score was 181 on a typical ten-point, 193-pound buck taken in 1977. QDS was initiated with two consecutive antlerless hunts in 1979–80 to protect adult bucks. Beginning in 1981, QDS restricted harvests of adult bucks by limiting hunter numbers. Antlerless harvests were used to maintain the overwinter herd at fifteen to twenty deer per square mile. During the early stages, annual harvests of adult bucks were kept conservative. Currently, annual hunts remove about one-third of the estimated prehunt adult bucks. Appropriate antlerless harvests maintain herd density.

About 5,700 people applied for the 1981–89 Sandhill hunts each year. By random drawing, 44 to 151 hunters were permitted to take one deer of either sex during a one-day hunt, but up to four people were allowed to apply and hunt together. These hunts were held a week before the statewide gun deer season and offered a greater opportunity for bagging an older and larger buck than elsewhere in the state.

Hunters averaged 32 percent success bagging adult bucks during the 1981–86 hunts, and 44 percent success in 1987–89, when about one-third of the hunters were allowed one deer of either sex and the remainder antlerless. Overall, hunters averaged 33 percent success during the 1981–89 either-sex and antlerless hunts.

On Sandhill, the harvest of bucks 1½ years and older averaged 3.4 per square mile of range compared with 6.2 per square mile in surrounding areas. For each buck in the harvest, 1.5 antlerless deer were removed. In surrounding management units, where overwinter density goals were higher than on Sandhill, 1.2 antlerless deer were harvested for each adult buck.

Harvest rates of adult bucks averaged about 35 percent. Of 403 bucks shot during 1981–89, 44 percent were 3½ years or older, compared with fewer than 5 percent in surrounding management units. As expected, hunters selected older bucks and does and tended to avoid fawns. Hunters shot 45 percent of the available bucks 2½ years or older and 20 percent of the yearlings. In comparison, hunters shot 37 percent of the does aged 2½ years or older and 23 percent of the yearlings.

Under this strategy, some impressive bucks were taken. Of the 403 bucks, 74 weighed more than 160 pounds; the largest was 206 pounds field-dressed. Two hundred bucks had eight or more antler points, 31 had ten or more, and 13 had outside antler spreads of 20 inches or more.

During 1982–87, we surveyed hunters with either-sex permits to determine their definition of a trophy deer and the type of deer they preferred. Ninety-five percent classified a trophy as a buck with at least eight antler points, a field-dressed weight of at least 175 pounds, and an outside antler spread at least 20 inches; how-

Getting first-time hunters off to a good start brings satisfaction and a quality deer-hunting experience. The future of deer hunting rests with us and first-time or young hunters. All hunters must behave ethically and respect landowners, as an example for youth. This should enhance hunting quality for everyone. Photograph by Wisconsin Department of Natural Resources.

ever, 20 percent of the successful hunters shot deer that ranked below what they had indicated they definitely would shoot.

Our surveys suggest that although management for a greater proportion of mature bucks may be an ideal, two-thirds of the hunters polled felt satisfied if they could take an adult buck with six or fewer antler points or an adult antlerless deer. At Sandhill, most hunters with either-sex permits attempted to shoot the first buck or large deer they saw.

At Sandhill, hunters strongly supported a restrictive adult buck harvest strategy where hunter numbers and the bag limit were closely regulated. The Sandhill experience clearly demonstrated that more large bucks were harvested under limited-access hunting, and populations were kept at desired goals through liberal removals of antlerless deer. These hunts also provided useful information on hunter attitudes and behavior and the application of similar harvest strategies on other areas.

IMPLEMENTATION OF QUALITY DEER MANAGEMENT ON OTHER AREAS IN WISCONSIN

Wisconsin deer hunters have long been used to a liberal buck-hunting policy and reasonable numbers of older bucks with large antlers. Though the current system is acceptable to most hunters, implementation of a more ambitious "formal" quality management program, particularly in southern Wisconsin, may include either a shorter buck season or restrictive harvest criteria coupled with liberal removals of antlerless deer. Hunters would have to be willing to harvest fewer yearling bucks and be satisfied with seeing more bucks while hunting. This quality management program would attempt to reduce exploitation of young antlered bucks and maintain overwinter deer densities at prescribed goals. Although most hunters have opposed the formal program, support for quality management is increasing. Currently, most hunters voluntarily forgo shooting small-antlered bucks on many areas of private land to allow more bucks to mature.

Support for this strategy was shown at Sandhill in 1989. Eighty-seven percent of 6,700 individuals who applied for the 1989 hunt indicated they would be willing to limit their buck hunting to a short period, provided antlerless hunting would be permitted during the rest of the statewide season.

Several issues would have to be addressed first:

1. Impact on hunting opportunity (limited access, fewer days to hunt bucks, or both).

2. Effect on total deer harvests.

3. Privatization of hunting.

4. Herd monitoring and accuracy of population estimates.

5. Harvest allocation among various user groups.

Although these issues have not been fully explored, several factors favor implementing a quality management program outside of Sandhill. These include the following:

1. The quality of the hunt should be enhanced under quality management, provided a concerted effort is made to improve hunter attitudes and behavior and regulate deer densities. This will require more responsible management of the herd. Hunters would have to exercise more self-restraint as custodians of the herd, seek good landowner relations, and exercise ethical hunting. Hunters also would have to forgo some bucks and accept more liberal removals of antlerless deer.

2. There will be lower deer harvests, but the magnitude would depend on harvest rates of adult bucks, herd density goals, recruitment levels, and the significance of poaching and woundings, among other factors. Rather than striving for very conservative removals of adult bucks, as practiced at Sandhill, harvest rates of adult bucks could be reduced only moderately below current levels to 60 percent to 70 percent. More 2½- and 3½-year-old bucks will become available under this strategy, plus a few older animals that would let hunters see trophy-class animals.

3. Privatization of hunting may increase regardless of har-

vest strategy, though quality management may accelerate the trend. Whatever, strategies should optimize hunting on private land while achieving adequate removals of antlerless deer.

4. Herd monitoring and existing population models should be refined within a few years. Given only minimal reduction in buck harvest rates, the accuracy of population estimates would not be appreciably affected, provided the annual mortality of bucks remains relatively stable. Refinements of population estimates also could be made if buck harvests were more conservative.

5. The adult buck harvest will be allocated to various groups (selected landowners, their friends or relatives, and bow and gun hunters who are willing to pay fees) irrespective of the harvest strategy, while hunter demand may continue to increase, at least in the short term.

It is uncertain how much hunter numbers and license sales would be altered in areas dominated by private land. It may require some hunters who currently hunt these areas to seek alternatives, particularly on larger tracts of public land that offer nearby hunting opportunities. Overcrowding could occur on some of the more accessible and smaller public lands, but this could be offset by regulating hunter density. These concerns may be negated by the projected long-term decline in Wisconsin deer hunters.

Organized efforts that encourage ethical behavior and better relations between landowners and hunters should improve the overall quality of the hunt. It should also enhance the perception of deer hunters and the deer management program among other hunters, landowners, and nonhunters. The outlook for quality management in Wisconsin is good, assuming widespread support among landowners and hunters. Sound direction from the Wisconsin Department of Natural Resources also will be required.

—JOHN F. KUBISIAK

contrast, south-central portions of the region carry high deer densities that unquestionably surpass the capacity of "core" wintering habitat to sustain healthy deer.

Northern Lower Michigan

Varied topography as well as cool and variable weather prevail in northern Lower Michigan. Annual snowfall ranges from 60 to 150 or more inches. Forest, agricultural, and urban land represent 61 percent, 29 percent, and 6 percent, respectively, of Region 2. Forty percent of the commercial forest land is under state and federal control, 7 percent is managed by private corporations, and the rest is privately held, primarily for recreation. Northern hardwoods dominate the more productive soils; oak, red pine, and jack pine occupy extensive tracts of drought-type soils.

A sandy, high plain, commonly referred to as the Club Country, occupies the east-central portion of this region. Much of this area is owned by private hunting clubs, where deer populations are maintained at artificially high levels through supplemental feeding and minimal harvesting of antlerless deer. Deer damage to farms presents special problems here because crops are intermixed with hunting club lands in many areas.

Southern Lower Michigan

Compared to northern sectors, southern Lower Michigan has a longer and less variable growing season with less annual snowfall. Soils are predominantly rich loams, clay, and some sand. Major crops include beans, corn, wheat, and alfalfa.

Region 3 contains many plant species that have a more southern affinity. Beech, sugar maple, and oak-hickory forests originally covered much of the region but now grow only in small, scattered lots in an agriculturally dominated landscape. Forested land represents approximately 18 percent of each county, equally distributed among state, federal, and private holdings, and the rest is in miscellaneous private ownership. Most of southern Lower Michigan has low-to-medium deer densities but high human population. As a result, thousands of deer-vehicle accidents occur annually.

BIOLOGICAL CONCERNS

Northern whitetails evolved to survive harsh winters. Typically, they are larger and have less surface area in proportion to body weight compared with deer living in warmer climates. This relationship enhances survival because it helps to reduce heat loss during cold weather. Most, if not all, of their seasonal physiological adjustments (including reproduction) are strictly controlled by changes in amount of daylight (photoperiod).

Herd Density and Composition

As of October 1, 1991, there were about 1.75 million deer in Michigan. They were most numerous in the Upper Peninsula (675,000), followed by northern Lower (575,000), and southern Lower Michigan (425,000).

In 1990, Michigan hunters harvested about 60 percent of the available antlered deer but only about 13 percent of the available does and fawns. Approximately 70 percent of the adult bucks and 35 percent of the adult females were yearlings. Fawns constituted 39 percent of the antlerless harvest (Hill 1991*a*). These data suggest that the Octo-

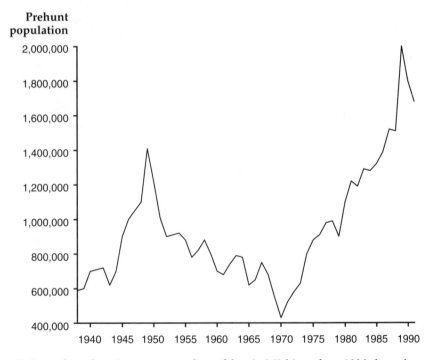

Estimated pre–hunting season numbers of deer in Michigan from 1938 through 1991 have ranged from a few hundred thousand in 1970 to about 2 million in 1990.

ber 1990 herd in Michigan was composed of about 2 does and 1.8 fawns for every adult (antlered) buck.

The sex and age structures of deer vary in different parts of the state. In general, deer in the UP are older and produce fewer fawns than in southern herds. The willingness of southern Michigan hunters to take antlerless deer has further accentuated differences in the sex and age structures.

Nutrition and Growth

White-tailed deer are selective feeders, so an abundance of deer may reduce preferred natural foods; other plants may increase because they are less palatable, resistant to grazing, or both (Ozoga and Verme 1982). As a result, overgrazed summer deer range may not have the stark overused appearance one would expect. Even so, the land's nutritional base and capacity to naturally support healthy deer steadily decline with continued overuse.

Fawns are particularly sensitive to unfavorable weather and food shortage in autumn because they do not achieve maximum growth and fatness until mid-December (Verme and Ozoga 1980*b*). Furthermore, autumn on northern deer range may switch to winterlike conditions overnight, accelerating body heat loss and forcing a shift from energy-rich foods to less nourishing, woody browse. This combination of low-quality diet and excessive heat loss may curtail growth among young deer and limit fat accumulation earlier than normal.

Storing fat in autumn enhances deer survival on northern range because the reserves can be used when forage is scarce. Like many other seasonal events, the accumulation of fat is cued to photoperiod and is hormonally controlled. Even poorly nourished fawns are physiologically compelled to store fat in autumn at the expense of additional skeletal growth (Verme and Ozoga 1980*a*, 1980*b*).

Energy levels in the autumn diet are especially important to northern fawns. Those that have access to high-energy foods (such as farm crops, beechnuts, or acorns) have greater body weight and skeletal size, and accumulate more fat, compared with fawns on poor diets (Verme and Ozoga 1980*a*, 1980*b*). Well-nourished northern fawns will be skeletally large as well as fat, whereas malnourished fawns may be fairly fat but skeletally small at onset of winter.

Another common phenomenon in high-density herds is the wide range in body sizes among young deer (fawns and yearlings) within the same sex-age class. For example, in the south-central UP, some autumn-harvested yearling males may be exceptionally large, whereas others may be as small as superior male fawns within the same herd. There is no evidence that these variable conditions are due to late breeding. Instead, they are most prevalent where nutrition is good but spotty, suggesting that high density contributes to intense competition among deer for space and food.

Normally, male whitetails are much larger than females of similar age (McCullough 1979; Ozoga and Verme 1982, 1984). When under nutritional or social stress, however, sex differences in body size decrease because male body size is more sensitive to malnutrition. Males and females may be uniformly small and have nearly identical average body weights on severely overbrowsed range, as occurs on North Manitou Island in Lake Michigan (Case and McCullough 1987).

Generally, in the northern Great Lakes region, any male fawn with a November field-dressed weight less than 57 pounds, or female fawn less than 53 pounds, likely experienced some nutritional shortage during the summer or autumn, or both (Verme and Ozoga 1980*b*). Likewise, autumn-harvested yearling bucks dressing out at less than 100 pounds or yearling does less than 90 pounds are indicative of inadequate diet. In Michigan, most undersized deer come from areas where densities exceed fifty deer per square mile, such as in northern Lower Michigan's Club Country and in the south-central UP.

Clearly, age-body size relationships among young males are good indicators of herd status on northern range. Small-bodied male deer, for their age, invariably reflect malnutrition because of depleted habitat and signal the need for accelerating the harvest of antlerless deer to balance numbers with available resources.

Breeding Season

Does seldom breed before mid- to late October in the Great Lakes region. In addition, the early onset of winter and associated nutritional stress inhibit ovulation and late-winter recycling. The length of the whitetail's breeding season in northern regions is much more constrained by environmental factors than in deer in southern ranges.

In northern Michigan, most (80 percent to 90 percent) of the healthy adult does breed in November, with peak breeding around midmonth (Verme 1965*a*, 1977; Ozoga and Verme 1982). Southern Lower Michigan adult does breed a few days earlier (McCullough 1979). Yearlings tend to breed a few days later than older individuals, as do 2½-year-olds that failed to raise fawns (Ozoga and Verme 1986). Poor nutrition (Verme 1965*a*) and density stress (Ozoga and Verme 1982) may cause delayed breeding among 1½- and 2½-year-old does. Where they achieve puberty and breed, doe fawns normally breed in December (Verme and Ozoga 1987).

Although small, even spotted, fawns are observed occasionally during October in Michigan, overexploitation of adult bucks apparently is not responsible for delayed breeding. This is because about half of the does in any given area are already pregnant before heavy buck harvesting starts. Furthermore, unlike reports from studies in southern states, well-nourished yearling bucks in northern Michigan can mate, despite their behavioral limitations, with no delay in conceptions or reduction in productivity (Ozoga and Verme 1985).

Even if late breeding and late birthing occurs in the northern Great Lakes region, when coupled with autumn nutritional shortage or inadequate winter range, these small fawns would be ill prepared to face winter. Such "poor quality" young deer normally are removed from the population during severe winters, except in special situations where they are fed artificially rich diets throughout the season.

Productivity
In Michigan, more than 95 percent of adult does normally breed (Freidrich and Hill 1982), but doe fawns achieve puberty and breed only under excellent nutrition and low herd density. Depending upon the year, 30 percent to 60 percent of the doe fawns in southern Michigan breed. Roughly 80 percent conceive single and 20 percent twin fetuses. In recent years, the proportion breeding has declined, presumably because of complex biosocial factors (Verme 1991). By comparison, only about 5 percent of the doe fawns breed in Upper Michigan and 10 percent in northern Lower Michigan, likely because of marginal nutrition and early onset of harsh weather (Verme and Ozoga 1987).

Yearling does are extremely stress sensitive and may fail to breed if subjected to nutritional shortage before the rut (Verme 1965*a*). In northern Michigan, blizzards in late November or early December may inhibit breeding among many yearlings (Verme and Doepker 1988).

The farmland-brush country of the Midwest generally provides excellent year-round nutrition for deer, contributing to their advanced rate of maturity, high conception rate, and minimal annual fawn mortality (Nixon et al. 1991). Hence, farmland does tend to be more productive than the northern forested areas.

The most important factor for a newborn's survival is its weight, which ultimately depends upon the mother's nutrition during the last three months of pregnancy (Verme 1962, 1963, 1977). Although lack of cover may sometimes lead to excessive predation of newborns in semi-arid regions, fawn losses to predators seldom exceed 25 percent in the Midwest (Huegel et al. 1985). On northern range, most newborn mortality occurs among fawns born to malnourished does. As many as 70 percent of the annual fawn crop may die in northern Michigan following a severe winter (Verme 1977).

On average, there is slightly less than one fawn recruited into the Michigan deer herd annually for each adult doe. Recruitment rates may vary widely from almost 0.4 fawns per doe in northern Michigan after a bad winter to 1.4 fawns per doe in the southern Michigan farmland. Normally, 30 percent to 40 percent of the fall deer herd in Michigan is composed of fawns.

Antler Development
Any dietary deficiency during spring, summer, and autumn can strongly hinder antler development in young bucks (Magruder et al. 1957, Cowan and Long 1962), because body growth takes precedence over antler growth. High protein and energy supplies in the month before the start of antler development are especially important (Ullrey 1983). Food restriction in midwinter has less effect (French et al. 1955).

Antler beam diameter and number of points have been recorded by the Michigan Department of Natural Resources since 1951 (Burgoyne et al. 1981). Average beam diameters, measured in millimeters, for 1½-year-old bucks with 3-inch or longer antlers from 1966 through 1980 were as follows: Region 1, 17.4; northeast Club Country, 17.8; balance of Region 2, 18.7; and Region 3, 21.7 (Ullrey 1983). In 1990, more than 50 percent of the yearling bucks harvested in the UP grew spike antlers, as compared with a 35 percent spike rate in northern Lower Michigan, and only 10 percent in southern Lower Michigan.

Yearling bucks with sublegal spikes (less than 3 inches) became more prevalent in parts of northern Michigan as the herd peaked during the late 1980s. For example, 23.7 percent and 15.3 percent, respectively, of the yearlings we examined from the south-central UP in 1986 and 1992 had sublegal spikes. These rates are comparable to those recorded (21.7 percent) among supplementally fed yearling bucks living in the Cusino enclosure at a density of 163 deer per square mile.

In recent years, most large Michigan bucks have come from areas of low-to-moderate deer density in the UP or southern Lower Michigan.

Some southern Michigan bucks have grown antlers of Boone and Crockett proportions by 3½ years. By comparison, trophy-sized bucks from the UP generally come from remote areas with less hunting pressure and tend to be older than southern trophies. Trophy bucks in southern Lower Michigan also may come from areas with restricted hunting opportunities that act as refuges and allow deer to survive to older ages. Few large-racked bucks currently come from northern Lower Michigan.

Nutrition, rather than late birth dates, is the most important factor limiting the antler quality of yearlings in areas of Michigan where deer live at high density. Buck fawns that are poorly nourished during summer and autumn, or those subjected to severe social stress because of overcrowding, tend to grow undersized antlers a year later. In some cases, bucks living on severely depleted summer range may not be able to recover sufficiently to grow respectable antlers at maturity.

Winter Adaptations

Normally, cold and wind prompt deer in northern regions to shift from scattered distribution on summer range to concentrations in conifer-dominated areas that provide shelter in winter (Verme and Ozoga 1971, Ozoga and Gysel 1972). Snow conditions govern freedom of travel once deer are in the wintering area (Verme 1968, Ozoga 1968). Such "yarding" behavior presumably evolved as an energy-conserving and predator-defense adaptation for winter survival (Marchinton and Hirth 1984).

In northern Michigan, deer often travel 8 to 9 miles to reach scattered wintering areas that represent less than 15 percent of the total range (Verme 1973). In south-central UP, however, deer may travel as much as 50 miles to reach a large wintering complex (Doepker and Ozoga 1991). Some deer in southern Lower Michigan travel more than 20 miles to reach favorable winter habitat, as do deer in Illinois (Nixon et al. 1991).

Because related does and fawns band together in autumn, fawns likely learn lengthy migration routes from female relatives (Nelson and Mech 1981). This doe-fawn social bond is important because such behavior increases the young animal's chances of finding tried-and-tested winter habitat and helps protect them from predation.

Northern white cedar is preferred in northern deeryards because it provides excellent protection from snow and wind and is the only browse that, by itself, will maintain deer over winter in good health (Verme 1965*b*). Cedar twenty to forty years old provides the most browse and dense stands eighty to two hundred years old provide the best shelter; therefore, the ideal conifer deeryard consists of blocks of mature dense conifers adjacent to young food-producing stands.

Even in Upper Michigan, however, prime shelter is not necessary if deer have access to plenty of nutritious food. They can withstand subzero temperatures when feeding on corn or alfalfa but bedding in only marginal cover. The high-energy diet plus some browse apparently provide sufficient energy to compensate for heat loss. If rich food becomes limited, however, many young deer exposed to cold will die from an energy deficit.

During winter, deer undergo several physiological changes, including reduced thyroid function and lowered metabolism (Silver et al. 1969). Less food is required to maintain body functions. By midwinter, deer reduce their food intake by about 30 percent, regardless of the quality or amount available (Ozoga and Verme 1970, 1982). They also decrease their movement by at least 50 percent (Ozoga and Verme 1970, Verme and Ozoga 1971), may restrict their travel to less than 60 acres of choice cover, and spend much time bedded (Nelson and Mech 1981).

The northern whitetail's impressive adaptation for winter diminishes around mid-March, when steadily increasing energy demands render deer once again exceedingly sensitive to environmental stress (Ozoga and Verme 1970). Thus, prolonged winters that overlap seasonal periods of high energy demand are devastating.

Deer from individual winter yards on northern range tend to represent distinct subpopulations. Adult deer from each yard usually occupy summer ranges in largely exclusive areas, with little overlap among deer from neighboring yards. A massive die-off within a given yard might greatly reduce densities upon the contingent ancestral summering grounds for years. Most cedar swamp deeryards in the northern Great Lakes region have been overbrowsed severely, have grown out of their reach, or have been cut and converted to other species (Doepker and Ozoga 1991). Few are currently managed specifically to rehabilitate them as deer wintering areas (Verme and Johnston 1986).

Because of overabundance and resultant nutritional shortage on summer range, deer in many parts of Michigan enter their first winter facing a greater-than-normal risk of death. Many stunted, lean fawns enter the winter season each year, ill prepared for survival when subjected to impoverished winter habitat already saturated with hungry deer. More than 100,000 deer died in northern Michigan during the

Starvation, which is relatively common in overpopulated northern deer wintering areas, is pathetic and slow. Small fawns are especially vulnerable to winter nutritional stress. Photograph by Michigan Department of Natural Resources.

severe winter of 1985–86, whereas 40,000 perished during the 1990–91 winter, one of the mildest on record.

The seasonal migrations of whitetails provide a special challenge for quality deer management efforts in northern environments. Where deer migrate long distances in winter, coordination among private landowners, hunters, and land management agencies is required, sometimes over vast areas, to effectively manage deer herd sex-age composition and improve habitat and quality of life for white-tailed deer.

ADMINISTRATIVE CONCERNS

In Michigan, deer are a public good, not property of the landowner. Thus deer management is a government function and public demand is important in formulating statewide deer management objectives.

Social Benefits and Costs of Deer

About 307,000 bow hunters, 753,000 firearm hunters, and 145,000 muzzle-loader hunters hunted deer in Michigan in 1990. They harvested about 433,000 deer and led the nation in days of deer hunting (11.7 million hunter-days), while spending around $350 million on food, lodging, transportation, and equipment.

In addition to hunting demand, the nonconsumptive interest in Michigan whitetails is high. Driving to view deer in summer is a major recreation. Incidental sightings of deer during other activities also have significant value.

Deer also produce some serious social costs. In 1990, there were forty-six thousand deer-vehicle accidents reported by Michigan motorists. On average, about five people per year die in deer-vehicle accidents and about fifteen hundred are injured. Costs of these accidents, including property damage and medical treatment, are about $100 million per year. About three thousand of the state's sixty thousand farms had serious crop damage from deer in 1990.

These benefits and costs of deer need to be weighed in establishing management objectives that meet people's needs as well as those of the herd and habitat.

Hunter Attitudes

Deer hunters in the UP tend to oppose antlerless harvest more than do hunters in Lower Michigan. There is a "bucks-only" hunting tradition in the UP that has been passed down among generations (Moncrief 1970). A 1982 survey showed that 43 percent of the deer hunters who live in the UP opposed antlerless deer hunting.

Although some of this opposition is due to beliefs that removing does will reduce the herd, much arises from tradition. In some years, more deer starved in the winter in the UP than were taken by hunters. Arguments that herds need to be reduced to prevent winter starvation have not been very useful in changing hunter attitudes. The unwillingness of UP hunters to take antlerless deer has had a serious impact on the ability to manage populations in this region.

Hunter densities may exceed eighty per square mile on opening day in northern Lower Michigan. Excessive demands on large blocks of public land may preclude quality deer management on most state and national forests, with the exception of a few islands in Lake Michigan. Most hunters using these public lands want to take the first buck they see, regardless of quality.

Landowner Attitudes

Most of the deer in Michigan live on private land. Thus, the attitudes of landowners toward hunting, public access, and antlerless deer hunting are important for meeting statewide objectives for deer management. Permission is required to hunt on private land in Michigan. The percentage of land hunted for deer has increased as deer populations have risen. In southern Michigan, the percentage of land hunted by an immediate family member has risen from 17 percent in 1960 to 36 percent in 1978. Willingness to grant permission for deer hunting to people outside the immediate family rose from 35 percent in 1960 to 51 percent in 1978 (Evans 1979).

Most landowners suffering severe crop damage still want deer on their property, although they want more freedom to remove nuisance animals (Nelson and Reis 1992). One useful step is the state's block permit program, where landowners with a history of agricultural damage work with biologists to establish management objectives.

Management Options

Michigan is divided into 158 deer management units. Management direction varies because of differences in soils, vegetation, climate, and attitudes. Michigan has a bonus antlerless-only license and other special regulations to encourage antlerless harvest. Under this system, a quota of antlerless-only licenses is issued by deer management unit. Antlerless-only licenses may be issued to landowners experiencing crop damage to help secure hunters to reduce deer on problem lands without hurting the herd in an entire management unit.

New regulations to reduce the exploitation of antlered bucks are being evaluated. A two-buck limit was established in 1991, regardless of the season in which the deer was taken.

These changes, along with a more knowledgeable public, had strong impacts. During the 1980s, the deer harvest in Michigan increased 207 percent. The harvest increased four times as much as the herd, which rose from 1.2 million to 1.7 million deer during this decade. By 1990,

44 percent of the harvest was antlerless deer, compared with 33 percent in 1981.

Public Information, Education, and Law Enforcement

Democratic management of wildlife resources demands an informed, educated, and involved public. Unfortunately, most people confuse quality deer management with trophy management, assuming that the primary goal of both strategies is large-antlered deer. In reality, quality deer management is primarily concerned with providing deer a healthful existence in reasonable harmony with the environment (McCullough 1984). We emphasize that human benefits are of secondary importance. Enhanced hunting experiences, more meat, better trophies, fewer human-deer conflicts, and other results of quality deer management merely reflect a system geared to accommodate the whitetail's inherent needs.

Quality deer management cannot be accomplished without self-disciplined hunters who understand and respect animals and who will be selective harvesters. Clearly, attitudes must shift from emphasis on personal goals to the value of participation in deer management (Decker and Connelly 1990). This will require special education designed to develop hunters' understanding of, and commitment to, their role in quality deer management.

Quality deer management requires law enforcement to protect antlered deer outside of the regular hunting season and to regulate hunters during the season. In Michigan, law enforcement is concentrated on areas where the recreational benefits of an additional deer are highest.

Research

With an increasing level of sophistication, tomorrow's deer hunter is destined to become a superb predator and an even more potent and potentially more selective influence on whitetails. The need to better understand harvest strategies will become even more important, as wildlife managers strive for quality deer management. Research must be conducted in a northern environment to assure that we have a firm basis for quality deer management in the Great Lakes region.

IMPLEMENTATION

In the past twenty years, Michigan has not had the luxury of managing for a quality deer herd. The mandate during the 1970s was to increase deer numbers through an aggressive program of habitat improvement and to meet rising recreational demands. Now that deer are abundant and well distributed statewide, we have the opportunity (if not the obligation) to improve the whitetail's quality of life.

Despite the complexities, one of the most influential factors governing deer welfare in the Great Lakes region is winter weather. The public seems to accept innovative approaches to deer management most readily in areas where winter weather is mild. It resists antlerless deer harvesting where severe winters contribute to low carrying capacity.

We propose that quality deer management in northern regions be geared to differences in winter weather severity, as determined by annual snowfall or other measures. As an example, we divided Michigan into three zones, based upon high, moderate, and low annual snowfall (1954–1985). We then examined annual trends (1959–1993) in deer abundance within these zones for a four-county area covering central Upper Michigan, using deer pellet surveys (Hill 1991*b*).

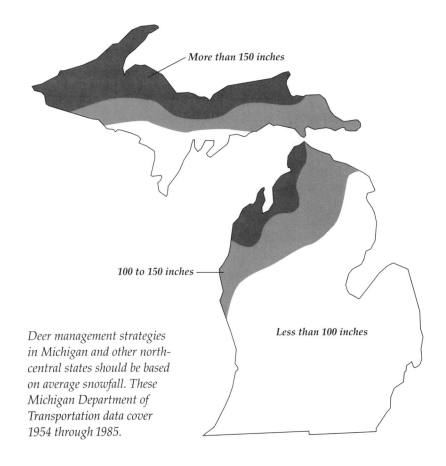

More than 150 inches

100 to 150 inches

Less than 100 inches

Deer management strategies in Michigan and other north-central states should be based on average snowfall. These Michigan Department of Transportation data cover 1954 through 1985.

Deer pellet groups

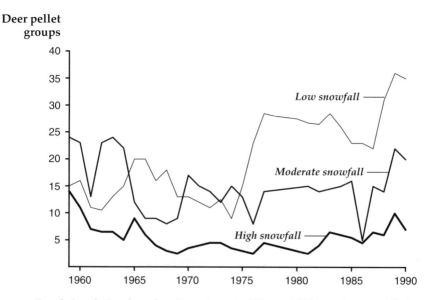

Trends in relative deer abundance in central Upper Michigan by snowfall zone from 1959 to 1990 demonstrate the influence of snowfall on populations. Herds in high snowfall zones are held at low levels; herds in areas with less snowfall can show dramatic growth. Data are based upon the mean number of deer pellet groups per survey.

Winter deer numbers in the low-snowfall zone are about 1.5 and 3 times higher, respectively, than in the moderate- and high-snowfall zones. In 1990, buck harvest rates in the low-snowfall zone were 3 and 5 times greater, respectively, than in the moderate- and high-snowfall zones. Furthermore, though deer numbers in the low-snowfall zone apparently increased about 2.5 times between 1960 and 1990, deer populations in the moderate- and high-snowfall zones have failed to return to the levels of the late 1950s and early 1960s.

Similar trends likely can be found throughout the region. A geographic breakdown, based upon winter weather severity, landscape vegetative patterns, and sociological factors, may help determine quality deer management opportunities and priorities in other northern environments.

High-Snowfall Zone

The welfare of deer in areas of heavy snowfall along Lake Superior in the UP and in northwestern Lower Michigan hinges upon quality of the winter habitat. Although these deer populations are below carrying capacity of the summer range, heavy winter kill and high mortality among fawns born to malnourished does contribute to low annual recruitment. Because of high natural mortality and comparatively light hunting, deer populations in this zone also have a more balanced buck-to-doe ratio and more structured buck population than other parts of the state.

Eastern hemlock, a conifer that provides excellent cover in winter, has all but disappeared from extensive tracts of northern hardwood where it was prevalent before logging in the 1930s and 1940s (Cunningham and White 1941). Also, large areas of white cedar, an unexcelled food and cover source for wintering whitetails in the eastern and central UP, reached peak food production between 1920 and 1950. These swamps have not regenerated and now are essentially protective "green barns" (Verme and Johnston 1986). As a result, whitetails in northern Michigan's deep-snow country suffer serious food and shelter shortages during prolonged winters, and some migrate south to areas of less snowfall.

Generally, few antlerless deer are taken in Michigan's high-snowfall zone, except on fruit-growing lands of Lower Michigan, where the potential for crop damage is high. Given this zone's severe winters and depleted winter range, increasing the harvest of antlerless deer would not reduce browsing pressure enough to stimulate deer winter habitat recovery. Fewer deer in these areas may not necessarily mean healthier, more productive animals.

In other areas of severe winter weather, it may be desirable to maintain hardy prime-age populations of deer with high reproductive potential, accomplished primarily through selective harvesting of fawns. Since many young deer do not survive their first year, their harvest has minimal effect on the population and would constitute wise use of a vulnerable and often wasted resource.

The first step toward quality deer management in this zone should be to improve wintering habitat. This will require diligent long-range planning, forestry techniques that consider deer behavior, strict herd control (through harvesting of antlerless deer, when necessary), and coordination among private landowners, hunters, and land management agencies.

Ironically, regardless of management emphasis, areas of heavy snowfall along Lake Superior will probably continue to produce some high-quality white-tailed deer, including mature bucks with sizable antlers, largely because of natural selection and relatively light hunting.

Moderate Snowfall Zone

Winter shelter requirements vary in the zone of moderate snowfall. During prolonged winters of more-than-normal snow, crowding of deer into areas of the best shelter leads to malnutrition, die-offs, and low fawn recruitment. Historically, the welfare of deer in this zone fluctuates from year to year, largely in response to alternating mild and severe winters, but other factors are involved.

White cedar–dominated lowlands, the principal wintering cover for whitetails, probably reached peak browse production forty to fifty years ago. Accelerated cutting of hardwood pulpwood near these wintering sites, plus logging of the conifer lowlands during the 1970s and 1980s, provided an abundance of reasonably nutritious browse each winter, and regrowth of deciduous trees temporarily improved browse availability. The long-term effects will probably be detrimental to deer, however, because logging has reduced the thermal cover. Cut areas are not adequately regenerating conifers.

Deer numbers in the moderate snowfall zone probably are comparable to levels in the 1950s but lower than in the 1930s and 1940s. Intensified pulpwood production, mild winters of the 1980s, supplemental feeding, and conservative harvesting of antlerless deer have resulted in high deer densities relative to the capacity of the winter range.

The increasing occurrence of small-bodied deer and yearling bucks with short-spike antlers suggests that some summer range in this zone is overstocked to the point of hindering deer nutrition and growth. Normally, these unthrifty individuals would be "weeded out" by winter stress, but recent mild winters have permitted more of them to survive to maturity, further depressing herd quality.

The first priority of quality deer management in this zone should be to reduce total deer density. Although there is a dire need to improve the winter conifer habitat, there is little chance of success when high deer numbers threaten to destroy cedar and hemlock regeneration.

Deer numbers already have declined in areas of northern Michigan with moderate snowfall, probably due to a higher antlerless harvest and altered vegetation patterns. In the future, winter die-offs and lower recruitment rates may reduce numbers to levels where deeryard management may become feasible.

We still expect resistance to quality deer management throughout this zone. It traditionally has been heavily hunted and recent success has been good. Hunters likely will not accept lower deer numbers graciously and will be reluctant to pass up antlered bucks.

Accelerated cutting of pulpwood in and around deer yards during the 1970s and 1980s provided abundant browse each winter and temporarily improved deer nutrition. The long-term effects of some of these operations, though, will probably be detrimental to deer because conifers have not adequately regenerated, resulting in a drastic reduction in thermal cover. PHOTOGRAPH BY MICHIGAN DEPARTMENT OF NATURAL RESOURCES.

If a sharp decrease in deer numbers coincides with accelerated antlerless deer harvesting, as most wildlife managers fear, the public will likely blame liberal harvesting policies, not severe winters and deterioration of winter habitat. Experience shows that unless hunters appreciate the ecological relationships involved, such controversy could lead to a prolonged moratorium on antlerless deer harvesting in portions of this zone. No one has come forth with a comprehensive solution.

Low-Snowfall Zones

Southern parts of the UP and roughly two-thirds of Lower Michigan receive less than 100 inches of snowfall annually. Although most of this zone had few deer before 1950, it now supports some of the state's highest densities. The deer-human relationships here are highly variable but, in some instances, favor quality deer management.

Effective habitat management can be difficult. The northern forested fringe of this zone contains conifer lowlands that attract large concentrations of deer from long distances during severe winters. As in the moderate snowfall zone, intense pulpwood harvesting has fostered temporarily favorable browse around deer yards and excellent summer range but has reduced thermal cover. Better wintering sites are still needed, but high deer numbers and mixed land ownership preclude effective swamp conifer management necessary to perpetuate cedar wintering areas.

The atmosphere for quality deer management is most favorable on private lands in southern portions of this zone. The public is aware that some private lands have unacceptably high densities, in which the physical condition of deer has declined, deer herd composition is skewed in favor of adult does, or both. Concerned citizens generally appreciate that such problems are not being resolved with current deer harvest tendencies.

Circumstances are unique in the Club Country of northeastern Lower Michigan, where deer populations are artificially high. The frequency of small-bodied deer and bucks with small antlers from this region of relatively poor sandy soils shows malnourished deer, not the results of late breeding and birthing as some believe. Large-scale winter feeding generally permits even physically inferior animals to survive in this area, where major starvation losses have been averted for more than a decade.

Since Club Country deer populations may be three to four times what the natural range could support, there is little opportunity for habitat rehabilitation or producing quality deer. The priority should be to reduce numbers. For clubs that insist upon feeding deer, half or more of the herd should be harvested for several years. Once the herds are under control, habitat rehabilitation may be possible. It also may be possible to increase the proportion of antlered bucks because selective harvesting can be regulated over fairly large areas, especially if adjacent clubs unite in their deer management goals.

The northward expansion of corn planting, beginning about 1970, appears to have boosted the herd considerably, especially where northern forest cover and southern agricultural lands meet. Corn now allows deer to survive winter in marginal cover, greatly increasing the capacity of the associated range. These highly productive populations require high levels of antlerless harvesting.

Compared with those living farther north, deer populations in the southern third of Michigan are less mobile and more productive because of good year-round nutrition. Despite the general shortage of mature bucks, these populations exhibit a fairly balanced adult sex ratio and their numbers are balanced by harvesting of both sexes. Heavy exploitation is offset by high fawn recruitment.

To implement quality deer management in these areas, 60 percent to 70 percent of the antlered bucks should be "saved" from harvest, and the winter herd should be reduced to about 75 percent of the carrying capacity. Generally, the antlerless harvest should slightly exceed the antlered harvest. Also, large cooperatively managed parcels must be committed to quality deer management to assure protection of antlered bucks. Development of regulations to protect young bucks, necessary to increase those 3½ years and older, will be an especially interesting challenge. Restrictive buck-harvesting procedures discussed in other chapters should be considered, especially on large private lands.

CONCLUSIONS

The complexity of quality deer management in the Great Lakes region has polarized biologists and managers. Advocates suggest that the white-tailed deer evolved with certain properties, such as a balanced sex ratio and a pyramidal age structure, and that management needs to simulate these natural conditions. Opponents of quality deer management in northern states usually stress the value of hunting recreation.

The hunting and nonhunting publics have not joined in the debate. Instead, there is a great deal of misconception about management programs. This lack of consensus has stymied development of policy guidelines. Based on the complexities in northern regions, deer management decisions should proceed as a series of steps that emphasizes the geographic differences in environmental conditions.

In some northern areas, deer habitat is deteriorating because of lack of adequate, or improper, timber harvesting, unreasonable agricultural practices, urban sprawl, and other factors. Elsewhere, habitat is stable or expanding, but it is increasingly difficult to control deer populations through recreational hunting. The highest priority for deer management in those areas should be to improve the habitat and to increase hunting access. This does not imply that restrictive buck harvests may not be an option. Rather, administrative action is needed in some areas to establish a base for management.

In other areas, there is an adequate habitat but overbrowsing and overgrazing are severe. The highest priority there should be to reduce numbers, in a publicly acceptable manner, and to balance them with habitat.

The most plausible area for quality deer management is on private lands in the southern Great Lakes region. They are highly productive and hunters are more willing to take antlerless deer. There is little impact of winter, compliance is easier on private lands, and the regulations can be more restrictive, if the landowners desire. In those areas, public education and incentives might help produce an older age structure of bucks. Then hunting can be improved through special regulations.

A stepwise approach may mean a gradual change in traditions. It may take decades to produce a quality life for deer and a quality experience for people in some northern regions.

Clearly, there is no "cookbook" formula to assure quality deer management success in a northern environment. There are no QDM data on free-ranging northern deer populations. We do have a wealth of biological knowledge on white-tailed deer that foster reasonably predictable results and current flexible regulations provide ways to regulate herd size and composition.

Landowners who wish to practice quality deer management will have to become true managers. They must know whitetail biology and be able to monitor herd health, or depend upon professional guidance. Still, poor-quality deer on northern range almost always are the product of inadequate nutrition associated with poor habitat and overabundance.

Above all, quality deer management advocates must maintain their convictions and be patient.

—John J. Ozoga,
Edward E. Langenau, Jr., and
Robert V. Doepker

CHAPTER 15

The Northeast

The art of wildlife management is to make possible the satisfaction of the needs of society within the biological constraints of the natural world. . . . the manager must find the place within those constraints in which human needs are best met. His success will be dependent upon his ability to listen. His finger must seek the pulse of society, and not his own.

—D. McCullough
The George Reserve Deer Herd

The sixteen states and provinces of the Northeast form a diverse region composed of coastal sand plains, remote mountaintops, forests, croplands, fields, wetlands, cities, and suburbs. White-tailed deer are found in all of the states and provinces, reflecting the species' adaptability. In some areas, deer coexist with humans among housing subdivisions, airport greenbelts, highway corridors, and urban parks. One city official has referred to them as "unrestrained urban cows" (Horton 1991).

Like the landscape, the climate varies greatly. In northern climates, severe winters can impact fawn production and survival to recruitment age (1½ years). In southern portions of the Northeast, summer droughts may reduce food availability before the drop of acorns.

The best deer ranges in the Northeast have minimal persistent snow accumulation, good interspersion of farm and forests, and mast-bearing forest stands. Populations on average are four times as dense in southern New England, New York, the mid-Atlantic states, Virginia, and West Virginia as those of northern New England and the Canadian provinces—29 deer per square mile of range versus 7.4.

Deer populations are at record levels in many states, particularly in southern and central sections of the Northeast. Fall population estimates for 1990 ranged from 4,500 deer in Rhode Island to 1.1 million in Pennsylvania. With 45 deer per square mile of range, Pennsylvania also has the densest population in the Northeast. Declining hunter numbers, limited access to private land, local hunting or firearms restrictions (Hesselton 1991), resistance to antlerless harvests, and less-than-desirable bag limits have made it increasingly difficult for deer managers to curtail population growth where needed. In 1990, total deer harvests ranged from 939 in Rhode Island to more than 415,000 in Pennsylvania. The region's harvest exceeded 1.1 million deer.

QUALITY MANAGEMENT IN THE NORTHEAST

There are two key criteria for determining to what extent quality deer management is being practiced: The consistent removal of antlerless deer to ensure that populations remain in balance with the habitat, and restraint in the harvest of male deer to promote a more natural age structure and sex ratio.

Public Programs

Each state or provincial deer biologist has a personal, professional desire to produce healthy or quality deer in balance with habitat and sociological constraints as well as good hunting. Yet, in most places, the application of one or both of the quality management criteria appears deficient.

The harvest of antlerless deer is the principal way to regulate population. Either-sex or permit-only systems are used, depending largely on tradition. In 1990, the percentage of does in the total harvest exceeded 30 percent in each of the states and provinces, with the exception of Quebec and Vermont. Although antlerless harvests are routinely prescribed in most places, they remain controversial in some areas. Often there is disagreement between hunters and managers over the level at which populations should be maintained. This, of course, fuels the debate about the need to harvest antlerless deer and in what numbers. The basic problem is that most hunters measure the success of a management program by the number of deer harvested, particularly bucks. Often, however, populations and consequently harvest goals need to be reduced for the long-term health of the herd.

Additionally, the ability to harvest enough antlerless deer has become a problem. In states and provinces with restrictive bag limits, where numbers of hunters have remained stable or declined, or where hunter attitudes promote the harvest of only adult males, it is difficult to harvest the number of antlerless deer necessary to control populations.

	Fall 1990 deer population	Deer per square mile of deer range	Does in total harvest	Yearling males in harvest
Southern				
Connecticut	50,000	13.8	43.9%	34–47%
Delaware	15,000	8.3	36.7	—
Maryland	140,000	15.7	38.0	35–89
Massachusetts	50,000	9.9	33.1	38–66
New Jersey	157,000	33.4	41.0	20–91
New York	825,000	17.0	36.5	25–80
Pennsylvania	1,175,000	44.7	46.1	45–95
Rhode Island	4,500	5.8	43.3	20–22
Virginia	850,000	34.6	35.5	29–85
West Virginia	1,000,000	43.7	37.0	55–75
	4,266,500	29.0		
Northern				
Maine	260,000	8.8	33.9	30–50
New Brunswick	130,000	4.9	33.7	—
New Hampshire	41,600	4.6	37.3	38–58
Nova Scotia	100,000	5.6	41.0	18
Quebec	270,000	9.0	27.1	40–50*
Vermont	90,000	11.4	6.1	35–85
	891,600	7.4		

*1976–1984

Deer population densities, percentage of yearling males in the harvest, and percentage of does in the harvest vary greatly among states and provinces in the Northeast. Yearling male harvest may also vary within a state.

Management also is impeded by the inability to even harvest deer in some circumstances. Some populations in urban or suburban settings with little or no hunting have grossly exceeded biological as well as cultural carrying capacity (Ellingwood and Spignesi 1987), so deer physical condition and survival have declined. In those areas, the issue is not quality management but management, period.

Harvest data from the Northeast indicate that yearlings make up a sizable portion of the buck harvest. Yearling frequencies exceeded 90 percent in some state management zones in 1990. Few bucks attain the

Food for deer on northern winter range generally is of poor quality and low quantity. Conifer needles, hardwood buds, twig ends, and the bark of young trees often are all that is available. After successive years of winter browsing, hardwood stems such as this one are deformed and broomy looking. Biologists use the evidence of heavy browsing to help identify winter habitat. PHOTOGRAPH BY JOHN HALL.

prime ages of 4½ and older. Only in areas with hunting restrictions or lack of access do male deer live longer.

Within the Northeast, no jurisdiction has the stated goal of producing older bucks except New Hampshire, where biologists want 8 percent of the buck harvest to exceed 3½ years of age. Nor do any states or provinces apply antler limits on any public management areas. Where older deer are more common, it is usually the result of luck and poor hunter access and density, not design. Given the opportunity, most hunters harvest the first buck seen. Without an extensive educational campaign, buck harvest limits (such as minimum antler spread) would likely be unacceptable to many sportsmen throughout the Northeast.

The Vermont Experience

Deer management has been controversial in Vermont for at least fifty years, with doe or antlerless hunting as the cornerstone of contention. A review of deer population trends in Vermont will help explain why.

European settlers relied heavily on venison for food. During the eighteenth and nineteenth centuries, deer populations dwindled because of extensive land clearing and liberal, poorly enforced hunting seasons. Hunting was banned from 1860 until 1897, when 103 bucks were harvested. Low deer populations fostered protectionism toward does and fawns that persisted for the next eighty years. Antlerless deer were harvested infrequently between 1897 and 1979. This occurred despite warnings from biologists as early as the 1940s that deer population growth needed regulation in some portions of the state (Foote 1945).

Record populations were reached in the 1960s; there was a record buck harvest of 17,384 in 1966. Simultaneously, physical condition declined and high winter mortality was recorded (Day 1964, Garland 1978). A controversial program of population management using antlerless harvests began in 1979. Through these, the population was reduced and held below the winter carrying capacity for more than a decade. Following sustained improvements in regional herd health, the population was allowed to increase, beginning in 1988.

In 1989, the public was asked to help set buck harvest objectives for each management unit. From the outset, biologists acknowledged that antlerless deer needed to be harvested to maintain populations that would meet buck harvest objectives. The five-year plan attempts to satisfy recreational demand without sacrificing herd health or habitat quality. This course is not without difficulty or challenge from sportsmen. Even though the emotional rancor of the 1960s over shooting does and fawns has all but disappeared, there is still some aversion to antler-less harvest.

During the planning, many issues were addressed but the Fish and Wildlife Department did not specifically ask Vermont sportsmen about restricting the buck harvest in one or more management units. Given the tradition of shooting any legal buck, this probably would not have been broadly supported. No state wildlife management area has been devoted to producing older bucks through antler size limits. For now, any such restrictions must be made on local private lands.

The Virginia Experience

Virginia has two harvest traditions. In the western mountains, contain-ing 1.5 million acres of national forest lands, there is a short season (twelve days). The eastern Piedmont and coastal plain region has a sea-son of forty days or more and allows the use of dogs.

Virginia deer managers had to overcome an aversion to antlerless harvests. Since the 1950s, Virginia has regulated populations by vary-ing the length of the antlerless season. This allows any licensed hunter to harvest antlerless deer. The bag limit of antlered and antlerless deer also can be varied geographically each year.

During the 1960s, the total harvest in the western counties declined following years when female harvest exceeded 40 percent of the total harvest. Such declines led to reduced confidence in the Department of Game and Inland Fisheries and antlerless harvests were subsequently restricted. Hayne and Gwynn (1977) later determined that if the per-centage of does in the total harvest is kept below a certain level, the population will not be overharvested. They recommended regulating the number of antlerless days to control the number of does harvested to achieve county management objectives, such as to increase, stabilize, or decrease populations.

Virginia's increasing harvest over the past three decades indicates a failure to stabilize populations, although herds have been stabilized in about a third of the counties. Management efforts will continue to emphasize expanded harvests to reduce and stabilize herd growth.

Since it is possible to underharvest a herd in one area of a county because of regulations set to properly harvest deer in another section of the same county, the Department developed two efforts, the Damage Control Assistance Program (DCAP) and the Deer Management Assis-tance Program (DMAP). DCAP allows every hunter who purchases a license to add an additional deer or bear to his bag limit when he cooperates with landowners who have crop-damage problems and have enrolled in the DCAP program.

DMAP allows hunt clubs and landowner groups to cooperate with state wildlife biologists to manage local deer populations. It is patterned after other programs in the Southeast and originated in Mississippi. The property owner–lessee provides information on kinds and quality of deer habitat, as well as sex, age, antler beam diameters, and weights of harvested deer. A management plan is developed to fulfill the objectives of the cooperator. Deer jaws and other harvest data must be collected for a year before a management plan is developed. When necessary, biologists issue antlerless deer permits for use on areas enrolled in the program. DMAP allows regulation of the buck harvest and improves communication between biologists and hunters. Innovative programs such as Virginia's DMAP allow site-specific deer management and are particularly exciting in that landowners and hunt clubs can actively participate in the management of the herds on their lands. They also expand opportunities for groups interested in quality deer management.

PRIVATE INITIATIVES

Most of the northeastern lands are privately owned. Regionwide, less than 6 percent of the land area is publicly owned and open to hunting. Timber companies, a key partner in quality management programs of southern states, own 9.7 million acres in Maine, New Hampshire, New York, and Vermont alone (Harper et al. 1990). Some companies do provide hunting leases to clubs, particularly in New York and Pennsylvania. Some of those clubs are seeking to implement quality deer management by creating food plots and to a lesser extent using harvest criteria to restrict the harvest of immature bucks.

Quality Deer Management in the Adirondacks—A Case Study

One private QDM initiative is by Weller Mountain Hunting Club, a 18,500-acre tract in the northwest corner of Adirondack State Park in New York. The area is mountainous and forested with northern hardwoods, spruce, and fir. Most of the timber is mature; recent (1985–90) logging has averaged fewer than 500 acres of selective cutting per year. Openings are limited to roadsides and log landings.

The club had 100 members until 1985, when it increased membership to 130. It averages 100 guests per year. By vote of the membership,

	Bucks harvested	4 or fewer points	Does harvested
1972	36	72.2%	0
1973	43	44.2	0
1974	59	57.6	0
1975	41	65.9	0
1976	66	27.3	0
1977	56	48.2	0
1978	47	48.9	0
1979	43	69.8	0
1980	54	55.6	0
1981	51	56.9	0
1982	55	54.5	0
1983	63	60.3	0
1984	69	43.5	0
1985	65	47.7	0
1986	95	51.6	0
1987	91	42.9	0
1988	85	51.8	0
1989	61	49.2	0
1990	48	52.1	0
1991	29	25.0	112
1992	24	58.3	73

Before quality management, no antlerless deer were harvested on Weller Mountain Hunting Club, New York. In 1991, antlerless harvests were begun to reduce herd density, and antler class restrictions were used to limit the harvest of young bucks. During 1991 and 1992, hunters refrained from harvesting bucks with an inside spread of less than 12 inches.

no antlerless harvest was allowed from 1959 to 1990. The number of deer harvested annually and number of points per buck were the only historical data recorded. Based on their observations, members believed that the adult sex ratio had become very unbalanced favoring does, few bucks were surviving to maturity, and the habitat's quality browse potential had decreased significantly. Weller Mountain's membership voted during spring 1991 to implement a quality deer management program aimed at improving herd and habitat conditions.

Spotlight censuses and daylight observations during summer 1991 indicated a density of approximately twenty-five deer per square mile with an adult sex ratio of 9:1 (does to bucks). Surveys also indicated Weller Mountain's deer density was greater than the habitat's capacity to produce browse on both summer and winter range. Key forage species had been heavily browsed and less-desirable species showed signs of light to moderate browsing pressure. Data from vegetation transects in 3- and 4-year-old harvest areas revealed no successful hardwood regeneration except for American beech.

The 1991 harvest goals for Weller Mountain's quality deer management program were based on the need to reduce density and balance the adult sex ratio, and a restriction on taking antlerless deer during a twenty-two-day archery season and seven-day muzzle-loader season only. The harvest goal consisted of one hundred adult does and a 12-inch minimum inside spread harvest criterion for bucks. Ninety-seven does and twenty-eight bucks were harvested at Weller Mountain during 1991. In addition, a scientific collection permit was obtained and fifteen does and one buck were collected during February 1992 to determine herd conditions in winter. Based on the data from fall- and winter-harvested deer and browse surveys during the summer of 1992, a harvest quota of one hundred adult does and a 14-inch minimum inside spread harvest criterion for bucks were recommended for the 1992 season. This resulted in a harvest of seventy-three does and twenty-four bucks.

Observations were recorded for 332 and 297 hunter-days during 1991 and 1992, respectively. The observed adult doe-buck ratio was 7.9:1 in 1991 and 7.3:1 in 1992. The fawn-doe ratio increased from 0.28:1 to 0.36:1 from 1991 to 1992. The average hunter observed 4.9 deer per hunt in 1991 and 5.5 in 1992. This was important to the hunters and local community, indicating the herd was not decimated by the 1991 doe harvest. It is helpful to document doe density when a doe harvest program is implemented in an area that has traditionally practiced bucks-only harvests. At Weller Mountain, adult doe observations decreased during archery and muzzle-loader seasons (the period when does were harvested), but increased during November, when does were protected.

Females 4½ years or older constituted 38 percent of the 1991 doe harvest and 41 percent of the 1992 doe harvest. All of the data indicate the 1991 doe harvest was conservative. The small number of mature bucks (3½ years or older) harvested during 1991 and 1992 was not surprising, considering the bucks-only harvest history at Weller Mountain. Male fawns born at the initiation of this project will not reach

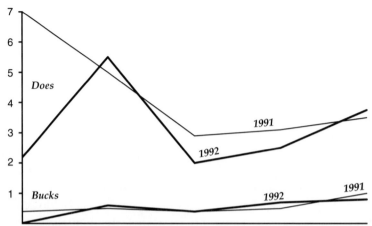

Study of the average number of deer seen per day per hunter during two-week blocks at Weller Mountain Hunting Club, New York, reveals that bucks become more evident as the season progresses. Observations of does declined as they were harvested, then increased slightly when doe season ended.

maturity until the fall of 1994. Although the average hunter observed slightly more bucks during 1992, most indicated they were yearlings. Average weights increased in every sex-age class during 1992. There were three obvious contributing factors to the improved weights: the harvest of 141 deer during the 1991–92 winter, the food plot program,

	Fawns	Dressed weight	Yearlings	Dressed weight	Adults	Dressed weight
Bucks						
1991	1	43 lbs.	4	78 lbs.	22	124 lbs.
1992	6	62	6	93	12	134
Does						
1991	6	47 lbs.	4	76 lbs	87	96 lbs.
1992	5	56	11	83	57	101

Field-dressed weights of deer harvested at Weller Mountain Hunting Club, New York, were much higher in 1992 following the heavy doe harvest in 1991 and the abundant cherry crop in 1992.

and an abundant black cherry crop. The cherry crop may have been the most important factor.

Ovaries were collected from twenty-two does during the third week of October in 1991 and 1992. Evidence of pregnancy, determined from the development of corpora lutea, was found in only three of the forty-four ovary pairs. Conception dates based on fetal data from mature does collected in February 1992 were from November 30, 1991, to January 10, 1992. A minimum range of conception dates, based on the ovarian and fetal data for winter 1991–92, was ninety-two days. Herds with an unbalanced adult sex ratio that favors females often have a delayed mean and an extended range of conception dates (Jacobson 1992). Based on Weller Mountain's data, the traditional bucks-only harvest apparently has resulted in a delayed and extended range of conception dates.

During 1991, a 12-inch minimum inside spread was used to prevent the harvest of immature bucks and to obtain data to determine more accurate harvest criteria for 1992. Twelve 2½-year-old bucks were harvested during 1991, of which five had an inside spread greater than 12 inches; however, only one had an inside spread larger than 14 inches. To reduce the number of 2½-year-old bucks harvested during 1992, a 14-inch inside spread was used and only six were taken in this age class.

Even more important than the herd's response to quality deer management was the membership's response. Weller Mountain is in the Adirondacks, where deer hunting is a part of the regional culture, so the change was a significant local event. Consider the initial doe harvest at Weller Mountain versus the total doe harvest for the regional deer management unit. During 1991, 97 does were harvested at Weller Mountain (28.9 square miles); only 346 were harvested in the entire management unit (1,337 square miles). Some local people were certain the deer herd at Weller Mountain had been decimated after the initial doe harvest. But as the program has progressed and members have shared their results with area hunters, the acceptance of quality deer management in the Adirondacks has grown. During 1993, quality deer management programs were being practiced on a minimum of 50,500 acres in the Adirondacks. In addition, a committee of private citizens has organized to pursue legislation that would allow for more liberal doe harvests as a deer management tool. Quality deer management has helped educate hunters about deer and habitat management in a region where a bucks-only harvest had been the only acceptable policy.

THE FUTURE OF QUALITY DEER MANAGEMENT
IN THE NORTHEAST

Quality deer management, particularly the need for consistent antler-less deer removal with a parallel decrease in harvesting young males, usually has been supported by northeastern deer managers. Valiant efforts have been, and continue to be, made to maintain populations in balance with habitat. Nevertheless, sufficient antlerless harvests may become difficult, particularly considering urbanized nonhunted land-scapes, a rise in opposition to hunting, and fewer hunters. Decker and Connelly (1990) acknowledge the "new" problems and suggest that deer biologists may need to recruit hunters to be managers through new educational initiatives.

We do not expect restricted buck harvests to be widely supported in a region or state, except perhaps where older bucks already are produced or there is an intensive educational effort demonstrating the benefits of such an approach. For now, buck harvest restrictions will be most easily implemented on large private lands where hunter cooperation can be realized. This raises an important point. Should agency biologists seek to implement or educationally promote buck harvest restrictions with the same fervor with which antlerless harvest systems have been advocated?

Some biologists fear that quality deer management programs on private lands will restrict hunter access. Private clubs and leased hunting lands are not as common as in the Southwest and Southeast. The fear is that if private ownerships are pooled on a large scale, thereby reducing the amount of land open to public hunting, it could hinder hunter recruitment, license sales, and wildlife management revenues over time. Whether this will occur is uncertain, but experiences in the Southeast suggest that the opposite may occur. Hunter surveys from Mississippi and South Carolina suggest that satisfaction and interest is greater on quality managed areas (Woods et al. 1992).

We believe quality deer management can counter some claims of the antihunting community. Some antihunting groups portray hunters as having an insatiable appetite for deer. Quality deer management offers a way to demonstrate a commitment to balanced, healthy popula-tions as a result of regulated antlerless harvests, even if that means fewer deer. An emphasis on quality deer, as opposed to quantity, could actually promote hunting as a management tool in areas with a strong traditional antihunting bias.

In summary, we believe deer biologists need to strongly promote healthy herds. Hunters need to know that quality deer management can work. Nonhunters need to be reassured that quality deer management is not synonymous with trophy management. In fact, we need to make sure that the hunting community does not turn quality deer management into nothing more than a program for large racks. Quality deer management should be viewed as stewardship.

—RONALD J. REGAN,
JACK V. GWYNN, AND
GRANT R. WOODS

PART IV

The Quality Hunting Experience

CHAPTER 16

A Proud Tradition

The pleasure of the sportsman in the chase is measured by the intelligence of the game and its capacity to elude pursuit and in the labor involved in the capture. It is a contest with sharp wits where satisfaction is mingled with admiration for the object overcome.

—JOHN DEAN CATON (1877)

Although quality deer management originated with Al Brothers and Murphy E. Ray in Texas in the 1960s, the origins of the quality deer hunting experience lie deep in our past. They are found in the adventures of such nineteenth-century deerslayers as John James Audubon, Oliver Hazard Perry, "Natty Bumppo," "Frank Forester," William Elliott, Philip Tome, John Dean Caton, T. S. Van Dyke, and Ernest Thompson Seton, among others. Their experiences offer a mixture of entertaining detail, curious facts, and colorful images on four major themes—adventure, romance, ethics, and natural history—that we need to put back into deer hunting, if the sport is to enter the twenty-first century with quality, style, and grace. This chapter traces these themes in the adventures of some of the giants among deer hunters. They achieved a deep intimacy with their surroundings and made natural history the focus of their lives.

In his great 1831 essay "Deer Hunting," John James Audubon (1785–1851) recorded his adventures with the American deer drive. Driving deer, Audubon wrote, is "the favourite pastime among the hospitable planters of the southern states. We have joined in on these hunts, and must admit that in the manner in which they were conducted, this method of deer hunting proved an exciting and very agreeable recreation." (Audubon 1972).

253

John James Audubon (1785–1851) clearly found excitement in deer hunting and considered it a very agreeable form of outdoor recreation. COURTESY AMERICAN MUSEUM OF NATURAL HISTORY.

Audubon greatly enjoyed deer hunting as a sport for many years, particularly the deer drive as customarily practiced in the Low Country of South Carolina with hounds, horns, and horses. Deer hunting was an essential part of Audubon's stock-in-trade as an artist and naturalist. His deeply engraved, double-barreled shotguns spoke often to the sight of fleeing deer in punctuation to the clamor of baying hounds, hunting horns, and galloping horses.

Audubon argued that the successful deer drive required great energy and activity, expert shooting, a thorough knowledge of the forest, and an intimate acquaintance with the habits of deer. While driving deer, Audubon noticed that whitetails frequently retreated from their home range but soon returned to their original haunts after the drive. In Audubon's day, as in ours, hunters designated the drives with names such as Crane Pond, Gum Thicket, the Pasture, the Oak Swamp, and so on. To his mortification, his colleagues named a bay after him, one where Audubon missed several deer.

Audubon's essay showed that man still-hunted, drove, fire-lighted, called, grunted, and decoyed deer for recreation as early as the 1830s. He gave one of the most picturesque and enthusiastic descriptions of the deer hunt ever penned: "Now, kind reader, prepare to mount a generous, full-blooded Virginian horse. See that your gun is in complete order, for hark to the sound of the bugle and horn, and the mingled clamor of a pack of harriers! Your friends are waiting for you, under the shade of the wood, and we must together go driving the light-footed deer. The distance over which one has to travel is seldom felt when pleasure is anticipated as the result; so galloping we go pell-mell through the woods, to some well-known place where many a fine buck has dropped its antlers under the ball of the hunter's rifle. The servants, who are called the drivers, have already begun their search. Their voices are heard exciting the hounds, and unless we put spurs to our steeds, we may be too late at our stand, and thus lose the first opportunity of shooting the fleeting game as it passes by. Hark again! The dogs are in chase, the horn sounds louder and more clearly. Hurry, hurry on, or we shall be sadly behind!

"Here we are at last! Dismount, fasten your horse to this tree, place yourself by the side of that large yellow poplar. . . . The deer is fast approaching; I will go to my stand, and he who shoots him dead wins the prize.

"The deer is heard coming. It has inadvertently cracked a dead stick with its hoof, and the dogs are now so near that it will pass in a moment. There it comes! How beautifully it bounds over the ground! What a splendid head of horns! How easy its attitudes, depending, as it seems to do, on its own swiftness for safety! All is in vain, however; a gun is fired, the animal plunges and doubles with incomparable speed. There he goes! He passes another stand, from which a second shot, better directed than the first, brings him to the ground. The dogs, the servants, the sportsmen are now rushing forward to the spot. The hunter who has shot it is congratulated on his skill or good luck, and the chase begins again in some other part of the woods.

"I hope that this account will be sufficient to induce you, kind reader, to go driving the light-footed deer in our western and southern woods." (Audubon 1972).

The cry of the deer hounds, the sight of galloping horses, and the sound of hunting horns obviously inflamed Audubon's imagination when he wrote this colorful account in *The Quadrupeds of North America* (1851): "No species of wild animals inhabiting North America, deserves to be regarded with more interest than the Common or Virginia deer; its symmetrical form, graceful curving leap or bound, and its rushing speed, when flying before its pursuers, it passes like a meteor by the startled traveller in the forest, exciting admiration though he be ever so dull an observer." (Audubon and Bachman 1851).

Oliver Hazard Perry (1817–1864), that rugged and robust deerslayer from Cleveland, Ohio, responded to Audubon's call. His annual deer hunts in Ohio and Michigan from 1836 to 1855 lasted two or three months at a time in the vast, unbroken wilderness of the North. After reading the *Hunting Expeditions of Oliver Hazard Perry* (1899), published posthumously, one can hear Perry's rifle belching out its thunderous notes as he tramped through the cedar swamps, eventually arriving at the Buck Horn Tavern, a log cabin, to dine on venison, potatoes, and snakeroot whiskey. His tales of how the deer "unfurled their white flags to the breeze" stir a deer hunter's heart. His backwoods jargon carries the reader along with great intensity. He didn't shoot deer; he "put their lights out"! After a stiff drink at the Buck Horn, he spent the evening playing Eure with the boys and talked of "flocks of deer." Yes, deer hunting must be fun.

On his hunting expeditions, Perry camped in tents for the most

Like Audubon, Oliver Hazard Perry (1817–1864) viewed deer hunting as part of a vigorous, manly, physical culture that actively led to literary pursuits in natural history. COURTESY LIBRARY OF CONGRESS.

part, although he frequently slept in large, hollow logs lined with straw, using large coonskin robes as bed clothing. En route to his favorite haunts, he traveled by steamship, train, horse and buggy, and during heavy snowfalls, by cutter. When weather curtailed his tramps afield, his group passed the time away merrily "with a good stock of tobacco, cigars, hard bread, rum, brandy, sugar and codfish." (Perry 1899).

He situated his deer camps so far back into the wilderness that he could hear no noise from any settlements. A dead silence reigned supreme around his camp, broken only by the hunting powwow music of Saginaw Indians or the occasional "nasal twang" of his hunting partners. After traveling for days on end over corduroy roads, roots of trees, and black, deep mud, this early deer stalker spent days just in the preparation of his camp. After a two-year absence from one of his favorite locations, Perry reflected in his journal on the ultimate meaning of deer camp life: "Sad and gloomy thoughts came into my mind when I viewed the well-known trees and other objects and witnessed the wild desolation, that deep and solemn silence. Here 2 years before a happy party of us, in the springtide of our existence, spent a portion of the most pleasant period of our lives. All was life and animation. The noise of singing, laughing, talking and hooting made the woods resound. But now how different! The great changer Time had intervened, and part of that merry Company were scattered to all portions of the earth, while two of them were then gazing in melancholy silence on the ruins of their old deserted Camp before them." (Perry 1899).

These early deer hunters, with tomahawks and knives belted to their sides, hunted like tireless hounds. With red faces sweating and begrimed with dust, they pursued their quarry with the deadly determination of Hiawatha. At the first ray of light, they "bent their course" through fields and thickets. Perry vividly described how one of his partners, D. W. Cross, headed for the deer forest: "Cross put a good quantity of his favorite 'bald eye' in his stomach, a few bullets in his pocket, shouldered his rifle, and turning over with ecstatic delight an old 'chaw' of Tobacco in his mouth, started into the woods, the sound of his footsteps reverberating back the exhilarated state of his mind and body." (Perry 1899).

Like Audubon, Perry viewed deer hunting as part of a vigorous and manly physical culture that actively led to literary pursuits in natural history. He embellished his deer-hunting journal with wildlife pictures engraved about 1800 by Dr. Alexander Anderson and kept detailed notes on all types of animal behavior.

It seems likely that during this period of time, James Fenimore Cooper (1789–1851) also read Audubon's spirited account of deer hunting. Cooper's depiction of Natty Bumppo in his classic novel *The Deerslayer* (1841) featured many of Audubon's hunter-naturalist ideas. Like Audubon and Perry, Bumppo is in tune with nature and hunts deer within the context of a strict code of ethics. Cooper was primarily a moralist who portrays Bumppo in opposition to the "wasty ways" of the settlers. His moral character and worth, Cooper argued, depended upon his degree of reverence and respect for deer, his direct relationship to nature, and the manner in which the hunter perceived his natural environment.

Bumppo killed deer only out of necessity and in a humane and reverent manner. "They call me Deerslayer. I'll own, and perhaps I deserve the name, in the way of understanding the creature's habits, as well as for the certainty in the aim; but they can't accuse me of killing an animal when there is no occasion for the meat or the skin. I may be a slayer, it's true, but I'm no slaughterer. . . . I never yet pulled a trigger on buck or doe, unless when food or clothes was wanting." (Cooper 1841). The Deerslayer's chief virtue was that he did not view the presence of a live deer as an insult to his powers. He hunted deer for food and the spiritual satisfaction of participating in the ennobling rite of the kill.

The Deerslayer's deep connection with the teachings of nature and his mastery of the intricate details of the deer forest create a rich, intensely exciting story filled with romance and theatricality. It is a story to be cherished by all deer hunters; Cooper invested the deer kill with an ennobling purpose. The chief virtues of the young Leatherstocking lay in his highly developed senses, his acute woodsmanship, and astonishing marksmanship with his rifle called Killdeer. As D. H. Lawrence noted, Bumppo "gets his deepest thrill of gratification when he puts a bullet through the heart of a buck." (Lawrence 1966).

In his novel, Cooper chastised the pioneers for unnecessary killing and urged restraint and moderation with regard to the natural resource. Bumppo deplored hunters who disrespect nature and usurp its gifts without proper reverence. He argued against the savage thrill of the hunt and declared that the hunter must view the kill with a spiritual and ennobling purpose. As deer populations declined, Cooper's adherence to an ecological consciousness became even more pervasive, as did his reverence for the hunt. In his study on hunting as a mode of environmental perception, historian Thomas Altherr observed that "Bumppo

Frank Forester (1807–1858) advocated English sporting ethics in the United States, taking a bitter and unrelenting stand against poachers and pothunters. In sporting journals, he demanded game laws and a sporting ethic. COURTESY ROBERT WEGNER.

advanced a sincere concern for the morality and natural right of hunting in America, and passionately advanced reverent hunting as proper ecological consciousness." (Altherr 1976). He viewed deer as a gift from God to be used within reason.

These ideas would eventually culminate in the thoughts of Frank Forester (Henry William Herbert, 1807–1858), and later in the century in the ecological consciousness of such hunter-naturalists as John Dean Caton, T. S. Van Dyke, and Ernest Thompson Seton, among others. Like Cooper, Forester constructed a brilliant portrait of the chase based on the ethical proposition "that there is not only much practical, but much moral utility in the Gentle Science of Woodcraft." (Herbert 1843). In *The Deer Stalkers* (1843), as well as in all of his writings, Forester preached the need for adapting English sporting ethics to the American scene, taking a bitter and unrelenting stand against poachers and pothunters. In the sporting journals of his time, he argued for game laws and a sporting ethic.

Forester's annual deer-hunting trips to the woodlands of Orange County, New York, and the lakes of the Adirondacks, especially an area known as Old John Brown's Tract, provided the background for this tale unequaled in the literature on American deer hunting. The following poem sets the stage for Forester's spirited portrait of the early American deer hunt:

Mark! How they file down the rocky pass,
Bright creatures, fleet, and beautiful, and free,
With winged bounds that spurn the unshaken grass,
And Swan-like necks sublime, their eloquent eyes
Instinct with liberty, their antlered crests,
In clear relief against the glowing sky,
Haughty and majestic!

When the kitchen clock struck four, Forester wrote, the deer stalkers were afoot. Breakfast was ham, eggs, and "not least, two mighty tankards smoking with a judicious mixture of Guinness's double stout, brown sugar, spice, and toast—for to no womanish delicacies of tea and coffee did the stout huntsmen seriously incline." (Herbert 1843). Frank's boys shouldered their rifles and struck forth while the stars were still in the sky.

The first flash of dawn in the east found two of Frank's boys, Harry Archer and Dolph Pierson, in the company of Smoker, their dog, hunting deer from a canoe while floating down the numerous narrow streams of the Adirondack country. After miles of floating in unbroken silence, they suddenly encountered two bucks. Forester recalled the scene:

"Under the shade of a birch stood two beautiful and graceful deer, one sipping the clear water, and the other gazing down the brook in the direction opposite to that from which the hunters were coming upon them.

"No breath of air was stirring in those deep, sylvan haunts, so that no taint, telling of man's appalling presence, was borne to the timid nostrils of the wild animals, which were already cut off from the nearer shore before they perceived the approach of their mortal foes.

"The quick eye of Archer caught them upon the instant, and almost simultaneously the hunter had checked the way of the canoe, and laid aside his paddle.

"Pierson was already stretching out his hand to grasp the ready rifle, when Archer's piece rose to his shoulder with a steady slow motion; the trigger was drawn, and ere the close report had time to reach its ears, the nearer of the two bucks had fallen, with its heart cleft asunder by the unerring bullet, into the glassy ripple out of which it had been drinking, tinging the calm pool far and wide with its life-blood.

"Quick as light, as the red flash gleamed over the umbrageous spot, long before it had caught the rifle's crack, the second, with a mighty bound, had cleared the intervening channel, and lighted upon the gray granite rock. Not one second's space did it pause there, however, but gathering its agile limbs again, sprang shoreward.

"A second more it had been safe in the coppice. But in that very second, the nimble finger of the sportsman had cocked the second barrel; and while the gallant beast was suspended in mid air, the second ball was sped on its errand.

"A dull, dead splash, heard by the hunters before the crack, announced that the ball had taken sure effect, and, arrested in its leap, the noble quarry fell.

"For one moment's space it struggled in the narrow rapid, then, by a mighty effort rising again, it dashed forward, feebly fleet, keeping the middle of the channel.

"Meanwhile the boat, unguided by the paddle and swept in by the driving current, had touched upon the gravel shoal and was motionless.

"Feeling this as it were instinctively, Harry unsheathed his long knife, and with a wild shrill cheer to Smoker, sprang first ashore, and then plunged recklessly into the knee-deep current; but ere he had made three strides, the fleet dog passed him, with his white tushes glancing from his black lips, and his eyes glaring like coals of fire, as he sped mute and rapid as the wind after the wounded game.

"The vista of the wood through which the brook ran straight was not at the most above fifty paces in length, and of these the wounded buck had gained at least ten clear start.

"Ere it had gone twenty more, however, the fleet dog had it by the throat. There was a stern, short strife, and both went down together into the flashing waters. Then, ere the buck could relieve itself, or harm the noble dog, the keen knife of Archer was in its throat—one sob, and all was over." (Herbert 1843).

Deer hunting for Forester, like Audubon, Perry, and Cooper, consisted of a manly adventure, a highly animated affair with pomp and spirit-arousing bustle, followed by social cheer and camaraderie. This was also especially true for William Elliott (1788–1863), one of the earliest Dixie deerslayers to respond to Audubon's inducement. Elliott, a contemporary of Audubon's and planter of the noblest South Carolina

Harvard-educated William Elliott (1788–1863) hunted deer with the gusto of starry-eyed generals engaged in sylvan warfare. COURTESY ROBERT WEGNER.

breed, carried deer hunting, Southern-style, to its climax. In his letters to the *Charleston Courier* signed "Venator," Elliott described his deer-hunting adventures. When he collected these hair-raising yarns in *Carolina Sports by Land and Water* (1846), the book became a classic on the subject, one of the few outdoor books to remain in print since its original publication.

Elliott hunted deer along the Chee-ha River, one of South Carolina's best deer-hunting grounds of its time, with the gusto of starry-eyed generals engaged in sylvan warfare.

Elliott referred to the drives as "raids against the deer." Those "sleek-skinned marauders," as he called them, had to be eliminated because they were ruining his crops. It was the beginning of modern pest control, with regard to deer management. Elliott waged havoc against bucks in particular, especially old, overgrown ones that had the insolence to baffle him and his boys.

For Elliott, deer hunting became an intense habit of mind. The noise of the shotguns, the aroma of gunpowder, the baying of hounds, and the echoes of horns set his heart to pounding as he galloped through the forest. When one buck miraculously escaped into the depths of a rapid stream, after fleeing the hounds and evading buckshot, wild Willie stood along the bank and vented his frustration by hollering at the buck, "Go, thou fool, no better than Napoleon, hast thou known the fitting time to die! The *devil* take thee, for thou hast needlessly kicked and thrust thyself beyond the reach of a *blessing!"* (Elliott 1967). With that grotesque verbiage, the Harvard-educated deerslayer spurred his horse and disappeared from the scene of ultimate disappointment. He found partial consolation later over venison steak at the campfire where Elliott decried all bucks as "luxurious rogues and the greatest epicures alive!"

These early American deer hunters not only sought wild scenes and wild adventures, but also hunted for the romance of natural history. By 1850, a small but growing group of concerned hunters put forth the image of the hunter-naturalist, who combined nostalgia and respect for nature with a code of ethics called sportsmanship. This idea emanated widely from William T. Porter's *Spirit of the Times,* the leading sportsmen's weekly journal published from 1831 to 1861 that peaked in circulation at 40,000 in 1856. In it, the great sporting authors of the day put forth highbrow prose on the virtues and romance of natural history for buckskin-clad backwoodsmen. Authors portrayed hunting, as historian Thomas Altherr observed, "as the best mode of environmental perception, the truest appreciation and apprehension of nature's ways and meanings. Most of them arrived at this philosophy through the combined influences of nature study and hunting experience. Preferring to look at the wilderness environment scientifically and dispassionately, the hunter-naturalists had little sympathy for pastoral visions or anthropomorphic stories of animals. The hunter-naturalists evinced a thorough understanding of the ecological bases of natural existence. The development of the hunter-naturalist ideal signified the emergence of an ecological consciousness." (Altherr 1976).

One of the most popular books of the time, Charles Wilkins Webber's *Romance of Natural History: or Wild Scenes and Wild Hunters* (1852), portrayed Audubon as the great hunter-naturalist and the mentor and guide that all hunters should emulate. In this work, a blend of fact and fiction, Webber created a metaphysics of hunting that contained adventures, discussion of ethics, spiritual communion with nature, and profound love for the romance of natural history. Webber's ultimate objective was "to produce a book . . . to instruct and amuse in the legitimate themes of natural history, *outside* the straight-laced mannerism of technical treatment." (Webber 1852). The hunting scenes in its illustrations gave it a romantic mystique that few hunters could forget.

The underlying theme of these hunter-naturalists perhaps was best

Philip Tome (1782–1855) was one of the greatest American hunters of his time. This indomitable, Indian-looking Nimrod had but one ambition: to challenge the brute force of nature in such a way that every hazard favored his adversary. Courtesy Warren County Historical Society.

summarized by Philip Tome (1782–1855) in his autobiography, *Pioneer Life: or Thirty Years a Hunter* (1854): "I never wantonly killed a deer, when I could gain nothing by its destruction. With the true hunter it is not the destruction of life which affords the pleasure of the chase; it is the excitement attendant upon the very uncertainty of it which induces men even to leave luxurious homes and expose themselves to the hardships and perils of the wilderness. Even when, after a weary chase, the game is brought down, he cannot, after the first thrill of triumph, look without a pang of remorse, upon the form which was so beautifully adapted to its situation, and which his hand has reduced to a mere lump of flesh." (Tome 1971).

Like Cooper and Frank Forester, Tome maintained a strong ethical code. It stands as a classic model for today's deer hunters, giving Tome a spiritual kinship across two centuries with the sportsman–deer hunter of today. Not surprisingly, the *Saturday Review of Literature* viewed Tome's autobiography as "a source book for the mores of the fringe of the first American frontier."

Tome seemingly had but one ambition: to challenge the brute force of nature in such a way that every hazard favored his adversary. Like his pioneer predecessors, he viewed deer and elk hunts as military campaigns to be waged through dense, virgin underbrush for miles at a time to be interrupted only by naps in hollow trees or in the skins of freshly killed bears. These Homeric deer hunts lasted for months at a time, frequently terminating only when the snow melted and the tracks could no longer be followed.

Never conquered by man or beast, Tome by the age of eighteen was clearly more conversant with the howl of the wolf and the snort of the deer than with the tones of civilized oratory. While hunting deer in October 1800 along Pine Creek in Potter County, Pennsylvania, the wolves flocked around him. "Their unearthly howling," Tome recalled in his autobiography, "mingled with the dismal screeching of the owls overhead made a concert of sound that banished sleep from my eyes the greater part of the night. I sat in my shanty, with my gun in one hand, a tomahawk in the other, and knife by my side. When the wolves became unusually uproarious, I would send the dog out to drive them away, and if they drove him back in, I would fire in among them. At length, toward morning, I fell asleep from sheer exhaustion and slept until daylight, when I arose, ate my breakfast and started again on tracking deer." (Tome 1971).

No one better epitomizes the hunter-naturalist than John Dean Caton (1812–1895), who also responded to Audubon's call. Throughout his life Caton combined the study of the natural history of the white-tailed deer and the thrilling incidents experienced while hunting them. All of his hunts became exercises in recording practical information about the whitetail's senses and habits, whether group-hunting them with the Pottawatomie Indians, coursing deer with greyhounds, floating the waterways, or still-hunting.

On one of his earliest recorded still-hunts in December 1847, Caton followed a large, antlered buck from daylight until around four o'clock in the afternoon over the bluffs of the Vermilion River. After tramping through 6 inches of dry, hard snow all day—"as difficult to walk in as dry cornmeal"—he stopped on a bluff. Too fatigued to go on, he rested his gun against a tree, feeling deeply chagrined at the dimming chance of getting the deer. Suddenly he heard the brush crack and the buck stopped not more than 30 feet from him, but the brush was too thick for a shot. Caton explained what happened in *The Antelope and Deer of America* (1877), the first scientific treatise on deer in America:

"The buck stared at me some seconds, as if something told him of

John Dean Caton (1812–1895) concluded, "To the cultivated mind capable of understanding and appreciating the works of the Divine hand, the pleasures of the pursuit are immeasurably enhanced by a capacity to understand the object taken." COURTESY ROBERT WEGNER.

danger; but at length he seemed to become reassured and bounded along in his original course as if he was in somewhat of a hurry, but not in manifest alarm. As I anticipated, on his third or fourth bound he gave me a chance, and I fired as he was descending. His heels flew into the air with a snap as if his hoofs would fly off, and he fell all in a heap. There was something in the size of the deer and his antlers, the way in which his hind legs, as quick as lightning, stretched almost perpendicularly in the air, and the mode of his falling, which produced a thrill of delight which I have never before or since experienced." (Caton 1877).

Caton found the prairies of Illinois the proper theater for coursing (running deer with greyhounds by sight, not scent). In commenting on this exhilarating sport, he classified it as by far the most dangerous, especially for the inexperienced rider. "To be the foremost in such a chase," Caton admitted, "to keep even with the leading hound, and see that each stride lessens the intervening space between the pursuers and the pursued, is the culmination of excitement only known to the ardent sportsman." (Caton 1877).

Most of Caton's deer hunts ended in camp with aging and weighing the harvested deer and preparing the skins and skeleton for mounting and research. "After our camp work was done," he wrote in his journal while deer hunting in the secluded valleys of California's Gaviota Pass, "we enjoyed a most leisurely feast of venison prepared in all the different modes most approved of in camp, sweetened by long absence and hard toil." (Caton 1877). The incidents of the day were then recounted in Caton's camp with such embellishments as were necessary for each companion to outdo the other with his own dazzling stories.

A complete knowledge of natural history and woodcraft meant many things to Caton. It meant knowing intimately the habits and movements of deer, being skilled in whatever weapon you chose, being able to prepare shelters along the trail and hearty venison meals in the field, and in general creating and maintaining a deer camp as a school for the beginner. Caton believed the hunter, above all, could study the habits of the animals he pursued and pass along the knowledge to the novice and scientist as well. "The hunter, who seeks and takes the game in its native fastnesses, may thus, I say, give the scientist valuable assistance," Caton wrote in his great essay "The Ethics of Field Sports." (Caton 1890).

In his essay on ethics, Caton urged hunters to go to the deer forest with partners of comparable tastes, for companionship remains indispensable for the full enjoyment of life in deer camp. Indeed, friendship and good feelings always prevailed in Caton's camp. "Between us there at once grew up a fraternal feeling; a cord of sympathy was drawn out between us which made us brothers and would have prompted us to make great sacrifices for each other, if need had been." (Caton 1890).

Caton only shot deer when he or others needed venison or when he needed the animal for research. He rightly argued that utility must be associated with the sport. "If the deer cannot be utilized, a pang of regret takes the place of gratification in the breast of the true sportsman." (Caton 1890). If you don't utilize the animal to the fullest, don't hunt. In conclusion, he wrote: "Let me beseech all sportsmen to maintain the dignity of the craft to which they belong and to exert all their influence to elevate the standing of that craft and to preserve our game." (Caton 1890).

When Caton shot a deer, he examined it with tremendous vitality, as he would a book full of knowledge. As an amateur naturalist with a vivid imagination and profound persistence, he selected and solved many of the earliest scientific natural history questions on deer. We have no finer guide and mentor than this all-time giant among American deer hunters. As long as the white-tailed deer roams the forests of this country and man pursues this marvelous and unique creature, we will always remember Caton's measure of what a quality deer hunt is all about:

"The pleasure of the sportsman in the chase is measured by the intelligence of the game and its capacity to elude pursuit and in the labor involved in the capture. It is a contest with sharp wits where satisfaction is mingled with admiration for the object overcome." (Caton 1877).

During his lifetime, T. S. Van Dyke (1842–1923), like his friend and colleague John Dean Caton, was often referred to as "one of the first authorities in the sporting world," and as "that prince of a sportsman." Indeed, he exhibited all of the qualities of a true sportsman, and these qualities are vividly revealed in his classic book, *The Still Hunter* (1882). First of these was his passionate love of nature in every form, which continually prompted him to study it patiently and faithfully. Consequently, he knew every tree and flower in the regions he hunted deer not only by their names but also by their minutest features. He had the same familiar acquaintance with the animals he pursued. "In the saddle at four o'clock and miles into the hills by the time it was light enough to shoot—such were the requirements" (Van Dyke 1923) of the quality deer hunter, Van Dyke believed, if he were ever to learn the habits of this unique animal.

T. S. Van Dyke (1842–1923) was a deer hunter, historian, naturalist, and author of The Still Hunter: A Practical Treatise on Deer Stalking *(1882).* Courtesy San Diego Historical Society, Title Insurance and Trust Collection.

Second of these sportsmanlike qualities was his aesthetic appreciation of the woods. After searching for deer in the woods of the East
Coast and after pursuing them in the old hardwood timber of Minnesota and Wisconsin as well as in the wild forests of Oregon, Mexico,
and California, Van Dyke gradually formulated a spiritual statement
on what the woods meant for the deer hunter. The woods, he maintained, give scope and deeper satisfaction to the hunter who values
game more for the skill required to bag it than as a thing to eat or boast
of. In 1907 he wrote, "No wonder Bryant called the woods God's first
temple. For nowhere else can you feel the mysterious power that rules
all. Not upon the prairie, though there are few places where you feel
smaller than on its vast sweep of loneliness. Nor on the sea with its still
more certain proof that there is no fellow man within many miles. Nor
yet on the mountain top where you can see even more plainly what a
trifling link you are in the mighty chain of being." (Van Dyke 1923).
Like his contemporary Aldo Leopold, Van Dyke viewed man as one of
the smallest minorities in the whole superstructure of life's forms.

This idea is no more evident than in his conception of the final stage
of deer hunting, the ultimate one he hoped all deer hunters would reach
sooner or later. In this stage, the mere act of killing, though it requires
the highest skill, becomes an inferior factor in the pleasure of those who
really love the woods and hills. "In this stage there is more real enjoyment than in any other. I never saw the time when I cared a cent for
records or anything of the sort and have always despised the 'trophy'
business which too often means beastly murder. I never had an Indian
or a guide hunt any game for me to pull the trigger on, and would far
rather do the hunting and let the Indian pull the trigger. What I wanted
from a deer hunt was not that particular bit of meat or that head of
horns, but to know whether I could get that buck or he get me. The pleasure in resolving this problem begins with the very first attempt to play
your wits against the wits of the game." (Van Dyke 1923). The number
of hunters who reach this stage, Van Dyke acknowledged, is greater
than many suppose, and many reach it early.

As a deer hunter, Van Dyke always believed that he belonged to a
hunting fraternity with a well-defined code of conduct and thinking.
In order to obtain membership in this ideal order of true sportsmanship, he believed, one had to practice proper etiquette in the field, give
game a sporting chance, and possess an aesthetic appreciation of the
whole context of the sport, which included a commitment to its per-
petuation. He also encouraged deer hunters above all to improve their

"mental furniture," to avoid drawing hasty conclusions from an insufficient number of instances, and to avoid inaccuracy of statement. As he put it in *The Still-Hunter*, "It's always and eternally that 'old buck' or 'big buck' that a writer kills (with his quill), until in the interest of philosophy one is almost tempted to offer a reward for any reliable information about the killing of a small doe or fawn." (Van Dyke 1923). He also came down hard on the braggart, on the man who talks of placing a bullet wherever he wishes to place it in a running deer and at any distance, or at one standing beyond 150 yards. This type of fellow hunter Van Dyke labeled as "an ignoramus who takes his listener for a bigger fool than he is himself." (Van Dyke 1923). Yes, as deer hunters we have a lot to learn from his lofty ideals of true sportsmanship.

Like his contemporary T. S. Van Dyke, Ernest Thompson Seton (1860–1946), viewed deer hunting as a school for manhood—and no one became a greater master of whitetail woodcraft than did Seton. In his *Book of Woodcraft* (1912), this hunter-naturalist noted not only that the hunter needed woodcraft in its highest form to outmaneuver the white-tailed deer, but also that woodcraft may very well save man from civilized decay.

Mastering whitetail woodcraft for Seton meant spending a lifetime in pursuit of every detail of this animal's remarkable natural history, whether with bow, rifle, camera, or sketch pad. He used all. No one worked more enthusiastically in sketching deer and making notes on their social behavior than this eccentric, strong-willed, eminent Victorian. The journals that he kept religiously for more than sixty years attest to his meticulous recording of deer behavior. His numerous drawings of antlers underscore his insatiable curiosity for understanding every facet of this animal's natural history; he became enamored with antlers and captured the spiritual essence of the animal in a way that few artists ever do.

Seton's deer-hunting tales are overwhelming with their wanderlust to hunt deer. His hunts during the early 1880s take on the dimensions of minor military campaigns. On one of the vigorous campaigns, known as "the Carberry deer hunt," Seton traveled about 300 miles on foot through deep snow. The hunt ended successfully, but only after nineteen days of toil.

The experiences of the Carberry hunt on the Big Plain of Manitoba had a lasting and profound impact on Seton. He referred to these days as the best of his life. The Carberry hunt surfaced in his great novella, *The Trail of the Sandhill Stag* (1899), one of the most thought-provoking,

No hunter-naturalist worked harder or more persistently to educate boys in quality deer hunting and woodcraft than Ernest Thompson Seton (1860–1946). COURTESY SETON MEMORIAL LIBRARY, PHILMONT SCOUT RANCH.

sensitive tales ever written of the long pursuit of a black-tailed buck. If you have not read this Seton story, you still have a lot to learn about the real meaning and significance of quality hunting, for the story challenges the basic philosophy of the chase to its foundations and teaches the deer hunter the virtues of allowing bucks to walk.

When Yan, the main protagonist of this tale, finally encounters the Sandhill Stag in his sights, after several years of intensive study and elusive chase, he refrains from shooting. He stands in front of the monarch of the woods with his nerves and senses taut and says to himself, "Shoot, shoot, shoot now! This is what you have toiled for!" But he does not shoot. Instead, he says to himself while staring into the soul of the stag:

"We have long stood as foes, hunter and hunted, but now that is changed and we stand face to face, fellow creatures looking into each other's eyes, not knowing each other's speech—but knowing motives and feelings. Now I understand you as I never did before; surely you at least in part understand me. For your life is at last in my power, yet you have no fear. I knew a deer once, that, run down by the hounds, sought safety with the hunter, and he saved it—and you also I have run down and you boldly seek safety with me. Yes! you are as wise as you are beautiful, for I will never harm a hair of you. We are brothers, oh, bounding Blacktail! only I am the elder and stronger, and if only my strength could always be at hand to save you, you would never come to harm. Go now, without fear, to range the piney hills; never more shall I follow your trail with the wild wolf rampant in my heart. Less and less as I grow old do I see in your race mere flying marks, or butcher-meat." (Seton 1899).

In his hunts, Seton pitted the wits of the deer against his, their strength against his, their speed against his Winchester's. He sketched their tracks and scat and measured them in great detail. He photographed deer at every opportunity and read everything he could find on deer behavior in the popular press and scientific journals. He compared his own enthusiasm for deer hunting to that of the instincts of the wolf in pursuit of whitetails.

Trigger itch, buck fever, or wanderlust—call it what you will—but Seton expresses it best of all in his story. "How the wild beast in his heart did ramp—he wanted to howl like a wolf on a hot scent; and away they went through the woods and hills the trail and Yan and the inner wolf." (Seton 1899).

Seton had read *The Deerslayer* and could quote whole passages of Natty Bumppo's hunting wisdom. Dressed in buckskin and moccasins, Seton played the role of the deerslayer to its full extent. Tall, active, and sinewy, with dark hair, dark eyes, and tanned skin, he looked more like an Indian than a white man. Seton actually desired to be an Indian and learned a great deal about deer hunting from his Indian friends. In the ritual of the hunt, Seton found himself to be spiritually at one with the deer and the wolves, with the Indians and the spirit of the land.

For more than two years, Black Wolf (Yan) followed the Sandhill Stag. The fascinating and endless tracks and behavior of this buck mesmerized the young hunter. No one can follow deer trails, he argued, "without feeling a wild beast prickling in his hair and down his spine. Away Yan went, a hunter-brute once more, all other feelings swamped." (Seton 1899). He likened the pursuit of this buck to the search for the

Holy Grail. After endlessly chasing this deer, Seton learned that a hardy man can, in fact, run a deer down.

"From a hunter, perfectly equipped, one who knows the secrets of the trail," he wrote in his *Animal Tracks & Hunter Signs,* published posthumously in 1958, "a deer cannot escape. The trail may seem to end, but the trailer knows that it does not, except at the victim. It may puzzle him by side tracks and doubles, and may distance him by sheer speed, but it cannot shake him off. Sooner or later the tracker will run it down." (Seton 1958). The mystery of this buck's trail overwhelmed Seton. He noticed that the buck often backtracked for 100 yards or more and then would bound off in another direction.

Like Aubudon, Van Dyke, and Caton, Seton wished to perpetuate the mystique of the stag that always gets away and fades into oblivion. In an article, "The Big Buck We Didn't Shoot," Seton indicated that often he preferred the animal to live so that it would continually tempt man to take up the chase:

"Again I see that glorious head against the sky, as often as I did— more often in early days than now, for he appears most often to the tyro in the woods—see him give one great bound when cracks the ready rifle, and know from the miraculous way in which the unerring ball was turned aside that this was indeed the Mighty Stag again, the Spirit of the Race, and that no bullet cast of lead can ever graze his hide—and again he fades away.

"Long may he roam and spurn the hill tops with his flying feet and dash the dew drops from the highest pine tops as he clears the valley at a bound; long may he live and tempt a perfect hail of harmless lead." (Seton 1891).

No hunter-naturalist worked more persistently to educate boys in quality deer hunting and woodcraft and in deciphering and recording the mysteries of deer tracks, trails, and behavior than did Ernest Thompson Seton. Seton, Audubon, Perry, Cooper, Frank Forester, Elliott, Tome, Van Dyke, and Caton are all giants among deer hunters; read their books and acquire the real meaning of the quality deer-hunting experience. For them it consisted of adventure, romance, natural history, and a code of ethics. Without these basic elements, deer hunting lacks substance, meaning, and integrity. Hunting must be viewed in the context of a spiritual bond between the hunter and the hunted.

—ROBERT WEGNER

CHAPTER 17

Stories around the Firepot

Without intangible values, life has no meaning.

—SIGURD OLSON (1980)

Campfires have always provided a focal point for outdoorsmen. Our distant forefathers relied on fires for warmth and to prepare food. To them, fire was the essence of survival. Through the ages, fire has remained as a bond among mankind. Regardless of age, creed, religion, or race, we are drawn to a fire for spiritual sustenance and guidance.

Many of the decisions that have shaped our lives originated from gatherings around a fire. Native Americans and European settlers would pass a peace pipe around a campfire. Franklin D. Roosevelt is remembered for his "fireside chats" from the White House. He knew the importance of "setting the stage" in maintaining his rapport with America.

Sigurd Olson, a naturalist and writer from the Minnesota-Wisconsin northwoods, began penning his philosophy in his later years. He, like Aldo Leopold, had a reverence for the outdoors and a unique ability to convince his readers of the necessity of serving as players rather than controllers in environmental concerns. Olson's philosophy was the product of his lifestyle. Only months before his death in 1982, he reminisced that his life was "a series of campfires."

Gazing into the flames and rising sparks is mesmerizing. The sights, sounds, and smells of a campfire allow one to explore and ponder one's deepest feelings. At fireside, we discover ourselves and develop lasting friendships with fellow fire gazers.

Campfires are synonymous with gatherings of hunters around the world. Methods of presenting the fire are as diverse as those who join to soak in the warmth. Many have moved the campfire inside their cabins, where the fire is presented via a potbellied stove. The ambience of a natural setting is replaced by memoirs hanging on the walls: sets of antlers connected by cobwebs, faded pictures of hunting scenes, a hornet nest found years ago and brought to the cabin for all to see, and a collection of other things. The decor of all hunting camps appears rather generic at a distance, but upon close observation each camp or cabin has its own personality, a reflection of its seasonal inhabitants. The same is true of conversations born of such surroundings. The focal point always seems to be the campfire, stove, or other source of warmth.

Several years ago, a group of hunters from South Carolina's deer-rich Lowcountry decided to create an outdoor gathering place. Pieces of weather-tolerant furniture of all descriptions found their way to the place and were arranged in a circle. This would not be complete without the appropriate presentation of the fire. We searched the countryside for a proper container to serve as our centerpiece. At long last we discovered a discarded, cast-iron cauldron measuring 5 feet across and 20 inches deep. It originally was used to cook cane syrup and later as a stock-watering trough. A long crack had rendered it useless until we came along. Our centerpiece was aptly named the Firepot. Once it was positioned atop four upright sections of railroad ties, the stage was set for hunters' stories.

A degree of peer pressure exists among hunters to describe hunts in detail. "How did it happen?" one hunter questioned his successful companion. The response: "Well, he just walked into an opening and I shot." This hunter missed a crucial element of the hunt. Fellow hunters are hungry for details. How long were you in the stand? Was the deer alone? Did it approach from upwind or downwind? Did you use any sort of scent? Was your stand chosen because it was near rubs and scrapes or did it overlook a game trail? Did you see other deer before shooting this one? The questions could be endless and usually are.

A seasoned hunter knows that campfires inspire detailed descriptions that provide chapters in many unwritten books on hunting each season. When told in detail, the story of a hunt answers all questions. Fellow hunters can learn from each encounter, as the storyteller extols

The stage has been set for a gathering of storytellers following the hunt. PHOTO-
GRAPH BY JOHN E. MORAN.

his prowess or bemoans his misfortune. Sharing the details of a hunt
bestows a mystique upon the quarry and pays tribute to the animal.

Stories around the Firepot are best presented seasonally because
deer hunters function that way, especially in the Southeast, where deer
seasons are so long. Here, a deer hunter's life is simple. One-third of
the year is spent preparing for hunting season, which lasts another
third, and the final portion of the year is for recuperation.

The Firepot's resting place is a 3,000-acre plantation along the
northern banks of Combahee River in Colleton County, South Carolina.
Traditional deer hunting, with dogs and bucks-only harvests, was the
norm into the 1980s. In 1985, a change in harvest strategy was implemented. Management recommendations were shifted to the harvest of
twenty-five adult does and no bucks. Also, pine trees were planted
around pastures and along the highway, and summer, fall, and winter
food plots were scheduled. Each year, management was adjusted to suit
the desires of the owners and the needs of the primary wildlife species:
deer, wild turkeys, and quail.

Initially, deer were hunted by owners, relatives, and friends. By
the fifth year, a club of seven members was formed to help defray some
of the management costs. The annual harvests were to consist of adult

does and bucks with at least eight points and a minimum outside spread of 16 inches. Naturally, mistakes were made each year, with button bucks (6 months old) and undersized adult bucks in the harvest. Mistakes can be valuable if something is learned. One approach is to use a mistake to show an individual or group the incident's significance. Hunters must recognize the immediate and long-term impacts of their actions. This ability should give a hunter more satisfaction from trips afield and this maturity enhances quality hunting experiences.

We thought that sharing some Firepot stories would be educational and entertaining. Stories are presented in order according to the three periods of a deer hunter's year.

PREPARATION

"Gettin' ready" usually involves some farm work. Fields have to be tilled and fertilized just before the spring-summer planting. Fertilization is based on results of soil testing. Decisions on what to plant often are made with the assistance of a wildlife biologist or agricultural agent.

A Visit to the Rifle Range

Summer afternoons provide a fine time to make sure the rifle, ammunition, and scope are performing well. Preseason shooting is absolutely necessary but checks during the season are advised. Once a suitable combination of bullet weight and style, powder, and casing is achieved, avoid changes during the season. This can have a noticeable effect on "point of impact."

Last hunting season, one of the club members returned to the Firepot rather long-faced after the evening hunt. As it was, his hunt had ended nearly two hours before dark. Accompanied by his wife for the first time in several years, Roger had packed too quickly for the hunting trip. His .270 shells were left at home. He could not find his usual brand, but a box of the same weight shells was purchased at a country store only a few miles from the hunting property. They arrived at the club, signed in for a particular stand, and were off to the woods. Why the hurry? October had arrived and the older bucks were in their seasonal courtship stupor. You've got to strike while the iron is hot!

In the elevated stand with the rifle propped in one corner, Roger and his sidekick were busy with their binoculars. No

Check the accuracy of your rifle, scope, and ammunition before and several times during the season. Rifle practice will enhance your confidence and efficiency.
PHOTOGRAPH BY JOE HAMILTON.

deer moving yet; only some masked warblers flitting among the pine limbs flanking the stand. "What kind of birds are they?" the hunter's wife asked. "Don't know, but I'll soon find out." As Roger leaned over to retrieve the Peterson's Field Guide from his day pack, he saw the dark form of a deer gliding quietly through the pines just 75 yards away. When the deer entered a clearing, Roger was propped against the side of the stand with rifle ready. There was no reason to glass this buck's antlers with binoculars. He had twelve points and main beams that extended well beyond his ear tips, probably a 21- or 22-inch spread. The crosshairs settled on the massive shoulders as naturally as a compass needle points northward. Take a deep breath, release most of it, squeeze . . . boom! The buck looked to the left, then to the right, lowered his head, and resumed feeding. "How could I have missed? I had a steady rest . . . oh, no! The ammunition! It must be the reason. I'm not going to risk a crippling shot. That's what I get for not testing my rifle with this new ammunition before hunting today." As luck would have it, a nice ten-pointer joined the other buck for an afternoon snack of lush wheat. He was studied through binoculars but the rifle remained in its corner, as if it were placed there for punishment. It was!

Incidentally, those feathered visitors were common yellowthroats. A lesson had been learned the hard way, but Roger also taught a lesson as he shared his hunt with us around the Firepot that evening. He gave both bucks the benefit of the doubt by refusing to fire a second "stray" bullet.

I sat there, gazing into the glowing coals and feeling proud to be a hunting companion, but wishing all the while that ten thousand deer hunters could have been at fireside to hear Roger's story. "I'll never switch ammunition again," he said, "and I'll always recognize a yellow-throat when we're face to face. It was a good hunt after all."

Learning birds by sight and sound can enhance hunting experiences. Bird activity and particularly alarm calls can alert hunters of an approaching deer.
DRAWING BY JOE HAMILTON.

Scouting

Scouting is a catch-all term that describes most nonhunting activities in the deer woods. It is a good excuse to get away from mundane things and go exploring, always in preparation for the hunting season.

I followed a set of human tracks once that took me in circles, back-tracking and zigzagging through the woods. Deer rubs, scrapes, droppings, beds, and trails were encountered during my search. Finally, the tracks led to a young fellow sitting on a log. He appeared to be staring at something far away. In fact, he was so intent that I caught myself glancing frequently toward whatever he was looking at as I approached.

Dry leaves covered the ground, so sneaking was out of the question. I made no effort to disguise my footsteps. When I was nearly arm's length away, he sprang to his feet, yelled, and assumed a semicrouched position. Somewhat startled by his response, I struck the same position. There we were, face to face, two predators ready for battle. The mood relaxed when I asked, "Scouting for deer?" A weak "Yep" came from the track maker. "Seen any promising sign?" was my attempt to strike up a conversation. "Nope," was his reply. What did he mean? I had been among continuous deer sign for the past hour—a hunter's dream!

I had some scouting of my own to do. Either this fellow was trying to protect a remote treasure, assuming I didn't recognize deer sign, or he was plain lost. I took a seat on the log, fetched a pipe from my coat pocket, and cast my attention to a distant woodpecker trying to wreck a rotten limb. My all-the-time-in-the-world attitude was in full swing. The track maker finally broke the silence: "You, uh, heading out of the woods anytime, you know, soon?" "Yep," was my reply. "Well, uh, if you wouldn't mind the company, I'll just tag along." He was definitely in a lost trance.

My scouting session had been successful on two counts. I had found a remote piece of property with an abundance of deer sign. Also, I would not be bothered by the track maker. He could never find this location again.

Scouting on an area that is being managed for quality deer is quite different from scouting on traditionally hunted lands. The difference is in determining where big bucks are, rather than bumping around, essentially in the dark, to discover if there are any around.

Scouting is not just a walk in the woods. An ardent scouter knows plants (for food and cover), soils, weather, and animal behavior. Hunters who are successful year after year usually are the ones who consider

Locating deer sign is the first part of the puzzle. Patience and knowledge of deer behavior will increase the chances of crossing paths with that elusive whitetail. Rubs like this one, made by a mature buck, can signal the progress of your quality management program. PHOTOGRAPH BY JOHN E. MORAN.

scouting an important part of their preparation for hunting. They do their homework and it pays off.

HUNTIN'

There are two ways to better appreciate privileges we often take for granted. One is to travel to other states or countries for firsthand experience. The other is to have visitors share their native culture through photographs and stories around the Firepot.

Each of three trips to the Land Down Under as a guest of the Australian Deer Association has been a dream come true. A lasting impression is Australian hunters' knowledge and reverence of nature. What I did not anticipate was the aftereffect of my travels. At home with senses honed to savor the sights, sounds, and smells of that faraway land, I discovered that I had been too casual an observer in my own land. Each venture afield now revealed treasures heretofore unappreciated.

Several years ago, Peter Stuart, past president of the Australian Deer Association and a native of Melbourne, visited me during October. The setting was perfect. This was the fourth year of quality deer management for my neighborhood and the rut was in full swing. Bucks were coming out of the woodwork. We hunted from stands, stalked, rattled, and grunted. Morning and afternoon hunts for six days yielded sightings of twenty-five bucks.

One morning, we sat 20 yards apart in a hardwood bottom and watched a beautiful sunrise. I began imitating the familiar grunt of a tending buck. Within minutes, we had been investigated by three bucks, including one that walked up to a mere dozen feet of me before making a rather indignant departure. The memory would be ours to relish, but we also had the entire sequence on videotape to share with friends and to document our conquest.

Two hours passed as we perched among the sprawling limbs of a live oak. The onslaught of mosquitoes signaled a prime activity period for whitetails, referred to locally as the shank of the evening. Eighty yards away and upwind, a nervous doe emerged from a patch of dog fennels. Her backward glance and hasty retreat put us on guard, Peter with gun in hand and me, the spotter, with my 10×40 binoculars. She was being chased by three suitors. They appeared in what I thought was reverse order with regard to age and dominance: first a six-pointer followed by a 14-inch eight-pointer, and then by one that Texans would call the "muy grande" or "papa cito" (big man).

Peter kept the large buck in his scope until it entered another thicket, still only 80 or 90 yards from us. "That was the size buck I've been looking for," Peter remarked, "but taking a shot at a moving target, especially with an unfamiliar rifle, is too risky." We returned the next morning at sunrise and saw a doe trot across the end of a long, narrow wheat patch. That same magnificent buck was on her heels. I grunted as I should have done the afternoon before and the buck stopped, stood broadside, and gazed at us through the early-morning mist. Peter shouldered the rifle, but an offhand shot at 120 yards was out of the question. The courtship was allowed to proceed. Spectacular sights like this are permanent in a deer hunter's memory.

He traveled 12,000 miles, purchased a nonresident hunting license, endured swarms of mosquitoes, watched the sun rise and set for six days, observed at least twenty-five bucks, and completed his visit without ever pulling a trigger. The intent was evident. He had taken game before and he has since, but he behaved as a true sportsman and always gave his quarry the benefit of the doubt. Peter Stuart returned to his native Australia with a storehouse of memories from our deer woods. We hope that his life will be enriched by those intangible values and thank him for the treasure he imparted upon us—a prime example to follow.

Incidentally, that big buck was taken by another friend of mine only two weeks after Peter's departure. That buck remains the best ever produced by the neighborhood deer population.

Silent Shots

One of the frequent visitors around the Firepot is John Moran, dubbed "the Phantom" by our group because of his unpredictable schedule and quiet demeanor. John is a dedicated and patient hunter. He chooses to shoot with a camera. His photos make thin gravy but provide a nutritious diet for the soul. The Phantom is an important member of our hunting group.

The One-Legged Stalker

Allowing more bucks to get older has affected buck sign on the property. The average size of rubbed trees has increased with buck age structure. These large rubs not only aroused the interest of hunters, but also snagged the attention of deer researchers. Grant Woods, while a doctoral candidate in wildlife biology at Clemson University, used automatic camera-computer systems mounted on metal posts to monitor the activity around these unusually large rubs. This one-legged stalker sprang into action each time its infrared beam was interrupted by a visitor to the signpost. Visits were tallied by time and date in the computer while the camera took mug shots of the animals—bucks, does, raccoons, opossums, bobcats, turkeys, and squirrels.

Nine cameras clicked away at passersby from late summer through fall of 1990 and 1991. Only the largest bucks were photographed rubbing; subordinate bucks apparently just visited to sniff the "signature" of those that had rubbed their antlers and foreheads on the signposts. One camera documented visits by twelve bucks. Nearly all of the buck activity was recorded during darkness. Aromatic species including sassafras, red cedar, and chinaberry were favorite rub trees. Many were rubbed during successive years and bore persistent scars.

Woods's research revealed a number of mature bucks that were seldom or never seen by hunters. What we can learn from this is that quality deer management means new hunting techniques. Through traditional hunting, we have become accustomed to hunting young, inexperienced bucks. Maintaining a reasonable harvest of older bucks will require hunters to use savvy, patience, and woodsmanship.

Woods also evaluated hunters' responses to an extensive questionnaire sent to selected members of the Quality Deer Management Association from South Carolina and participants in the Anderson-Tully Company deer management program in Mississippi. Respondents agreed that quality deer management enhanced the quality of deer on their hunting lands and that it was not frustrating to change from traditional management. Hunters from South Carolina and Mississippi placed a high value on *knowing* that mature bucks were on their property. Additional advantages of quality deer management included the opportunity to mature as a deer hunter, the importance of teaching youngsters to appreciate wildlife and the right to hunt, producing something of value for our children, and observing young bucks and looking forward to next season.

Rainy Day Stalk

This story is a love affair involving a veteran hunter, a Marlin 30-30, 10×40 binoculars, and ideal stalking conditions: a light drizzle with a gentle northeast breeze.

The setting is a South Carolina Lowcountry plantation bisected by extensive rice fields. Heavy rains marked the beginning of this November morning. Deer season had been going strong since August 15. Eleven weeks of hunting and nasty weather would certainly keep deer in the most remote recesses of the property all day.

By noon, the rain had diminished to a drizzle, so the time was right for a stalk. An aerial photograph solved the question of where to hunt. The rice fields contain miles of canals flanked by densely vegetated banks. Deer use these canal banks as travel lanes and bedding areas, especially during foul weather.

I began my quest at the southern end of a north-south bank. The breeze, barely perceptible at times, was quartering from the northeast. An hour passed and only a couple hundred yards were traversed. Each step of the way was preceded by careful and methodical study of both canal banks through my binoculars.

As a learning stalker, I had hunted without binoculars. In those days, the forays were fruitless, yielding only glimpses of white flags and indignant snorts. Eagle eyes are useless on fleet feet! Stalking deer is a slow man's sport.

Thirty minutes later and another hundred yards, still nothing was seen but a few startled gallinules scooting across the 15-foot-wide canal and into cattails along the opposite bank. Such distractions can break one's train of thought. I knew deer were here and maintained my composure and a snail's pace.

The binoculars were trained on a small opening in the brush about 20 yards away and on the other bank. Gently adjusting the focus allowed my eyes to penetrate the cover one twig at a time. An antler tip emerged from the blur. A little fine tuning and a main beam with two points and a brow tine developed. Jubilation overwhelmed me. I had stalked to within a stone's throw of a bedded buck, possibly an eight-point monarch. Davy Crockett, my childhood hero, would have been proud, I said to myself.

Taking a buck was out of the question. A mature doe was the order of the day. Nevertheless, I was numbed by my accomplishment. Two carefully placed steps produced a better view. Seven points and a 17-inch spread. What a magnificent buck! I can't believe how tight he's holding. He doesn't even know I'm here.

A good pair of binoculars cannot compensate for a hunter's eyes blurred with excitement. Suddenly, reality sobered me. I could see nasal bones. That's a cotton-pickin' skull! All my stealth had been wasted on a pile of bones. If old bucks go to the happy hunting grounds, I'll bet he smiled, if that's possible.

Before taking another step, I peered through a keyhole opening on my bank. Two does were standing under the spindly branches of a young live oak, just 12 yards away. I quickly realized my purpose and the doe with the longest head became an entry in our season's hunting data.

Once the necessary biological information was recorded (98 pounds, 3½ years old), the object of my quest was field-dressed and placed on a hook in the cooler for ten days of aging. I returned to the rice field late that afternoon to collect my other trophy—the buck's skull. As I approached the scattered bones, a small basket-racked eight-point buck sprang from his bed only 10 yards from me. His oval bed was dry! Each of us was a bit wiser when that day ended because we shared a ringside seat in the drama. He, too, will remember my rainy day stalk.

Bending the Rules for Beginners
Several hunters had gathered around the Firepot one crisp fall afternoon to prepare the evening's fire. This practice has become a prehunt ritual so that we will have a nice bed of coals to greet our return. One hunter asked if the rules could be flexible enough to allow his son to take any size buck as his first deer. All eyes turned to me, the scapegoat. The question was not unreasonable, although the response came with some difficulty and not immediately. I considered the situation from a variety of angles. Is it fair to ask a young hunter to refrain from shooting a yearling buck? Is it fair to the club members if ten young hunters take bucks from the "protected" category in one season? Would the young hunter feel cheated later when he realized that an exception to the grownups' rules had been made? Should youngsters have to adhere to the rules of the older, experienced hunters? After all, how many of us have harvested small bucks during our years of hunting?

Hunting groups will have to address these questions individually. Long-term goals are important, but the path should be enjoyable as well as educational. Management guidelines should be rigid enough to produce desired results, yet have the flexibility to maintain relaxed attitudes of the participants.

PERSPECTIVE
Hunters end the hunting season with mixed emotions. Seasons usually are closed with a sigh of relief. The alarm clock and coffeepot can be given a rest until next season. Certain events that occurred during the season will be recalled and told with a degree of embellishment. Most of

all, the season will be logged into history as a package—a measuring stick to gauge seasons past and those yet to come.

Barometers

The close of one season marks the beginning of another. This time of reflection is also an opportunity to read the sign for next year. Harvest data collected throughout the season must be delivered to the area wildlife biologist. Try to observe deer on a regular basis through winter to determine when the antlers are dropped, or cast. When stressed physically by diseases, parasites, or poor nutrition, bucks will lose their antlers early—sometimes before the hunting season is over. Bucks in good condition, on the other hand, will retain their antlers as long as mid- to late March. The combination of harvest analysis and field observations can serve as a gauge for the coming fawning and hunting seasons.

The Annual Antler Roundup

My collection of Native American artifacts is testimony of many hours spent searching the rain-washed furrows of plowed fields. My annual collection of deer antlers reflects hours of searching as well, but it also provides a measure of management success. There are other similarities in finding arrowheads and antlers. Seeing such treasure lying on the ground, especially at a distance, immediately quickens your pace. You rush to claim your find as if someone were competing. The first touch of a newly found arrowhead is exhilarating. A gap of hundreds, perhaps thousands, of years has been bridged. Questions begin to flow. Who made this arrowhead? How did he live? Was the arrowhead lost during a hunt where I now pursue descendants of the same deer? If so, time has melted away the cultural differences and we have something in common.

Finding an antler is an educational process as well. Survey the dimensions: main beam length, number and lengths of points, and basal circumference. These characteristics will enable the seasoned woodsman to determine the owner's age class. Cataloging each antler according to date of find and location can indicate the animal's condition and habitat preference. My experience has been that most antlers are found in food plots, especially patches of wheat, rye, and oats. Are antlers more visible in closely cropped green patches than in woods? Collectively, the antlers found on a property each winter provide a storehouse of knowledge. These "artifacts" prove that the deer sur-

This is one year's collection of antlers from a 3,000-acre property. Based on characteristics, they have been arranged in yearling, 2½-year-old, and 3½ years and older age classes. The antlers will be one year larger next year. PHOTOGRAPH BY JOE HAMILTON.

vived the hunting season and, barring misfortune, these bucks should enter the fall with larger antlers. When a particularly large or unique antler is found, that portion of the property is imparted with a certain mystique. You know he is there; the challenge is on!

The '90 Season Was One to Remember

Expectations were high for our sixth season of quality deer management. Last winter's antler roundup yielded thirty-two sheds, with some impressive matched sets. Those bucks will be a year larger and smarter this season. During the summer, several groups of large-antlered, mature bucks were observed in food plots. It's comforting and exciting to know they are still around.

September 30 saw the first of many memorable visits to our skinning shed. Two bucks had been taken that afternoon: a 3½-year-old eight-pointer with an 18-inch outside spread and a 4½-year-old ten-pointer measuring 19 inches outside and weighing 180 pounds live weight. By neighborhood standards, these were top-of-the-line bucks.

At season's end, the harvest totaled fifty-six deer, including thirty-six does, five button bucks, and fifteen antlered bucks. The '90 harvest appeared bittersweet at first glance. Too many button bucks had been taken. They represented 12 percent of the antlerless harvest and that number should have been less than 10 percent, ideally 7 percent or 8 percent.

A couple of "management" bucks were included in the antlered harvest. We prefer that term to "cull." Just because an animal falls short of our expectations for its age class does not mean it cannot provide a quality hunting experience. In fact, recognizing an animal that the deer population can do without (thus, a "management" deer) is among the ultimate challenges of the quality manager.

One of those bucks was 2½ years old with only three antler points, certainly substandard for that age class. The deer was observed to stagger slightly before it was taken by an archer. At the skinning shed, a large abscess was found between its antlers, a chronic condition that probably affected antler growth and explained his unusual gait. The observations of a seasoned hunter resulted in a plausible explanation for poor antlers. Incidentally, it was the archer's first deer. That distinction rendered the three-pointer unforgettable and the hunt a quality experience.

The other "management" buck sported a malformed four-point rack that bent backward along the deer's neck. Dentition revealed 9½ years of wear. His gaunt, 146-pound frame and freak antlers made him the perfect specimen of a "spent" buck and an obvious candidate for the "management" category.

Among the remaining antlered bucks were three that scored high enough to be placed on the South Carolina Record Buck List (minimum of 125 Boone and Crockett score for typical antlers). This is the only time an individual property or club has produced three entries in one year since the record program began in the early 1970s. Finally, the combination of management plan, genetics, and soil quality has enabled our deer to exhibit their potential.

Did I say the '90 season was bittersweet? We did deviate a bit from our course, though our intentions were steadfast. To expect the ideal situation is human nature, but to criticize performance when all participants share dedication to the long-range program is neither fair nor warranted.

The '90 season was one to remember after all. When examined hunt by hunt, each season becomes unique, a treasure to be remembered

Results of the sixth year under quality deer management include three bucks that scored more than 125 Boone & Crockett points. What could not be shown or measured were the hours of quality experiences that hunters enjoyed during the 1990 season. PHOTOGRAPH BY JOHN E. MORAN.

The Firepot has become a permanent fixture in our lives. We hope the stories and friendships developed at fireside will guide our future. PHOTOGRAPH BY JOHN E. MORAN.

by its own merits. As hunts are the building blocks of seasons, they also build the character of participants. This is the importance of quality hunting and its role in nurturing quality hunters. This is a reciprocal arrangement with quality, whether it originated from a hunting experience or from a hunter. Perhaps from this revolutionary development in hunters' values a legacy will be ensured.

—JOE HAMILTON

CHAPTER 18

Ethics for the Future

Ten thousand years ago that hunter would have stood by a fire and recounted the great deed to his clan brothers. . . . It hasn't changed much . . . the ethical killer of the great stag or the great bear still commands attention by the fire as he recites his deeds. His peers still salute him, the old men still nod and remember, and young boys still dream of tomorrow's hunts.

—JOHN MADSON

The past four summers have seen some very significant events regarding the future of American deer hunting. The first event was in Godollo, Hungary, in August 1991, when more than three hundred scholars from twenty-seven countries assembled at the Twentieth Annual Congress of the International Union of Game Biologists. One theme of this meeting was "World-Wide Trends in Hunting: Are They on the Decline?"

Boguslau Bobeck, a Polish wildlife researcher, concluded that without radical changes in management, "the isolation of hunters as a social group will deepen . . . and in the not-far future, the silhouette of the hunter will disappear from our forests and fields."

While attending this congress, Professor Tom Heberlein, a rural sociologist and die-hard hunter from the University of Wisconsin, echoed similar predictions: "The percentage of hunters is declining in the United States and by the middle of the next century, assuming current trends and effects, will show much lower levels of participation. It is not out of the question that there will be no sport hunting, or a dramatic change in the character of sport hunting, in the United States by the middle of the twenty-first century. Hunting is decreasing for males because of rural to urban population change, increasing education, a reduction in skilled manual workers, a decrease in family size, and decreasing white population."

Researchers from Canada agreed: "It is clear that participation in hunting in Canada is not increasing."

In July 1992, Montana played host to the first Governor's Symposium on North America's Hunting Heritage. Its purpose was to examine the motivation to hunt from cultural and historic standpoints. Hunter and cultural anthropologist Richard Nelson suggested that we return to the spiritual dimensions of hunting as found in Native American culture: "I have always hunted for staple foods, especially black-tailed deer on the northwest Pacific coast where I make my home. Like many people, I am passionate in my love for deer, but I also kill them. And, I appreciate that fact that I am made in part from the animal I love— that I am given body and sight and voice by the deer who feed me. In turn, I know my body will eventually nourish plants that provide food for deer, so the cycle will come around. We do not own life; we only take its shape for a time and then pass it along."

Claus Chee Sonny, a Navajo elder, expressed this relationship simply and profoundly: "Animals are our food. They are our thoughts."

If we are to justify deer hunting to nonhunters, we need to return to the wisdom and inspiration of our Native American elders; we need to return to our hunting heritage. Are we doing this? At the second Governor's Symposium on North America's Hunting Heritage in Pierre, South Dakota, in August 1993, Jody Enck of the Human Dimensions Research Unit at Cornell University asked this very question: "Will we pass on the hunting heritage?"

The future for hunting looks bleak. Nearly every published report of trends indicates that the number of participants declined during the 1980s and forecasts continued decline. Certainly without, and perhaps even with, extraordinary intervention, hunting is going to continue to decline over the foreseeable future.

We hope that interest in hunting in America early next century will not be restricted to the domain of historians. We are convinced that hunting is at a crossroads. Either advocates will get ahead of the problem with innovative programs or we will watch painfully as our heritage fades. We hope we will not be the generation responsible for allowing hunting to pass away, rather than passing it on in good health to future generations.

In the summer of 1994, the Izaak Walton League of America published a report, "Hunter Behavior in America." In a survey of state fish and wildlife agencies, the league concluded:

"The responding agencies expressed concern for the future of hunting and its contribution to wildlife management. . . . As more people question the validity of hunting, as anti-hunting protests become more common, and as land open to hunting decreases, understanding and tolerance is needed between hunters and non-hunters to keep public wildlife management programs working successfully."

Concern for the future of hunting is unquestionably in the minds of many agency personnel, as reflected in the following comments by representatives of a large western and a southern state, who are less concerned with the behavior of hunters than with the perceptions of nonhunters:

"Positive public perception of hunters has not improved in this state. There are local pockets where landowners are now more receptive to hunters and hunting, but overall hunting and support for same is slipping. The majority of people do not hunt and increasingly question its validity. Antihunting protests are becoming more frequent, more organized, and more militant. Areas open to hunting are decreasing."

Historically, the relationship between man and white-tailed deer has passed through three distinct phases: coexistence, exploitation, and reconstruction. We now enter the present-day phase, one of stewardship, in our relationship with the whitetail.

We should not be surprised that deer hunting is a major concern of wildlife biologists, managers, and hunters. Our voices are drowned by those of the majority in our society who are affected by the highest deer densities in history. The adaptable whitetail is causing many problems, including damage to crops, suburban ornamental plants, and forest regeneration. Habitats of other wildlife species and domestic livestock are being degraded by deer populations that are increasing in number and expanding their range. Deer-vehicle collisions are on the rise, although this cannot be attributed solely to changes in deer populations. The ever-increasing human population pushes highways to capacity while demanding that more be added to a system that already fragments deer habitat. Affluent people are moving en masse to the countryside to establish their small estates in an attempt to escape the city, yet their financial umbilical cords remain attached and commuting becomes necessary. The stage is set for calamity. Bambi has become the Achilles' heel for his own species by fueling the emotions of antihunters and animal rights advocates.

Sport hunting has taken on a new meaning at the hands of slob hunters, game hogs, poachers, and the like to the point that all honor, mystique, and pride are lost. Contests have driven too many to unsports-manlike or even illegal acts. Somehow, even gun control enters the equation. This is a knee-jerk and ill-directed attempt to solve an esca-lating violent crime rate. Our society is too liberal to tackle this cancer head-on.

With this in mind, it is difficult for true sportsmen to seek higher fines and penalties (such as restitution or "replacement" fees) for chronic or flagrant game law violators. The real problem is that it is dif-ficult to severely penalize someone for illegally taking an animal that is being referred to in the news media as a hooved rat. The whitetail has become more of a liability than an asset to our society.

Why has the issue of deer hunting been such a dilemma for its supporters? The basic problem is threefold. We are running out of space, so people and deer are being forced together. Fewer than 10 per-cent of Americans hunt; our age-old tradition has lost its ability to attract youngsters, resulting in attrition. In the last decade of the twen-tieth century, most Americans have lost that all-important direct tie to the land. Unfortunately, many young professionals charged with man-aging our natural resources have a one- or two-generation gap in their land heritage. Most of the problems encountered in natural resource management, including hunting as one of its tools, come from misun-derstanding and lack of exposure.

The white-tailed deer has a definite role in our lives now and we can almost guarantee that its adaptability will ensure a position of prominence in our future. But what about people who pursue the whitetail as a game animal? The authors of this book had a strong enough commitment to the future of deer and hunting that they spent years developing and compiling these management guidelines. The quality deer management approach does not have all of the answers but we feel that it is addressing most of the current problems.

We must strive to regain and maintain the integrity of our favored game animal. This must be accomplished through a recognized, legiti-mate organization—the Quality Deer Management Association. Even though young by most standards, the association has a remarkable record. The universal interest in quality deer management testifies to hunters' interest in becoming active managers. Considering the social, political, and economic influences wrought on our natural resources by current society, this "change of the guard" is timely. Aldo Leopold best expressed our line of thought: "At what point will governmental conservation, like the mastodon, become handicapped by its own dimensions? The answer, if there is any, seems to be in a land ethic, or some other force which assigns more obligation to the private landowner."

Twenty years ago, two young Texas wildlife biologists ended their book, *Producing Quality Whitetails,* with this paragraph: "There will be many challenges, opportunities, accomplishments and failures in the future, and only when individuals are armed with factual information and knowledge, acquired through a concerned effort, can they be prepared for ensuing events."

If there is one simple answer to the management of deer in the future, it lies in education among everyone affected by them. The Quality Deer Management Association fosters stewardship by educating those who pursue this noble animal in the age-old tradition of hunting. Enlightened hunters will be the stewards of our white-tailed deer.

—JOE HAMILTON,
AL BROTHERS, AND
ROBERT WEGNER

Acknowledgments

The authors gratefully acknowledge the support of the following individuals for their contribution to this book:

T. J. Allen, *West Virginia Department of Natural Resources*

S. Atwater, *Stackpole Books*

C. L. Bennett, Jr., *Michigan Department of Natural Resources*

J. Beringer, *Missouri Department of Conservation*

T. Breault, *Florida Game and Fresh Water Fish Commission*

D. Brewster, *Saskatchewan Parks and Renewable Resources*

D. Burke, *New Jersey Division of Fish, Game and Wildlife*

M. E. Cahill, *Vermont Fish and Wildlife Department*

D. M. Carlock, *Georgia Department of Natural Resources*

M. Cartwright, *Arkansas Game and Fish Commission*

J. Crum, *West Virginia Division of Natural Resources*

S. R. Darling, *Vermont Fish and Wildlife Department*

N. Dickinson, *New York Department of Environmental Conservation (ret.)*

R. Dressler, *Maine Department of Inland Fisheries and Wildlife*

T. Duke, *Nova Scotia Department of Lands and Forests*

G. Dusek, *Montana Department of Fish, Wildlife and Parks*

M. R. Ellingwood, *New Hampshire Fish and Game Department*

R. E. Eriksen, *New Jersey Division of Fish, Game and Wildlife*

J. Farrar, *Louisiana Department of Wildlife and Fisheries*

D. Freddie, *Colorado Department of Natural Resources*

R. Fugate, *Texas Parks and Wildlife Department*

V. Gittings, *Stackpole Books*

W. Glasgow, *Alberta Forestry, Lands and Wildife*

H. Harden, *Florida Game and Freshwater Fish Commission*

H. Harju, *Wyoming Game and Fish*

I. Hatter, *British Columbia Wildlife Branch*

T. Howard, *Wisconsin Department of Natural Resources*

W. Ishmael, *Wisconsin Department of Natural Resources*

R. Johnson, *Washington Department of Wildlife*

E. Kautz, *New York Department of Environmental Conservation*

I. L. Kenyon, *Virginia Department of Game and Inland Fish (ret.)*

J. Kube, *Illinois Department of Conservation*

L. Kuck, *Idaho Fish and Game*

R. Larche, *Manitoba Natural Resources*

G. R. Lavigne, *Maine Department of Inland Fish and Wildlife*

R. Lee, *Arizona Game and Fish*

B. Les, *Wisconsin Department of Natural Resources*

E. L. Marchinton, *Bloody Creek Hunting Club*

K. McCaffery, *Wisconsin Department of Natural Resources*

J. McKenzie, *North Dakota Game and Fish Department*

K. Menzel, *Nebraska Game and Parks Commission*

D. Nelson, *Alabama Department of Conservation and Natural Resources*

D. A. Osborn, *University of Georgia*

W. L. Palmer, *Pennsylvania Game Commission*

S. G. Parren, *Vermont Fish and Wildlife Department*

A. E. Patton, *Nova Scotia Department of Natural Resources (ret.)*

J. Phillips, *Kentucky Division of Wildlife*

F. Potvin, *Quebec Ministry of Loisir, Chasse et Peche*

G. W. Redmond, *New Brunswick Department of Natural Resources and Energy*

M. Regan, *Texas Parks and Wildlife Department*

M. Reynolds, *Delaware Division of Fish and Wildlife*

L. Rice, *South Dakota Department of Game, Fish and Parks*

D. Riehlman, *New York Department of Environmental Conservation*

J. L. Sandt, *Maryland Forest Park and Wildlife Service*

D. Schad, *Minnesota Department of Natural Resources*

A. Schultz, *International Paper Company*

W. H. Sell, *Georgia Agricultural Extension Service (ret.)*

K. Sexson, *Kansas Investigations and Inventory Office*

M. Shaw, *Oklahoma Department of Wildlife Conservation*

D. Shipes, *South Carolina Wildlife*

*and Marine Resources
Department*
W. Shope, *Pennsylvania Game
Commission*
R. Stoll, *Ohio Division of Wildlife*
W. Suchy, *Iowa Department of
Natural Resources*
L. Suprock, *Rhode Island Fish and
Wildlife Division*
W. Thomason, *Mississippi Depart-
ment of Wildlife, Fisheries, and
Parks*
S. Titshaw, *Scott Hudgens
Properties*

R. Vander Linden, *Canton, Georgia*
R. Vanderhoof, *Florida Game and
Fresh Water Fish Commission*
G. Vecellio, *Massachusetts Division
of Fisheries and Wildlife*
G. Wathen, *Tennessee Wildlife
Resource Agency*
M. M. Welch, *Vermont Fish and
Wildlife Department*
S. A. Williams, *Pennsylvania Game
Commission*
S. J. Williamson, *Wildlife Manage-
ment Institute*

About the Authors

AL BROTHERS, formerly a wildlife biologist for Texas Parks and Wildlife Department and manager of the H. B. Zachry Company Ranches, is senior author of the book *Producing Quality Whitetails*, which initiated the quality management movement. He remains one of its philosophical leaders.

JAMES F. BULLOCK, JR., wildlife manager for Union Camp Corporation, is a long-time proponent of quality deer management and responsible hunter behavior. In recent years, he has focused attention on the development of a management ethic that integrates the biological, ecological, and sociological values of quality deer management.

ROBERT V. DOEPKER is a wildlife habitat biologist with the Michigan Department of Natural Resources. His professional interests are in forest ecology and history, investigating and modeling wildlife and forest habitat relationships, and applying ecological principles to forest management.

DAVID C. GUYNN, JR., is a professor of forest wildlife management at Clemson University. His research has focused on harvest strategy and population dynamics. An avid deer hunter and advocate of quality deer management, he directs most of his research efforts to on-the-ground management.

JACK V. GWYNN recently retired from the Virginia Department of Game and Inland Fisheries, where he was employed since 1956. He has worked extensively on whitetail research and harvest management programs. He participates in the Northeast Deer Technical Committee and the Southeast Deer Study Group.

R. JOSEPH HAMILTON is a wildlife biologist with the South Carolina Wildlife and Marine Resources Department. He founded the Quality Deer Management Association and is editor of its journal, *Quality Whitetails*. Hamilton has received a number of awards and wide recognition for his dedication to wildlife conservation.

HARRY A. JACOBSON, professor of wildlife management at Mississippi State University, has spent his career researching all aspects of white-tailed deer behavior, biology, and ecology. His studies have demonstrated that quality deer management works in many areas of the country.

KENT E. KAMMERMEYER is a senior wildlife biologist with the Georgia Department of Natural Resources. He compiles, analyzes, and models deer data for all the state's forty-four wildlife management areas and has published many scientific and popular articles on whitetails.

W. MATT KNOX was a wildlife biologist for the South Carolina Wildlife and Marine Resources Department and is currently deer program leader for the Virginia Department of Game and Inland Fisheries. He strongly supports quality deer management.

JAMES C. KROLL is a professor at Stephen F. Austin State University's College of Forestry and founded the Institute for White-Tailed Deer Management and Research. He has written many articles as well as three reference books on whitetail management and hunting.

JOHN F. KUBISIAK, a forest biologist with the Wisconsin Department of Natural Resources, was instrumental in implementing a quality deer strategy at Wisconsin's Sandhill Wildlife Area. He is the lead author of a book encompassing twenty-seven years of research on deer and hunter management at Sandhill.

EDWARD E. LANGENAU, JR., is big-game specialist for the Michigan Department of Natural Resources. He manages the state's deer, elk, and moose programs and coordinates habitat management, data collection, hunting regulations, and public information.

R. LARRY MARCHINTON, professor of wildlife biology at the University of Georgia, has studied and published on white-tailed deer for more than thirty years. His research has focused on behavior, ecology, and, in recent years, quality management.

J. SCOTT MCDONALD is a biologist with the Georgia Department of Natural Resources. His graduate research at the University of Georgia focused on plantings for white-tailed deer. His expertise on this helps clubs and landowners with quality management.

KARL V. MILLER is a research scientist and instructor in wildlife biology at the University of Georgia. He has conducted extensive research on the physiology, behavioral ecology, and habitat requirements of white-tailed deer.

J. SCOTT OSBORNE has been deer project leader for North Carolina's Wildlife Resources Commission since 1981. He earned a master's degree from the University of Georgia in 1976 and strongly supports quality deer management.

JOHN J. OZOGA is a former research biologist for the Michigan Department of Natural Resources. He spent nearly thirty years conducting deer research at the Cusino Wildlife Research Station in Upper Michigan and now devotes much of his time to writing about the importance of proper deer management.

RONALD J. REGAN is Director of the Wildlife Division for the Vermont Fish and Wildlife Department deer management team. He has been embroiled in the debate over managing deer populations through regulated antlerless harvests. Regan also has served as chairman of the Northeast Deer Technical Committee.

STEPHEN M. SHEA was a wildlife biologist with the Florida Game and Fresh Water Fish Commission for five years and now works as a biologist at Tyndall Air Force Base. He has written several scientific papers on management of white-tailed deer in poor habitats.

REGGIE E. THACKSTON has worked as a wildlife biologist with the Oklahoma Department of Wildlife Conservation, the South Carolina Wildlife and Marine Resources Department, and now the Georgia Department of Natural Resources. He has been extensively involved in all aspects of whitetail management.

MIKE D. VAN BRACKLE is a wildlife biologist with the South Carolina Wildlife and Marine Resources Department. His graduate research at the University of Georgia was on biological markers to determine deer movements. He now helps landowners in the South Carolina Lowcountry develop wildlife management plans.

HARMON P. WEEKS, JR., is associate professor of wildlife ecology at Purdue University. He began studying the behavior and physiology of white-tailed deer in relation to mineral licks in 1969 and is evaluating the impact of mineral supplementation on antler size.

ROBERT A. WEGNER was formerly senior editor and co-owner of *Deer & Deer Hunting* magazine. Trained as a historian, he received his doctorate from the University of Wisconsin. He spends most of his time reading, researching, and writing about white-tailed deer and the American deer-hunting experience.

GRANT R. WOODS owns a consulting firm offering site-specific management plans to landowners and hunting groups. His doctoral research at Clemson University included the human dimensions and harvest results associated with quality deer management.

Literature Cited

Abrahamson, W.G., and D.C. Harnett. 1990. Pine flatwoods and dry prairies. Pages 103–149 *in* P.L. Meyers and J.J. Ewel, eds. Ecosystems in Florida. Univ. Florida Press, Gainesville.

Adams, D.J. 1984. A computer model for deer-forage-timber interactions in the loblolly–shortleaf pine–hardwoods ecosystem of east Texas. M.S. Thesis, Stephen P. Austin St. Univ., Nacogdoches, Tex. 150pp.

Albert, D.A., S.R. Denton, and B.V. Barnes. 1986. Regional landscape ecosystems of Michigan. School Nat. Res., Univ. Michigan, Ann Arbor. 32pp.

Allee, W.C., A.E. Emerson, O. Park, T. Park, and K.P. Schmidt. 1949. Principles of animal ecology. W. B. Saunders Co., Philadelphia, Pa. 837pp.

Allen, R.H., Jr. 1965. History and results of deer restocking in Alabama. Alabama Dep. Conserv., Div. Game and Fish, Bull. 6. 50pp.

Altherr, T.L. 1976. The best of all breathing: hunting as a mode of environmental perception in American literature and thought from James Fenimore Cooper to Norman Mailer. Ph.D. Dissert., Ohio St. Univ., Columbus. 354pp.

Ammann, A.P., R.L. Cowan, C.L. Mothershead, and B.R. Baumgardt. 1973. Dry matter and energy intake in relation to digestibility in white-tailed deer. J. Wildl. Manage. 37(2):195–201.

Arman, P., R.N.B. Kay, E.D. Goodall, and G.A.M. Sharman. 1974. The composition and yield of milk from captive red deer (*Cervus elaphus* L.). J. Reprod. Fert. 37:67–84.

Armstrong, R.A. 1950. Fetal development of the northern white-tailed deer (*Odocoileus virginianus borealis* Miller). Am. Midl. Nat. 43(3):650–666.

Audubon, J.J., and J. Bachman. 1851. The quadrupeds of North America. Vols. I & II, V.G. Audubon, New York.

Audubon, M.R. 1972. Audubon and his journals. Peter Smith, Mass. 554pp.

Baker, D.L., and N.T. Hobbs. 1985. Emergency feeding of mule deer during winter: tests of a supplemental ration. J. Wildl. Manage. 49(4):934–942.

Ball, D.M., C.B. Hoveland, G.D. Lacefield. 1991. Southern forages. Potash and Phosphate Inst., Norcross, Ga. 256pp.

Banks, W.J. 1974. The ossification process of the developing antler in the white-tailed deer *(Odocoileus virginianus)*. Calc. Tissue Res. 14:257–274.

Beck, D.E. 1977. Twelve-year acorn yield in Southern Appalachian oaks. USDA For. Serv., Res. Note SE-244. 8pp.

Bell, B.C. 1974. A comparison of age determination techniques for white-tailed deer (*Odocoileus virginianus,* Zimmerman) from differing Louisiana soils. M.S. Thesis, Louisiana State Univ., Baton Rouge. 156pp.

Blackard, J.J. 1971. Restoration of the white-tailed deer in the Southeastern United States. M.S. Thesis, Louisiana State Univ., Baton Rouge. 171pp.

Blair, R.M., R. Alcaniz, and A. Harrell. 1983. Shade intensity influences the nutrient quality and digestibility of southern deer browse leaves. J. Range Manage. 36:257–264.

Blair, R.M., and E.A. Epps, Jr. 1969. Seasonal distribution of nutrients in plants of seven browse species in Louisiana. USDA For. Serv., Res. Pap. SO-51.

Blouch, R.I. 1984. Northern Great Lake states and Ontario forests. Pages 391–410 *in* L. K. Halls, ed. White-tailed deer: ecology and management. Stackpole Books, Harrisburg, Pa. 870pp.

Botkin, D.B., P.A. Jordan, A.S. Dominski, H.S. Lowendorf, and G.E. Hutchinson. 1973. Sodium dynamics in a northern ecosystem. Proc. Natl. Acad. Sci. 70:2745–2748.

Bridges, R.J. 1968. Individual white-tailed deer movement and related behavior during the winter and spring in northwest Florida. M.S. Thesis, Univ. Georgia, Athens. 86pp.

Brothers, A., J. Hamilton, D.C. Guynn, Jr., and R.L. Marchinton. 1990. Spike bucks: should we shoot or protect? Deer & Deer Hunting 13(77):13–17.

Brothers, A., and M.E. Ray, Jr. 1975. Producing quality whitetails. Caesar Kleberg Wildl. Res. Inst., Kingsville, Tex. 246pp.

Brown, R.D. 1990. Nutrition and antler development. Pages 426–441 *in* G.A. Bubenik and A.B. Bubenik, eds. Horns, pronghorns, and antlers. Springer-Verlag, N.Y.

Brown, R.D., R.L. Cowan, and L.C. Griel. 1978. Correlation between antler and long bone relative bone mass and circulating androgens in white-tailed deer *(Odocoileus virginianus)*. Am. J. Vet. Res. 39:1053–1056.

Bubenik, A.B. 1972. North American moose management in light of European experiences. North Am. Moose Conf. Workshop 8:276–295.

Bubenik, A.B. 1988. An immodest proposal. Bugle 4(1):68–70.

Bubenik, G.A. 1990a. Neuroendocrine regulation of the antler cycle. Pages 265–297 *in* G.A. Bubenik and A.B. Bubenik, eds. Horns, pronghorns, and antlers. Springer-Verlag, N.Y.

Bubenik, G.A. 1990b. The role of the nervous system in the growth of antlers. Pages 339–358 *in* G.A. Bubenik and A.B. Bubenik, eds. Horns, pronghorns, and antlers. Springer-Verlag, N.Y.

Bubenik, G.A., and A.B. Bubenik. 1986. Phylogenic and ontogenic development of antlers and neuroendocrine regulation of the antler cycle—a review. Saugetierkudl. Mitt. 33:97–123.

Buckner, J.L., and J.L. Landers. 1980. A Foresters guide to wildlife management in southern industrial pine forest. Int. Paper. Co., Southlands Exp. For. Tech. Bull. 10. 16pp.

Burgoyne, G.E., Jr., J. Meister, and M. Alexander. 1981. Deer checking station data—1980. Michigan Dept. Nat. Res., Wildl. Div. Rep. 2888. 36pp.

Byford, J.L. 1970. Movements and ecology of white-tailed deer in a logged floodplain habitat. Ph.D. Dissert., Auburn Univ., Auburn, Ala. 157pp.

Carlock, D.M., K.E. Kammermeyer, L.E. McSwain, and E. J. Wentworth. 1993. Deer movements in relation to food supplies in the Southern Appalachians. Proc. Annu. Conf. Southeast. Assoc. Fish and Wildl. Agencies 47:in press.

Carlsen, J.C., and R.E. Farmes. 1957. Movements of white-tailed deer tagged in Minnesota. J. Wildl. Manage. 21(4):397–401.

Cartwright, M.E. 1975. An ecological study of white-tailed deer in northwestern Arkansas: home range, activity and habitat utilization. M.S. Thesis, Univ. Arkansas, Fayetteville. 147pp.

Carver, G. 1989. An evaluation of linear wildlife openings. P.R. Proj. W-35-33 Study IV, Alabama Game and Fish Comm. 13pp.

Case, D.J., and D.R. McCullough. 1987. The white-tailed deer of North Manitou Island. Higardia 55:1–57.

Casscles, K.M. 1992. Effects of harvest strategies on breeding season timing and fecundity of white-tailed deer. M.S. Thesis, Mississippi State Univ., Mississippi State. 124pp.

Caton, J.D. 1876. A new California deer. Am. Nat. 10:465–468.

Caton, J.D. 1877. The antelope and deer of America. Forest and Stream, New York. 426pp.

Caton, J.D. 1890. The ethics of the field sports. Pages 567–581 *in* G.O. Shields, ed. Big game of North America. Sampson Low, London.

Caughley, G. 1966. Mortality patterns in mammals. Ecology 47(6):906–918.

Caughley, G. 1977. Analysis of vertebrate populations. John Wiley and Sons, Inc., N.Y. 234pp.

Cheatum, E.L. 1949. The use of corpora lutea for determining ovulation incidence and variations in fertility of the white-tailed deer. Cornell Vet. 39(3):282–291.

Cook, H.W., R.A. Rausch, and B.E. Baker. 1970. Moose *(Alces alces)* milk. Gross composition, fatty acid, and mineral constitution. Can. J. Zool. 48:213–215.

Cook, R.S. and W.F. Harwell. 1979. Refinements of white-tailed deer census techniques. Texas Parks and Wildl. Dep., P-R Proj. W-109-R-2. 23pp.

Cook, R.S., M. White, D.O. Trainer, and C.W. Glazener. 1971. Mortality of young white-tailed deer fawns in south Texas. J. Wildl. Manage. 35(1):47–56.

Cooper, J.F. 1841. The deerslayer. A.L. Burt Co., Chicago. 564pp.

Cowan, R.L., and T.A. Long. 1962. Studies on antler growth and nutrition of white-tailed deer. Proc. Nat. white-tailed Deer Dis. Symp. 1:54–60.

Crawford, H.S. 1984. Habitat management. Pages 629–646 *in* L.K. Halls, ed. White-tailed deer: ecology and management. Stackpole Books, Harrisburg, Pa. 870pp.

Creed, W.A. 1964. Calculating deer populations by the sex-age-kill method. Rep. to Wisconsin Dept. Nat. Resour., Bur. Res., Rhinelander. 2pp.

Cunningham, R.N., and H.E. White. 1941. Forest resources of the Upper Peninsula of Michigan. USDA For. Serv., Lake States For. Exp. Stn., Misc. Publ. 429.

Cushwa, C.T., E.V. Brender, and R.W. Cooper. 1966. The response of herbaceous vegetation to prescribed burning. USDA For. Serv., Southeast. For. Exp. Stn., Res. Note SE-53. 2pp.

Cushwa, C.T., R.L. Downing, R.F. Harlow, and D.F. Urbston. 1970. The importance of woody twig ends to deer in the Southeast. USDA Forest Serv., Res. Pap. SE-67. 12pp.

Davidson, W.R., F.A. Hayes, V.F. Nettles, and F.E. Kellogg, editors. 1981. Diseases and parasites of white-tailed deer. Tall Timbers Res. Stn., Tallahassee, Fla., Misc. Publ. 7. 458pp.

Day, B.W., Jr. 1964. The white-tailed deer in Vermont. Vermont Fish and Game Dep., Wildl. Bull. 64–1. 25pp.

Decker, D.J., and N.A. Connelly. 1990. The need for hunter education in deer management: insights from New York. Wildl. Soc. Bull. 18:447-452.

Degayner, E.J., and P.A. Jordan. 1987. Skewed fetal sex ratios in white-tailed deer: evidence and evolutionary speculations. Pages 178–188 *in* C.M. Wemmer, ed. Biology and management of Cervidae. Smithsonian Inst. Press, Washington, D.C.

Denton, D.A. 1957. The study of sheep with permanent unilateral parotid fistulae. Quant. J. Exp. Physiol. 42:72–95.

DeYoung, C.A. 1989. Mortality of adult male white-tailed deer in south Texas. J. Wildl. Manage. 53(3):513–518.

Dobie, D. 1986. Georgia's greatest whitetails. Bucksnort Publ., Marietta, Ga. 440pp.

Dobson, J.W., and E.R. Beaty. 1980. Contributions of white clover to the N,P, and Ca Concentration of perennial grasses. J. Range Manage. 33:107–110.

Doepker, R.V., and J.J. Ozoga. 1991. Wildlife values of northern white-cedar. Pages 15–34 *in* D.O. Lantagne, ed. Northern white-cedar in Michigan. Michigan State Univ., Rep. 512. 122pp.

Downing, R.L. 1980. Vital statistics of animal populations. Pages 247–267 *in* S.D. Schemnitz, ed. Wildlife management techniques manual. 4th ed. The Wildlife Soc., Washington, D.C.

Downing, R.L., and D.C. Guynn, Jr. 1985. A generalized sustained-yield table for white-tailed deer. Pages 95–104 *in* S.L. Beasom and S.F. Robertson, eds. Game harvest management. Caesar Kleberg Wildl. Res. Stn., Kingsville, Tex.

Downing, R.L., B.S. McGinnes, R.L. Petcher, and J.L. Sandt. 1969. Seasonal changes in movements of white-tailed deer. Pages 19–24 *in* White-tailed deer in the southern forest habitat. Proc. Symp., Nacogdoches, Tex. USDA For. Serv., South. For. Exp. Stn., New Orleans.

Downing, R.L., W.H. Moore, and J. Kight. 1965. Comparison of deer census techniques applied to a known population in a Georgia enclosure. Proc. Annu. Conf. Southeast. Assoc. Fish and Wildl. Agencies 19:26–30.

Dusek, G.L., R.J. Mackie, J.D. Herriges, Jr., and B.B. Compton. 1989. Population ecology of white-tailed deer along the lower Yellowstone River. Wildl. Monogr. No. 104. 68pp.

Eiben, B., S.T. Scharla, K. Fisher, and H. Schmidt-Gayk. 1984. Seasonal variations of serum 1,25-dihydroxyvitamin D_3 and alkaline phosphatase in relation to the antler formation in the fallow deer (*Dama dama* L.). Acta Endocrinol. 107:141–144.

Elder, W.H. 1965. Primeval deer hunting pressures revealed by remains from American Indian middens. J. Wildl. Manage. 29(2):366–370.

Ellingwood, M.R., and J.V. Spignesi. 1987. Management of an urban deer herd and the concept of cultural carrying capacity. Trans. Annu. Northeast Deer Tech. Comm. Meet. 22:42–3.

Elliott, W. 1967. Carolina sports by land and water. Arno Press, N.Y. 172pp.

Evans, C. 1989. The hunting club as a management unit: extent of current involvement in wildlife management in east Texas. M.S.F. Thesis, Stephen F. Austin St. Univ., Nacogdoches, Tex. 52pp.

Evans, R.A. 1979. Changes in landowner attitudes toward deer and deer hunters in southern Michigan, 1960–1978. M.S. Thesis., Univ. Michigan, Ann Arbor. 45pp.

Eve, J.H. 1981. Management implications of disease. Pages 413–423 *in* W.R. Davidson, F.A. Hayes, V.F. Nettles, and F.E. Kellogg, eds. Diseases and parasites of white-tailed deer. Tall Timbers Res. Stn., Tallahassee, Fla., Misc. Publ. 7.

Fennessy, P.F., and J.M. Suttie. 1985. Antler growth: nutritional and endocrine factors. Pages 239–250. *in* P.F. Fennessy and K.R. Drew, eds. Biology of deer production. Roy. Soc. New Zealand, Bull 22.

Foote, L.E. 1945. The Vermont deer herd: a study in productivity. Vermont Fish and Game, State Bull., P-R Ser. No. 13. 125pp.

Forbes, G.B. 1962. Sodium. Pages 1–72 *in* C.L. Comar and F. Bronner, eds. Mineral metabolism. Vol. 2, Part B. Academic Press, N.Y.

Fraser, D. 1979. Sightings of moose, deer, and bears on roads in northern Ontario. Wildl. Soc. Bull. 7(3):181–184.

Freidrich, P.D., and H.R. Hill. 1982. Doe productivity and physical condition: 1982 spring survey results. Michigan Dep. Nat. Res., Wildl. Div. Rep. 2926. 11pp.

French, C.E., L.C. McEwen, N.D. Magruder, R.H. Ingram, and R.W. Swift. 1955. Nutritional requirements of white-tailed deer for growth and antler development. Pennsylvania Agric. Exp. Sta. Bull. 600. 50pp.

French, C.E., L.C. McEwen, N.D. Magruder, R.H. Ingram, and R.W. Swift. 1956. Nutrient requirements for growth and antler development in the white-tailed deer. J. Wildl. Manage. 20(2):221–232.

Fuller, T.K. 1990. Dynamics of a declining white-tailed deer population in north-central Minnesota. Wildl. Monogr. 110. 37pp.

Garland, L.E. 1978. Vermont's experience with a bucks-only hunting season since 1897. Vermont Fish and Game. 27pp.

Gavin, T.A., L.H. Suring, P.A. Vohs, Jr., and E.C. Meslow. 1984. Population characteristics, spatial organization, and natural mortality in the Columbian white-tailed deer. Wildl. Monogr. 91. 41pp.

Geist, V. 1986. Super antlers and pre–World War II European research. Wildl. Soc. Bull. 14(1):91–94.

Gilbert, F.F. 1966. Aging white-tailed deer by annuli in the cementum of the first incisor. J. Wildl. Manage. 30(1):200–202.

Goodrum, P.D., V.H. Reid, and C.E. Boyd. 1971. Acorn yields, characteristics and management criteria of oaks for wildlife. J. Wildl. Manage. 35(3):520–532.

Goodrum, W.B., Sr. 1990. Implementation of an optimum sustained yield harvest system for white-tailed deer: an eight year case history study. M.S.F. Thesis, Stephen F. Austin State Univ., Nacogdoches, Tex. 47pp.

Goss, R.J. 1983. Deer antlers: regeneration, function, and evolution. Academic Press, N.Y. 316pp.

Grasman, B.T., and E.C. Hellgren. 1993. Phosphorus nutrition in white-tailed deer: nutrient balance, physiological responses, and antler growth. Ecology 74:2279–2296.

Gross, J.E. 1972. Criteria for big game planning: performance measures vs. intuition. Trans. North Am. Wildl. Nat. Resour. Conf. 37:246–259.

Gruver, B.J., D.C. Guynn, Jr., and H.A. Jacobson. 1984. Simulated effects of harvest strategy on reproduction in white-tailed deer. J.Wildl. Manage. 48(2):535–541.

Gruver, B.J., D.C. Guynn, Jr., H.A. Jacobson, and R.N. Griffin. 1980. Possible effects of harvest strategy on the reproduction biology of white tailed deer in Mississippi. Annu. Meet. Southeast Deer Study Group 3:11–12.

Guynn, D.C. 1991. October's balance—harvest for the resource. The Signpost 2(4):6–7.

Guynn, D.C., Jr., J.R. Sweeney, and R.J. Hamilton. 1986. Adult sex ratio and conception dates in a South Carolina deer herd. Annu. Meet. Southeast Deer Study Group 9:13.

Guynn, D.C., J.R. Sweeney, R.J. Hamilton, and R.L. Marchinton. 1988. A case study in quality deer management. S.C. white-tailed Deer Manage. Workshop 2:72–79.

Hamilton, R.J., W.M. Knox, and L.O. Rogers. 1991. An evaluation of antlerless deer harvest trends in the South Carolina Coastal Plain. Annu. Meet. Southeast Deer Study Group 14:12.

Harlow, R.F. 1959. An evaluation of white-tailed deer habitat in Florida. Florida Game and Fresh Water Fish Comm., Tech. Bull. 5. 64pp.

Harlow, R.F., and F.K. Jones, Jr., editors. 1965. The white-tailed deer in Florida. Florida Game and Fresh Water Fish Comm., Tech. Bull. 9. 240pp.

Harlow, R.F., J.B. Whelan, H.S. Crawford, and J.E. Skeen. 1975. Deer foods during years of oak mast abundance and scarcity. J. Wildl. Manage. 39(2):330–336.

Harmel, D.E. 1982. Effects of genetics on antler quality and body size in white-tailed deer. Pages 339–348 *in* R.D. Brown, ed. Antler development in Cervidae. Caesar Kleberg Wildl. Res. Inst., Kingsville, Tex.

Harper, S.C., L.L. Falk, and E.W. Rankin. 1990. Northern forest lands study of New England and New York. USDA For. Serv. and Governor's Task Force on Northern Forest Lands. 206pp.

Haugen, A.O. 1975. Reproductive performance of white-tailed deer in Iowa. J. Mammal. 56(1):151–159.

Havera, S.P., and K.E. Smith. 1979. A nutritional comparison of selected fox squirrel foods. J. Wildl. Manage. 43(3):691–704.

Hayne, D.W., and J.V. Gwynn. 1977. Percentage does in total kill as a harvest strategy. Joint Meet. Northeast-Southeast Deer Study Group 1:117–123.

Herbert, H.W. 1843. The deer stalkers. T.B. Peterson & Brothers, Philadelphia, Pa. 198pp.

Hesselton, W.T. 1991. How governmental wildlife agencies should respond to local governments that pass antihunting legislation. Wildl. Soc. Bull. 19(2):222–223.

Hesselton, W.T., and L.W. Jackson. 1974. Reproductive rates of white-tailed deer in New York. New York Fish and Game J. 21:135–152.

Higginbotham, B.J., Jr, and J.C. Kroll. Warm season supplemental forages for white-tailed deer in the piney woods of east Texas. Proc. Annu. Conf. Southeast. Assoc. Fish and Wildl. Agencies. In press.

Hill, H.R. 1991*a*. Deer checking station data—1990. Michigan Dept. Nat. Res., Wildl. Div. Rep. 3137. 73pp.

Hill, H.R. 1991*b*. Instruction for deer pellet group survey—spring 1991. Michigan Dept. Nat. Res., Wildl. Div., Unpubl. Rep. 3pp.

Holter, J.B., H.H. Hayes, and S.H. Smith. 1979. Protein requirement of yearling white-tailed deer. J. Wildl. Manage. 43(4):872–879.

Holzenbein, S., and R.L. Marchinton. 1992. Emigration and mortality in orphaned male white-tailed deer. J. Wildl. Manage. 56(1):147–153.

Hood, R.E. 1971. Seasonal variations in home range, diel movement and activity patterns of white-tailed deer on the Rob and Bessie Welder Wildlife Refuge (San Patricio County, Texas). M.S. Thesis, Texas A&M Univ., College Station. 173pp.

Horton, T. 1991. Deer on your doorstep. The New York Times Magazine. April 28, 1991:29–31, 38, 40, 42, 74.

Hoskinson, R.L., and L.D. Mech. 1976. white-tailed deer migration and its role in wolf predation. J. Wildl. Manage. 40(3):429–441.

Hoveland, C.W., M.W. Alison, G.V. Calvert, and J.F. Newsome. 1986. Performance of annual clovers in north Georgia. Georgia Agric. Exp. Sta., Res. Rep. 510. 4pp.

Huegel, C.N., R.B. Dahlgren, and H.L. Gladfelter. 1985. Mortality of white-tailed deer fawns in south-central Iowa. J. Wildl. Manage. 49(2):377–380.

Hurst, G.A. 1979. Deer food on slash pine plantations and a longleaf pine forest. Annu. Meet. Southeast Deer Study Group 2:13.

Hurst, G.A., and R.C. Warren. 1981. Enhancing white-tailed deer habitat of pine plantations by intensive management. Mississippi Agric. and For. Exp. Sta., Tech. Bull. 107. 8pp.

Hyvarinen, H., R.N.B. Kay, and W.J. Hamilton. 1977. Variation in weight, specific gravity and composition of antlers of red deer *(Cervus elaphus)*. Br. J. Nutr. 38:301–311.

Jackson, J.J., G.D. Walker, R.L. Shell, and D. Heighes. 1984. Managing timber and wildlife in the southern piedmont. Univ. Georgia, Coop. Ext. Serv. Bull. 845. 51pp.

Jacobson, H.A. 1984*a*. Investigation of phosphorus in the nutritional ecology of white-tailed deer. Fed. Aid Wildl. Rest. Prog. W-48-31, XXIII, Mississippi Dep. Wildl. Conserv.

Jacobson, H.A. 1984*b*. Relationships between deer and soil nutrients in Mississippi. Proc. Annu. Conf. Southeast. Assoc. Fish and Wildl. Agencies 38:1–12.

Jacobson, H.A. 1992. Deer condition response to changing harvest strategy, Davis Island, Mississippi. Pages 48–55 *in* R.D. Brown, ed. The Biology of Deer. Springer-Verlag, N.Y.

Jacobson, H.A. 1994*a*. Reproduction. Pages 98–108 *in* D. Gerlach, S. Atwater, and J. Schnell, eds. Deer. Stackpole Books, Mechanicsburg, Pa.

Jacobson, H. A. 1994*b*. Quality deer management: a public lands experiment. Quality Whitetails Summer/Fall:8–12.

Jacobson, H.A., and D.A. Darrow. 1992. Effects of baiting on deer movements and activity. Annu. Meet. Northeast Deer Tech. Comm. 28/Southeast Deer Study Group 15:23–24.

Jacobson, H.A., D.C. Guynn, and S.P. Mott. 1981. Investigations to improve the management of white-tailed deer in Mississippi (1976–1981). Fed. Aid in Wildl. Restor., W-48-27, Mississippi Dep. Wildl. Conserv. 138pp.

Jacobson, H.A., C. Lunceford, and E.J. Jones. 1985. Supplemental food plantings for deer in the Southeastern United States. Mississippi State Univ., Coop. Ext. Serv. Pub. 85-2. 5pp.

Jefferies, L. 1975. Deer stocking program in Georgia 1928–1974. Georgia Dep. Nat. Resour., Fed. Aid Wildl. Restor. 39pp.

Johnson, A.S., P.E. Hale, J.M. Wentworth, and J.S. Osborne. 1986. Are we really managing deer populations? Annu. Meet. Southeast Deer Study Group 9:9–10.

Johnson, A.S., H.O. Hillestad, S.F. Shanholtzer, and G.F. Shanholtzer. 1974. An ecological survey of the coastal region of Georgia. U.S. Nat. Park Serv., Sci. Monogr. Ser. 3. 233pp.

Johnson, A.S., and J.L. Landers. 1978. Fruit production in slash pine plantations in Georgia. J. Wildl. Manage. 42(3):606–613.

Johnson, M.K., B.W. Delaney, S.P. Lynch, J.A. Zeno, S.R. Schultz, T.W. Keegan, and B.D. Nelson. 1987. Effects of cool-season agronomic forages on white-tailed deer. Wildl. Soc. Bull. 15(3):330–339.

Jones, R.L. and H.C. Hanson. 1985. Mineral licks, geophagy, and biogeochemistry of North American ungulates. Iowa State Univ. Press, Ames. 301pp.

Jones, R.L., and H.P. Weeks, Jr. 1985. Ca, Mg, and P in the annual diet of deer in south-central Indiana. J. Wildl. Manage. 49(1):129–133.

Jordan, P.A., D.B. Botkin, A.S. Dominski, H.S. Lowendorf, and G.E. Belovsky. 1973. Sodium as a critical nutrient for the moose of Isle Royale. Proc. North Am. Moose Conf. Workshop 9:1–28.

Kammermeyer, K., J. Kurz, D. Whittington, K. Grahl, S. Johnson, W. Abler, C. Allen, and L. McSwain. 1988. Deer herd management for Georgia hunters. Georgia Dep. Nat. Resour., Game and Fish Div., Social Circle. 19pp.

Kammermeyer, K.E., and R.L. Marchinton. 1976. Notes on dispersal of male white-tailed deer. J. Mammal. 57(4):776–778.

Kammermeyer, K.E., and E.B. Moser. 1990. The effect of food plots, roads, and other variables on deer harvest in Northeastern Georgia. Proc. Annu. Conf. Southeast. Assoc. Fish and Wildl. Agencies 44:364–373.

Kammermeyer, K.E., E.A. Padgett, W.M. Lentz, and R.L. Marchinton. 1992. Production, utilization, and quality of three ladino clovers in northeastern Georgia. Joint Annu. Meet. Northeast Deer Tech. Comm. 28/Southeast Deer Study Group 15:15.

Kay, R.N.B., M. Phillippo, J.M. Suttie, and G. Wenham. 1981. The growth and mineralization of antlers. J. Physiol. 322:4P.

Knox, W.M., M.O. Bara, and K.V. Miller. 1991. Effect of estimated fawning date on physical development in yearling male white-tailed deer. Proc. Annu. Conf. Southeast. Assoc. Fish and Wildl. Agencies 45:30–36.

Korschgen, L.J. 1962. Foods of Missouri deer, with some management implications. J. Wildl. Manage. 26(2):164–172.

Kroll, J.C. 1991. A practical guide to producing and harvesting white-tailed deer. Stephen F. Austin State Univ. Press, Nacogdoches, Tex. 590pp.

Larson, J.S. 1969. Agricultural clearings as sources of supplemental food and habitat diversity for white-tailed deer. Pages 46–50 *in* White-tailed deer in the southern forest habitat. Proc. Symp. Nacogdoches, Tex. USDA For. Serv., South. For. Exp. Stn., New Orleans.

Lawrence, D.H. 1966. Studies in classic American literature. Dell Publ., N.Y.

Lay, D.W. 1956. Some nutrition problems of deer in the southern pine type. Proc. Annu. Conf. Southeast. Assoc. Game and Fish Comm. 10:53–58.

Lay, D.W. 1967. Browse palatability and the effects of prescribed burning in southern pine forest. J. For. 65:826–828.

Lennerts, L. 1989. Sesambuchen/-expeller und sesamextraktionsschrot. Die Muhle + Mischfuttertechnik 126:240–241.

Leopold, A. 1933. Game management. Charles Scribner's Sons, N.Y. 481pp.

Lewis, D.M. 1968. Telemetry studies of white tailed deer on Red Dirt Game Management Area, Louisiana. M.S. Thesis, Louisiana State Univ. and A&M College, Baton Rouge. 65pp.

Likens, G.E., and F.H. Bormann. 1970. Chemical analyses of plant tissues from the Hubbard Brook ecosystem in New Hampshire. Yale Univ., School For., Bull. 79.

Lockard, G.R. 1972. Further studies of dental annuli for aging white-tailed deer. J. Wildl. Manage. 36(1):46–55.

Ludwig, J. 1980. An evaluation of pelleted feed vs. corn for feeding deer. Minnesota Wildl. Res. Q. 40:61–74.

Magruder, N.D., C.E. French, L.C. McEwen, and R.W. Swift. 1957. Nutritional requirements of white-tailed deer for growth and antler development II. Pennsylvania State Agric. Exp. Stn. Bull. 628. 21pp.

Marchinton, R.L. 1968. Telemetric study of white-tailed deer movement-ecology and ethology in the Southeast. Ph.D. Dissert., Auburn Univ., Auburn, Ala. 138pp.

Marchinton, R.L., and L.K. Jeter. 1966. Telemetric study of deer movement ecology in the Southeast. Proc. Annu. Conf. Southeast. Assoc. Game and Fish Comm. 20:189–206.

Marchinton, R.L., J.R. Fudge, J.C. Fortson, K.V. Miller, and D.A. Dobie. 1991. Genetic stock and environment as factors in production of record class antlers. Pages 315–318 *in* B. Bobek, K. Perzanowski, and W.L. Regelin, eds. Global trends in wildlife management. Vol. 1. Trans. 18th Congr. Int. Union Game Biol. 1987. Swiat Press, Krakow-Warszawa.

Marchinton, R.L., and D.H. Hirth. 1984. Behavior. Pages 129–168 *in* L.K. Halls, ed. White-tailed deer: ecology and management. Stackpole Books, Harrisburg, Pa. 870pp.

Marchinton, R.L., K.V. Miller, R.J. Hamilton, and D.C. Guynn. 1990. Quality deer management: biological and social impacts on the herd. Pages 7–15 *in* C. Kyser, D.C. Sisson, and J.L. Landers, eds. Proc. Tall Timbers Game Bird Seminar, Tallahassee, Fla.

Marshall, A.D., and R.W. Whittington. 1968. A telemetric study of deer home ranges and behavior of deer during managed hunts. Proc. Southeast. Assoc. Game and Fish Comm. 22:30–46.

Marshall, C.M., J.F. Smith, and A.J. Weber. 1964. A simple technique for removing mandibles of deer without trophy defacement. Proc. Annu. Conf. Southeast. Assoc. Game and Fish Comm. 18:137–140.

Mayr, E. 1947. Ecological factors in speciation. Evolution 1:263–288.

McCaffery, K.R., J.E. Ashbrenner, and J.C. Moulton. 1981. Forest opening construction and impacts in northern Wisconsin. Wisconsin Dep. Nat. Res., Tech. Bull. 120. 42pp.

McCaffery, K.R., and W.A. Creed. 1969. Significance of forest openings to deer in northern Wisconsin. Wisconsin Dep. Nat. Res., Tech. Bull. 44. 104pp.

McCullough, D.R. 1979. The George Reserve deer herd: population ecology of a K-selected species. Univ. Michigan Press, Ann Arbor. 271pp.

McCullough, D.R. 1982. Antler characteristics of George Reserve white-tailed deer. J. Wildl. Manage. 46(3):821–826.

McCullough, D.R. 1984. Lessons from the George Reserve, Michigan. Pages 211–242 *in* L. K. Halls, ed. White-tailed deer: ecology and management. Stackpole Books, Harrisburg, Pa. 870pp.

McEwen, L.C., C.E. French, N.D. Magruder, R.W. Swift, and R.H. Ingram. 1957. Nutrient requirements of the white-tailed deer. Trans. North Am. Wildl. Conf. 22:119–132.

McGinnes, B.S. 1969. How size and distribution of cutting units affect food and cover of deer. Pages 66–70 *in* White-tailed deer in the southern forest habitat. Proc. Symp. Nacogdoches, Tex. USDA For. Serv., South. For. Exp. Stn., New Orleans.

Millar, C.E., L.M. Turk, and H.D. Foth. 1966. Fundamentals of soil science. John Wiley & Sons, Inc., N.Y. 491pp.

Miller, K.V., K.E. Kammermeyer, R.L. Marchinton, and E.B. Moser. 1987. Population and habitat influences on antler rubbing by white-tailed deer. J. Wildl. Manage. 51(1):62–66.

Miller, K.V., R.L. Marchinton, J.R. Beckwith, and P.B. Bush. 1985. Variations in density and chemical composition of white-tailed deer antlers. J. Mammal. 66(4):693–701.

Miller, K.V., R.L. Marchinton, and W.M. Knox. 1991. white-tailed deer signposts and their role as a source of priming pheromones: a hypothesis. Pages 455–460 *in* B. Bobek, K. Perzanowski, and W.L. Regelin, eds. Global trends in wildlife management. Vol. 1. Trans. 18th Congr. Int. Union Game Biol. 1987. Swiat Press, Krakow-Warszawa.

Miller, S.K. 1988. Reproductive biology of white-tailed deer on Cumberland Island, Georgia. M.S. Thesis, Univ. Georgia, Athens. 57pp.

Moncrief, L.W. 1970. An analysis of hunter attitudes toward the state of Michigan's antlerless deer hunting policy. Ph.D. Dissert., Michigan State Univ., East Lansing. 283pp.

Moreland, R. 1969. Emergency wildlife feeding and herding. P.R. Proj. W-77-D-1. Washington State Game Dep. 19pp.

Morrison, P.A. 1985. Habitat utilization by white-tailed deer on Davis Island. M.S. Thesis, Mississippi State Univ., Mississippi State. 62pp.

Mossman, H.W., and K.L. Duke. 1973. Comparative morphology of the mammalian ovary. Univ. Wisconsin Press, Madison. 461pp.

Mott, S.E., R.L. Tucker, D.C. Guynn, and H.A. Jacobson. 1985. Use of Mississippi bottomland hardwoods by white-tailed deer. Proc. Annu. Conf. Southeast. Assoc. Fish and Wildl. Agencies 39:403–411.

Muir, P.D., A.R. Sykes, and G.K. Barrell. 1987. Calcium metabolism in red deer *(Cervus elaphus)* offered herbages during antlerogenesis: kinetic and stable balance studies. J. Agric. Sci. 109:357–364.

Murphy, B.P., R.L. Marchinton, and K.V. Miller. 1992. Supplemental feed preference, consumption and cost in a free-choice situation. Joint Annu. Meet. Northeast Deer Tech. Comm. 28/Southeast Deer Study Group 15:13–14.

Murphy, D.A., and J.A. Coates. 1966. Effects of dietary protein on deer. Trans. North Am. Wildl. and Nat. Resour. Conf. 31:129–139.

Nelson, C.M., and T.F. Reis. 1992. Michigan deer crop damage block permit study. Trans. North Am. Wildl. and Nat. Resour. Conf. 57:89–95.

Nelson, M.E., and L.D. Mech. 1981. Deer social organization and wolf predation in northeastern Minnesota. Wildl. Monogr. 77. 53pp.

Nelson, M.E., and L.D. Mech. 1992. Dispersal in female white-tailed deer. J. Mammal. 73(4):891–894.

Nesbitt, W.H., and P.L. Wright, editors. 1981. Records of North American big game. 8th ed. The Boone and Crockett Club, Alexandria, Va. 409pp.

Nesbitt, W.H., and P. L. Wright. 1985. Measuring and scoring North American big game trophies. Boone and Crockett Club, Missoula, Mont. 176pp.

Nesbitt, W.H., and J. Reneau, editors. 1986. Boone and Crockett Club's 19th big game awards 1983–1985. Boone and Crockett Club, Dumfries, Va. 410pp.

Nixon, C.M., L.P. Hansen, P.A. Brewer, and J.E. Chelsvig. 1991. Ecology of white-tailed deer in an intensively farmed region of Illinois. Wildl. Monogr. 118. 77pp.

O'Pezio, J.P. 1978. Mortality among white-tailed deer fawns on the Seneca Army Depot. New York Fish and Game J. 25(1):1–15.

Osborne, J.S. 1981. Population dynamics of white-tailed deer in northeastern North Carolina. North Carolina Wildl. Resour. Comm. 53pp.

Osborne, J.S. 1990. The white-tailed deer in North Carolina. P.R. Proj. W-57-R-3, North Carolina Wildl. Res. Comm. 32pp.

Osborne, J.S., A.S. Johnson, P.E. Hale, R.L. Marchinton, C.V. Vansant, and J.M. Wentworth. 1992. Population ecology of the Blackbeard Island white-tailed deer. Tall Timbers Res. Stn., Tallahassee, Fla., Bull 26. 108pp.

Ozoga, J.J. 1968. Variations in microclimate in a conifer swamp deeryard in northern Michigan. J. Wildl. Manage. 32(3):574–585.

Ozoga, J.J. 1972. Field trial of maintaining deer under artificial conditions. P.R. Proj. W-117-R-5, Michigan Dep. Nat. Res. 8pp.

Ozoga, J.J., and L.W. Gysel. 1972. Response of white-tailed deer to winter weather. J. Wildl. Manage. 36(3):892–896.

Ozoga, J.J., and L.J. Verme. 1970. Winter feeding patterns of penned white-tailed deer. J. Wildl. Manage. 34(2):431-439.

Ozoga, J.J., and L.J. Verme. 1982. Physical and reproductive characteristics of a supplementally-fed white-tailed deer herd. J. Wildl. Manage. 46(2): 281–301.

Ozoga, J.J., and L.J. Verme. 1984. Effect of family-bond deprivation on reproductive performance in female white-tailed deer. J. Wildl. Manage. 48(4): 1326–1334.

Ozoga, J.J., and L.J. Verme. 1985. Comparative breeding behavior and performance of yearling vs. prime-age white-tailed bucks. J. Wildl. Manage. 49(2):364–372.

Ozoga, J.J., and L.J. Verme. 1986. Initial and subsequent maternal success of white-tailed deer. J. Wildl. Manage. 50(1):122–124.

Ozoga, J.J., L.J. Verme, and C.S. Bienz. 1982. Parturition behavior and territoriality in white-tailed deer: impact on neonatal mortality. J. Wildl. Manage. 46(1):1–11.

Parmalee, P.W. 1965. The food economy of Archaic and Woodland peoples at the Tick Creek Cave Site, Missouri. Missouri Archeologist 27(1):1–34.

Perry, O.H. 1899. Hunting expeditions of Oliver Hazard Perry. Privately printed. 246pp.

Petrick, C.J., R.E. Vanderhoof, and S.M. Shea. 1994. Relationship of in utero productivity to population indices of white-tailed deer in the Florida sandhills. Annu. Meet. Southeast Deer Study Group 17:30.

Pletscher, D.H. 1987. Nutrient budgets for white-tailed deer in New England with special reference to sodium. J. Mammal. 68(2):330–336.

Robbins, C.T. 1983. Wildlife feeding and nutrition. Academic Press, N.Y. 343pp.

Robbins, C.T., and A.N. Moen. 1975. Milk consumption and weight gain of white-tailed deer. J. Wildl. Manage. 39(2):355–360.

Rogers, M.J. 1980. Sylamore deer and forest game management study. P.R. Proj. W-53-R Arkansas Game and Fish Comm. 151pp.

Rongstad, O.J., and J.R. Tester. 1969. Movements and habitat use of white-tailed deer in Minnesota. J. Wildl. Manage. 33(2):366–379.

Ruth, C.R., Jr. 1990. A comparison of three white-tailed deer management strategies in the coastal plain of South Carolina. M.S. Thesis, Clemson Univ., Clemson, S.C. 63pp.

Rutske, L.H. 1969. A Minnesota guide to forest game habitat improvement. Minnesota Dep. Conserv., Div. Game and Fish, Tech. Bull. 10. 68pp.

Sadleir, R.M.F.S. 1980. Milk yield of black-tailed deer. J. Wildl. Manage. 44(2):472–478.

Sauer, P.R. 1973. Seasonal variation in physiology of white-tailed deer in relation to cementum annuli formation. Ph.D. Dissert., State Univ. of New Yourk, Albany, 85pp.

Scanlon, J.J., and M.R. Vaughan. 1985. Movements of white-tailed deer in Shenandoah National Park, Virginia. Proc. Annu. Conf. Southeast Assoc. Fish and Wildl. Comm. 39:397–402.

Schultz, S.R. 1990. Effects of artificial mineral licks on white-tailed deer. Ph.D. Dissert., Louisiana State University, Baton Rouge.

Sell, W.H. 1976. Alfalfa. Agronomy facts, forage, crops. Univ. Georgia, Coop. Ext. Serv. Bull. 476. 2pp.

Segelquist, C.A., and R.E. Pennington. 1968. Deer browse in the Ouachita Forest in Oklahoma. J. Wildl. Manage. 32(3):623–626.

Segelquist, C.A., and M.J. Rogers. 1975. Response of Japanese honeysuckle to fertilization. J. Wildl. Manage. 39(4):769–775.

Seton, E.T. 1891. The buck we didn't shoot. Forest and Stream 37:143

Seton, E.T. 1899. The trail of the sandhill stag. C. Scribner's Sons, N.Y. 93pp.

Seton, E.T. 1921. The book of woodcraft. Garden City Publ. Co., Garden City, N.Y. 590pp.

Seton, E.T. 1958. Animal tracks and hunter signs. Doubleday and Co., N.Y. 160pp.

Severinghaus, C.W. 1949. Tooth development and wear as criteria of age in white-tailed deer. J. Wildl. Manage. 13(2):195–216.

Sharpe, G.W., C.W. Hendee, and W.F. Sharpe. 1986. Introduction to forestry. 5th ed. McGraw-Hill Book Co., N.Y. 629pp.

Shea, S.M., and T.A. Breault. 1989. Implications of deer harvest management in northwest Florida pine flatwoods. Annu. Meet. Southeast Deer Study Group 12:9–10.

Shea, S.M., T.A. Breault, and M.L. Richardson. 1992a. Herd density and physical condition of white-tailed deer in Florida flatwoods. J. Wildl. Manage. 56(2):262–267.

Shea, S.M., T.A. Breault, and M.L. Richardson. 1992*b*. Relationship of birth date and physical development of yearling white-tailed deer in Florida. Proc. Annu. Conf. Southeast. Assoc. Fish and Wildl. Agencies 46:in press.

Short, H.L. 1971. Forage digestibility and diet of deer on southern upland range. J. Wildl. Manage. 35(4):698–706.

Short, H.L. 1975. Nutrition of southern deer in different seasons. J. Wildl. Manage. 39(2):321–329.

Short, H.L., R.M. Blair, and E.A. Epps, Jr. 1975. Composition and digestibility of deer browse in southern forests. USDA For. Serv., Res. Pap. SO-111. 10pp.

Silver, H. 1961. Deer milk compared with substitute milk for fawns. J. Wildl. Manage. 25(1):66–70.

Silver, H., N.F. Colovos, J.B. Holter, and H.H. Hayes. 1969. Fasting metabolism of white-tailed deer. J. Wildl. Manage. 33(3):490–498.

Simmons, H.L., and C.R. Ruth. 1990. white-tailed deer management at the Cedar Knoll Club. Annu. Meet. Southeast Deer Study Group 13:8.

Simmons, H.L., C.R. Ruth, Jr., and T.T. Fendley. 1991. Cedar Knoll Club: an update. Annu. Meet. Southeast Deer Study Group 14:28.

Smart, C.W., R.H. Giles, Jr., and D.W. Guynn, Jr. 1973. Weight tape for white-tailed deer in Virginia. J. Wildl. Manage. 37(4):553–555.

Smith, M.H., R.K. Chesser, E.G. Cothran, and P.E. Johns. 1982. Genetic variability and antler growth in a natural population of white-tailed deer. Pages 365–387 *in* R.D. Brown, ed. Antler development in Cervidae. Caesar Kleberg Wildl. Res. Inst., Kingsville, Tex.

Smith, R.P. 1991. Baiting for deer. Deer and Deer Hunting 15(1):60–68.

Smith, S.H., J.B. Holter, H.H. Hayes, and H. Silver. 1975. Protein requirement of white-tailed deer fawns. J. Wildl. Manage. 39(3):582–589.

Sparrowe, R.D., and P.F. Springer. 1970. Seasonal activity patterns of white-tailed deer in eastern South Dakota. J. Wildl. Manage. 34(2):420–431.

Spencer, G.E. 1981. Pineywoods deer management. Texas Parks and Wildl. Dep., Bull. 7000-88. 34pp.

Stephenson, D.C., and R.D. Brown. 1984. Calcium kinetics in male white-tailed deer. J. Nutr. 114:1014–1024.

Stockstad, D.L., M.S. Morris, and E.C. Lory. 1953. Chemical characteristics of natural licks used by big game animals in western Montana. Trans. North Am. Wildl. Conf. 18:247–258.

Stransky, J.J. 1980. Forage produced by clearcutting and site preparation in east Texas. Annu. Meet. Southeast Deer Study Group 3:3.

Stransky, J.J., and L.K. Halls. 1976. Nutrient content and yield of burned vs. mowed japanese honeysuckle. Proc. Annu. Conf. Southeast. Assoc. Game and Fish Comm. 29:403–406.

Stransky, J.J., and L.K. Halls. 1980. Fruiting of woody plants affected by site preparation and prior land use. J. Wildl. Manage. 44(1):258–263.

Stransky, J.J., and R.F. Harlow. 1981. Effects of fire on deer habitat in the Southeast. Pages 135–142 *in* G.W. Wood, ed. Prescribed fire and wildlife in southern forests. Belle W. Baruch For. Sci. Inst., Georgetown, S.C.

Suttie, J.M., and P.F. Fennessy. 1985. Regrowth of amputated velvet antlers with and without innervation. J. Exp. Zool. 234:359–366.

Swayngham, T., T. Fendley, L. Rogers, and D. Shipes. 1988. Juvenile white-tailed deer dispersal on Webb Wildlife Center, South Carolina. Annu. Meet. Southeast Deer Study Group 11:23–24.

Tanner, G.W., and W.S. Terry. 1982*a*. Vegetation inventory in the longleaf/slash pine forest type, Apalachicola National Forest, Florida. Final Rep. Coop. Agreement No. 19-306. U.S. For. Serv., South. For. Exp. Stn., Alexandria, La. 242pp.

Tanner, G.W., and W.S. Terry. 1982*b*. Inventory of nutritional quality of major dietary components of domestic herbivores on the Apalachicola National Forest, Florida. Final Rep. Coop. Agreement No. 19-342. U.S. For. Serv., South. For. Exp. Sta., Alexandria, La. 48pp.

Teer, J.G. 1984. Lessons from the Llano Basin, Texas. Pages 261–290 *in* L.K. Halls, ed. white-tailed deer: ecology and management. Stackpole Books, Harrisburg, Pa. 870pp.

Thackston, R.E. 1991. Artificial mineral licks: longevity and use; public and professional opinion. Georgia Dep. Nat. Res., Annu. Rept. W-47, 91-11.

Thomas, J.W., J.G. Teer, and E.A. Walker. 1964. Mobility and home range of white-tailed deer on the Edwards Plateau in Texas. J. Wildl. Manage. 28(3):463–472.

Thompson, C.B., J.B. Holter, H.H. Hayes, H. Silver, and W.E. Urban, Jr. 1973. Nutrition of white-tailed deer. I. Energy requirements of fawns. J. Wildl. Manage. 37(3):301–311.

Tome, P. 1971. Pioneer life; or, thirty years a hunter. Arno, New York. 238pp.

Tyson, E.L. 1952. Estimating deer populations from tracks. Proc. Annu. Conf. Southeast. Assoc. Game and Fish Comm. 6:507–517.

Tyson, E.L. 1959. A deer drive vs. track census. Trans. North Am. Wildl. Conf. 24:457–464.

Ueckermann, E. 1951. Die Einwirkung des Standortes auf Korpergewicht und Gehornbildung des Waldrehes. Doc. Thesis, Hann., Munden.

Ullrey, D.E. 1982. Nutrition and antler development in white-tailed deer. Pages 49–59 *in* R.D. Brown, ed. Antler development in Cervidae. Caesar Kleberg Wildl. Res. Inst., Kingsville, Tex.

Ullrey, D.E., W.G. Youatt, H.E. Johnson, A.B. Cowan, L.D. Fay, R.L. Covert, W.T. Magee, and K.K. Keahey. 1975. Phosphorus requirements of weaned white-tailed deer fawns. J. Wildl. Manage. 39(3):590–595.

Ullrey, D.E., W.G. Youatt, H.E. Johnson, L.D. Fay, and B.L. Bradley. 1967. Protein requirement of white-tailed deer fawns. J. Wildl. Manage. 31(4): 679–685.

Ullrey, D.E., W.G. Youatt, H.E. Johnson, L.D. Fay, B.L. Schoepke, and W.T.

Magee. 1970. Digestible and metabolizable energy requirements for winter maintenance of Michigan white-tailed does. J. Wildl. Manage. 34(4): 863–869.

Ullrey, D.E., W.G. Youatt, H.E. Johnson, L.D. Fay, B.L. Schoepke, W.T. Magee, and K.K. Keahey. 1973. Calcium requirements of weaned white-tailed deer fawns. J. Wildl. Manage. 37(2):187–194.

U.S. Forest Service. 1981. Wildlife habitat management handbook. USDA For. Serv. Southern Region, FSH 2609.23R

Urbston, D.F. 1967. Herd dynamics of a pioneer-like deer population. Proc. Annu. Conf. Southeast. Assoc. Game and Fish Comm. 21:42–50.

Urbston, E.F., C.W. Smart, and P.P. Scanlon. 1976. Relationship between body weight and heart girth in white-tailed deer from South Carolina. Proc. Annu. Conf. Southeast. Assoc. Game and Fish Comm. 30:471–473.

Vanderhoof, R.E., and H.A. Jacobson. 1988. Influence of food plots on deer, hunter success and distributions. Annu. Meet. Southeast Deer Study Group 11:18–19.

Vanderhoof, R.E., and H.A. Jacobson. 1989. Effects of agronomic plantings on white-tailed deer antler characteristics. Annu. Meet. Southeast Deer Study Group 12:20.

Vanderhoof, R.E., and H.A. Jacobson. 1991. Production and use of agricultural food plantings by deer on the Marion County Wildlife Management Area. P-R Proj. Rep. W-48, Study XXIV. Mississippi Dep. Wildl. Fish. Parks. 90pp.

VanDyke, T.S. 1923. The still-hunter. Macmillan Press, N.Y. 389pp.

Verme, L.J. 1962. Mortality of white-tailed deer fawns in relation to nutrition. Proc. Nat. White-tailed Deer Dis. Symp. 1:15–38.

Verme, L.J. 1963. Effect of nutrition on growth of white-tailed deer fawns. Trans. North Am. Wildl. and Nat. Res. Conf. 28:431–443.

Verme, L.J. 1965*a*. Reproduction studies of penned white-tailed deer. J. Wildl. Manage. 29(1):74–79.

Verme, L.J. 1965*b*. Swamp conifer deeryards in northern Michigan: their ecology and management. J. For. 63(7):523–529.

Verme, L.J. 1967. Influence of experimental diets and white-tailed deer reproduction. Trans. North Am. Wildl. and Nat. Resour. Conf. 32:405–420.

Verme, L.J. 1968. An index of winter weather severity for northern deer. J. Wildl. Manage. 32:(3)566–574.

Verme, L.J. 1973. Movements of white-tailed deer in Upper Michigan. J. Wildl. Manage. 37(4):545–552.

Verme, L.J. 1977. Assessment of natal mortality in Upper Michigan deer. J. Wildl. Manage. 41(4):700–708.

Verme, L.J. 1983. Sex ratio variations in *Odocoileus:* a critical review. J. Wildl. Manage. 47(3):573–582.

Verme, L.J. 1985. Progeny sex ratio relationships in deer: theoretical vs. observed. J. Wildl. Manage. 49(1):134–136.

Verme, L.J. 1991. Decline in doe fawn fertility in southern Michigan deer. Can. J. Zool. 69:25–28.

Verme L.J., and R.V. Doepker. 1988. Suppression of reproduction in Upper Michigan white-tailed deer, *Odocoileus virginianus*, by climatic stress during rut. Can. Field-Naturalist 102:550–552.

Verme, L.J., and W.F. Johnston. 1986. Regeneration of northern white cedar deeryards in Upper Michigan. J. Wildl. Manage. 50(2):307–313.

Verme, L.J., and J.J. Ozoga. 1971. Influence of winter weather on white-tailed deer in Upper Michigan. Pages 16–28 *in* A.O. Haugen, ed. Proc. snow and ice in relation to wildlife and recreation symp. Iowa Coop. Wildl. Res. Unit, Iowa St. Univ., Ames. 280pp.

Verme, L.J., and J.J. Ozoga. 1980*a*. Influence of protein-energy intake on deer fawns in autumn. J. Wildl. Manage. 44(2):305–314.

Verme, L.J., and J.J. Ozoga. 1980*b*. Effects of diet on growth and lipogenesis in deer fawns. J. Wildl. Manage. 44(2):315–324.

Verme, L.J., and J.J. Ozoga. 1981. Sex ratio of white-tailed deer and the estrus cycle. J. Wildl. Manage. 45(3):710–715.

Verme, L.J., and J.J. Ozoga. 1987. Relationship of photoperiod to puberty in doe fawn white-tailed deer. J. Mammal. 68(1):107–110.

Verme, L.J., J.J. Ozoga, and J.T. Nellist. 1987. Induced early estrus in penned white-tailed deer does. J. Wildl. Manage. 51(1):54–56.

Vogt, F. 1948. Das Rotwild. Osterreichischer Jagd und Fischereiverlag, Vienna, Austria. 207pp.

Webber, C.W. 1852. Romance of natural history; or, wild scenes and wild hunters. Lippincott, Grambo, and Company, Philadelphia, Pa. 610pp.

Weber, S.J. 1986. white-tailed deer habitat management guidelines in Vermont. Pages 29–41 *in* Blodgett et al., Model habitat management guidelines for deer, bear, hare, grouse, turkey, woodcock and non-game wildlife. P.R. Proj. W-46 D, Vermont Fish and Wildl. 64pp.

Weber, S.J. 1987. white-tailed deer habitat management guidelines in Vermont. Page 107 *in* Proc. Symp. Deer, For., and Agric.: Interactions and Strategies for Management. Allegheny Soc. Am. For., Warren, Pa. 183pp.

Weeks, H.P., Jr. 1974. Physiological, morphological, and behavioral adaptations of herbivorous mammals to a sodium-deficient environment. Ph.D. Dissert., Purdue Univ., W. Lafayette, Ind. 421pp.

Weeks, H.P., Jr. 1978*a*. Variation in the sodium and potassium content of food plants of wild Indiana herbivores. Purdue Univ. Agric. Exp. Stn. Res. Bull. 957.

Weeks, H.P., Jr. 1978*b*. Characteristics of mineral licks and behavior of visiting white-tailed deer in southern Indiana. Am. Midl. Nat. 100:384–395.

Weeks, H.P., Jr., and C.M. Kirkpatrick. 1976. Adaptations of white-tailed deer to naturally occurring sodium deficiencies. J. Wildl. Manage. 40(4):610–625.

Weeks, H.P., Jr., and C.M. Kirkpatrick. 1978. Salt preferences and sodium drive phenology in fox squirrels and woodchucks. J. Mammal. 59(3):531–542.

Wegner, R. 1991. Deer management. Deer and Deer Hunting. November:18–25.

Weichert, C.K. 1970. Anatomy of the chordates. McGraw-Hill Book Co., St. Louis. 814pp.

Wentworth, J.M., A.S. Johnson, and P.E. Hale. 1990. Influence of acorn use on deer in the Southern Appalachians. Proc. Annu. Conf. Southeast. Assoc. Fish and Wildl. Agencies. 44:142–154.

Wentworth, J.M., A.S. Johnson, P.E. Hale, and K.E. Kammermeyer. 1992. Relationships of acorn abundance and deer herd characteristics in the Southern Appalachians. South. J. Appl. For. 16(1):5–8.

White, M. 1973. The white-tail deer of the Aransas National Wildlife Refuge. Tex. J. Sci. 24(4):457–489.

Williams, J.D. and D.E. Harmel. 1988a. Heritability estimates in white-tailed deer—Progress report. Annu. Meet. Southeast Deer Study Group 11:12–13.

Williams, J.D., and D.E. Harmel. 1988b. Predicting mature antler characteristics for yearling white-tailed deer. Annu. Meet. Southeast Deer Study Group 11:10.

Wood, J.M., and G.W. Tanner. 1985. Browse quality response to forest fertilization and soils in Florida. J. Range Manage. 38:432–435.

Woods, G.R., D.C. Guynn, Jr., and J.G. Williams. 1992. Attitudes and experiences of quality deer management participants in Mississippi and South Carolina. Joint Annu. Meet. Northest Deer Tech. Comm 28/Southeast Deer Study Group 15:8.

Yantis, J.H., C.D. Frentress, W.S. Daniel, and G.H. Veteto. 1983. Deer management in the post oak belt. Tex. Parks and Wildl. Dep., Bull. 7000–96. 28pp.

Zaiglin, R.E. 1977. The effects of a supplemental feed on free-ranging white-tailed deer. M.S. Thesis, Texas A&I Univ., Kingsville. 56pp.

Zwank, P.J., and J.A. Zeno. 1986. Weight gain of white-tailed deer relative to fawning date. Proc. Annu. Conf. Southeast. Assoc. Fish and Wildl. Agencies 40:424–429.

QUALITY DEER MANAGEMENT ASSOCIATION
P.O. Box 707 • Walterboro, SC 29488•1-800-209-DEER

MEMBERSHIP APPLICATION

Name: _____

Address: _____

City: _____ State: _____ Zip: _____

County of Residence: _____ Telephone: (home) _____ (office) _____

Type of Hunting: ___ Gun ___ Archery ___ Muzzleloader ___ Other (___)

Counties Hunted: _____

Club Member: ___ Yes ___ No   Name of Club: _____   No. of Acres: _____

Membership Fee: $15.00 (enclose with this Membership Application)
Make check payable to *Quality Deer Management Association*
By joining this Association, I hereby agree to adopt this Code of Ethics
Signature: _____

QDMA CODE OF ETHICS

1. Members should know and obey all hunting rules and regulations. Any conviction for the willful violation of a game law will result in immediate expulsion from the QDMA.
2. Members should learn as much as possible about wildlife management, recreational hunting and hunter ethics.
3. Members should act in a manner that would bring credit to recreational deer hunting and to the QDMA.
4. Members should foster good relations among hunters by setting an example as responsible hunters.
5. Members should participate in hunter education and safety courses and encourage other hunters to do the same.
6. Members should respect the activities of other hunters, landowners and the general public.
7. Members should support the objectives of the QDMA.
8. Members should adopt this CODE OF ETHICS.